JAZZ IN REVOLUTION

JAZZ
IN REVOLUTION

Constable · London

First published in Great Britain 1998
by Constable and Company Limited
3 The Lanchesters, 162 Fulham Palace Road
London W6 9ER
Copyright © John Dankworth 1998
ISBN 0 094 77570 2
The right of John Dankworth to be identified as author
of this work has been asserted by him
in accordance with the Copyright, Designs and Patents Act 1988
Set in Monotype Photina 11pt
by Servis Filmsetting Ltd, Manchester
Printed in Great Britain by
St Edmundsbury Press Ltd
Bury St Edmunds, Suffolk

A CIP catalogue record for this book
is available from the British Library

Contents

Acknowledgements

My grateful thanks to Sheila Gray and Becky Stevenson for their inde-fatigable assistance in copying and correcting, as well as assembling photos, facts and dates galore.

Also to Dan Morganstern and his colleagues at the Jazz Archives of Rutgers University in Newark, New Jersey for information on my 1949 Paris trip.

Lastly to my darling wife, Cleo, who remains not only one of the great singers but one of the most vigilant proof readers this world has to offer.

Prologue

The course of true jazz has never run smoothly.

Jazz, to its eternal credit, is a hybrid which owes its very beginnings to a series of fusions of music from a variety of sources. Thus 'true jazz' is hard to define and 'pure jazz' does not exist. Yet this process of taking in elements of a diversity of musical styles is precisely why jazz has survived, and why its practitioners and followers are such passionately devoted and fervent advocates of their chosen music.

The history of jazz covers something short of a century at the time of writing. In other words, something vaguely resembling the jazz of today seemed to begin to emerge in the early 1900s, and by about 1917 the Original Dixieland Jazz Band had begun making recordings which seem sufficient evidence to bear that out. The evolution of the music made rapid strides after that, and by 1927 a large and ever-increasing number of recordings were being made which, although restricted to morsels of around three minutes' duration, were pretty good indications of what was happening in jazz. All the indications were that it had truly come of age – in fact some say its Golden Age.

1927 was the year I was born – a child of the Golden Age of jazz, perhaps. Thus it was natural that my talents for music emerged in the language of jazz, and that the events of my entire musical career are directly or indirectly attributable to jazz. I feel that since childhood I have watched, observed and participated in many of the events that have shaped the music and have a special story to tell.

What's this – an Englishman with something to say about jazz, an undeniably American music?

I feel that the very fact of my being an Englishman could have contributed to making me a better, more dispassionate observer of the scene than someone nearer it or with more national or ethnic involvement. This could certainly be argued in the case of the late Leonard Feather, an Englishman who not only became the world's best-known and perhaps most respected jazz critic of his day, but actually wrote many jazz pieces, including traditional blues items, which were performed by prominent jazz artistes. It could also be argued that those active in other musical backgrounds, and thus far enough away to view the entire scene, can more effectively assess the strengths and weaknesses of jazz than its actual participants; Leonard Bernstein, Gunther Schuller and André Previn all seem to bear that out.

But I feel I have another valid qualification. My active career in jazz began in about 1944, almost precisely the time of the greatest upheaval in the history of the music. Both my work and my views have been shaped by musical events and artists on both sides of that phenomenal divide, the advent of the bebop style in jazz.

But whether you, the reader, be an avid jazz enthusiast, someone who would wish to learn more about the music, or just a passing reader with no particular affiliations at all, perhaps I have revealed enough to entice you to continue with my story and said enough about my arguments to retain your interest. Perhaps the confusion of snippets of information you have so far gleaned about the development of jazz in the last half-century seem more akin to a flood than a river. If so, perhaps the ensuing story of my personal experience of it all may help control the flow and make the scene a little easier to comprehend. I certainly hope so.

1

Younger than springtime

'Never trust a foreigner, son – they're all mad.'

The words had come from my father's lips when I was quite small. I can remember them so vividly that I can recall the part of our house we were in when he uttered them. It was the corner of the dining-room of our semi-detached 'between wars' villa on the edge of the east London suburb of Walthamstow. This contribution to urban sprawl, then in the process of further enlarging the already bloated Greater London metropolis (and threatening to swallow up yet more Essex countryside, including large sections of beautiful Epping Forest, which almost reached our back garden), was home for me from my fourth to about my thirtieth birthday. Its red-tiled roof, complete with a mock-Tudor dormer window section typical of the times, and its pebble-dashed walls concealed an interior of modest proportions.

We were four – my parents, my sister Avril and me. My father was a sales manager for an electrical insulation firm on the other, more industrial side of Walthamstow. He was a dapper man of moderate height, whose constantly worn glasses – in my early childhood they were pince-nez but later changed to horn-rimmed – gave him a studious appearance and the air of a well-educated man. In fact he left school in his early teens to help out with money for the family, and thus his education was basic – though well imbibed and utilised –

rather than extensive. He was a kind man of whom my early recollec-
tions are nothing but pleasant. However, I suspect that he also had a
moody, uncommunicative side, which he tended to cover up in front
of the children and saddle his wife with more frequently; I occasionally remember my mother tearfully accusing him of such tactics.
Nevertheless, my mother and father otherwise made an acceptable
pair by the standards expected of the day, and, although their relationship was never an overtly warm one, they both showed great love
of their kids in those formative days of our early youth.

The words of fatherly wisdom referred to earlier were addressed to
me when I was beside a circular free-standing ashtray (it was about
as tall as I was at the time) which stood by the fireplace. My father was
the lone smoker in the household, sometimes smoking cigarettes but
occasionally devoting himself to one of the many pipes bought for
him by one of us for a birthday or Christmas present. Not that he
smoked very much, or drank very much for that matter. My father
was not, as far as I could tell, a man who had ever been given to
excesses of any sort. Except sometimes with words. And at my tender
age at the time I took him literally when he dismissed the vast majority of the world's inhabitants as being insane.

What I didn't know then (and if I had known it would surely have
only confused me more) was that my father's parents were both
foreigners. My grandfather was one of four brothers, the sons of a
German portrait artist named August Dankworth. Their father, by
the evidence he left, was a successful and talented man whose skills
obviously earned him many commissions from the moneyed families
who engaged him in order to perpetuate (and perhaps occasionally
adorn) their likenesses. Many oils with his signature are on view in
several museums in Germany. But in spite of their father's ability the
sons apparently chose to quit their homeland. Just why is not docu-
mented, but, since they were a Lutheran family at a time when the
surrounding population was mainly Catholic, one might divine that
they elected to leave for an easier life, or even for their own personal
safety. Two brothers made for the United States, one went to
Scandinavia, and my grandfather decided on England.

There may be another reason that my grandfather chose London.
A recently unearthed family chronicle seems to indicate that he was

married, with a young child, in Germany. Not long after his arrival in England he is discovered indeed to be married – but not to the same woman, which on the face of it seems to point to some bigamous goings-on! He died when my father was about fifteen and of course long before I was born, but I clearly remember his wife (or 'wife' as the case may be), who was certainly my grandmother, and who survived her husband by many years. This dignified lady spoke with a heavy accent, so that it could be that Grandad fled Germany having pre-arranged a rendezvous with his German lover in London. But, being ignorant of any of these goings-on, it never entered my mind to ask her any leading questions.

My grandmother bore her husband five sons and two daughters. Most of my uncles and aunts visited 16 Hollywood Way (our exotic address in a somewhat less than exotic setting) with varying frequency. One, however, didn't visit at all, simply because he had left Britain for Australia some time before – under a cloud, according to my mother, who made it her business to know such things. Many years later I would get to meet this missing link in the family. My uncles Bob and, especially, Arthur (also known as Sep, short for Septimus, since he was the seventh-born) were the most frequent callers – usually on a weekend. My father and his two brothers were also keen snooker players, and on a couple of nights a week met at a local Conservative club, or on occasions at a pub, to improve their game and compete with each other for stakes of a half-crown or so. On these nights Dad occasionally came home a wee bit 'merry', as Mother described it. But we kids had to take her word for it, as only she could tell. Dad was a relatively quiet man, and I can honestly say I never saw him the worse for drink. As for Mother, she would start giggling – and then roaring with laughter – after anything more than a sip of alcohol; she consequently seldom touched a drop save on high days and holidays.

There were further bits of fatherly advice which I remember being given, sometimes at bedtime, sometimes while Dad was scrubbing my back during the weekly bath, or sometimes at the table during meals. Most of them were far more predictable than the warning about folks from overseas, however, like: 'speak the truth and fear not', 'honesty is the best policy' and 'neither a borrower nor a lender be'. But most of these other gems of potted morality were covered by my lessons at Winchester Road Methodist Sunday school. Here was also to be found the source of some of my musical inspiration, in the form of the hymns that were part of Sunday school ritual. The succulent harmonies and well-crafted melodies of some of the better ones stand the test of time extremely well and retain their appeal to me to this day.

But it was my mother who was the main musical influence in our household. She came from a family with several professional musicians in its ranks – one a church organist, another a pianist for the silent movies. Her connections with the Methodist church and Townswomen's Guild choirs – first as a mezzo-soprano and later as a choir leader – meant that she was constantly searching through songbooks for new material and roping us young 'uns in to practise it. As far back as I can recall I was expected to look over her shoulder at the piano music-stand and keep my end up. I struggled manfully to sight-read unfamiliar notes, coupling them with unfamiliar words, which were often nowhere near the notes but at the bottom of the page.

Thus I became, almost before I was aware of it, initiated into the world of musical performance – and the die was cast. I suppose it slowly and imperceptibly dawned on me that here was the foundation of a job, a job that would beat the daylights out of a daily trek to an office on a bicycle. But I had to reason all this out for myself gradually over the years, because even though my father was full of good advice about some things he was a hopeless counsellor for others. Nothing my father ever said to me led me even to suspect that there was any other way to earn a living than his way – to hop on a bike or bus to go to work in the mornings every weekday, and return in time for supper and the 6 o'clock evening news on BBC radio. The possibility that anyone on this earth led a normal and solvent life performing music did not exist – as far as my father was concerned.

Life was sweet. True, Wall Street had not long ago crashed and left millions destitute and homeless. Hitler was beginning to take over Germany and Mussolini was already in charge of Italy. The Japanese were raping China. Spain was racked with bitter divisions which would lead to a bloody civil war . . . but all of these were of small concern to a young lad living in a genteel suburb of a country at peace.

I could go out of the back door of our garden to a strip of waste land by a stream and play with the other kids of the neighbourhood. I could get out my bike and cycle all over the area without meeting a car. But if I did see a parked car I would dismount and inspect the vehicle meticulously, whether it be a Rolls, a Morris Cowley or a Trojan van. I could go to the level-crossing by the station and watch the steam trains go by. I could go along to the Regal cinema (we used to call them picture palaces in those days) and look at the pictures in the display cabinet outside. There were a hundred things to do without spending any money at all – there had to be, for we so often had no money to spend. But even just a little money went a very long way. Tuppence bought a quarter of a pound of sweets, quite a long ride on a bus, a couple of hours seeing films in the Regal on Saturday morning, a comic paper such as *Film Fun*, an adventure magazine such as *Hotspur* or *Wizard*, or even a kid's science paper such as *Modern Wonder*.

My first five years or so of school involved a fifteen-minute dawdle through side streets and along footpaths, and necessitated crossing only one road with any appreciable amount of traffic. The daily routine at school was much the same as it had been for years – kids drank their school milk in the morning break and ate their sandwiches at lunch time, if they didn't go home for lunch. They played in the playgrounds before and after school and during breaks much as they had since time immemorial. Occasionally playground ditties would reflect the goings-on of the outside world:

> *Roll along, Mussolini, roll along*
> *You won't be in Abyssinia very long*
> *You'll be lying on the grass*
> *With a bullet up your arse,*
> *Roll along, Mussolini, roll along.*

That particular one demonstrated which side British kids were on at the time of the Italian invasion of Abyssinia, long before we were at war with them in 1940.

My sister Avril was five years ahead of me – at junior school, at high school and eventually at earning a living. Avril and I were always good friends. In some ways she was my guiding light, my advisor in moments of unhappiness or doubt. Yet in some ways she was a bit of a millstone round my neck (a tiny one from a peppermill perhaps, but a millstone nevertheless) because, as an exemplary student, she created a model for me which I found very hard to live up to. She was a staunch and enthusiastic Girl Guide, so I was enrolled in the Cubs. She took music lessons, so I was sent to music lessons. That wasn't so bad, but Avril practised, and I (in common with millions of young boys coerced into taking up a musical instrument) hated practising. All in all, Avril was much too good an example of what can be done with a young life for me to be able to get away with anything at all. Which made me occasionally wish I had been an only child – and a spoilt brat, no doubt. Avril and I were nevertheless bosom buddies and spent countless happy hours together. Some of the happiest were when she rattled out popular songs of the day on our front-room piano from sheet music she had somehow acquired, and I played along on a toy drum kit. As a duo we were hard to beat.

And so life went on for us in the 1930s, day after day, year after year. Father plied to and from his office and played his snooker, Mother did the shopping and went to her choir practices, while Avril and I wafted to school and music lessons and Guide or Cub meetings. Nothing much seemed to change.

However, around my eleventh birthday came the inevitable school selection exams. To my parents' delight I found myself chosen for the Sir George Monoux Grammar School for Boys in Walthamstow. The Monoux was a good school, and I was proud to have been selected for it. It boasted a reputation for entrances to Oxford, Cambridge and others of the more venerable universities that was far and away above the national average. My contemporaries included ballet critic John Percival, England cricketer Doug Insole, symphony conductor John Pritchard and several others who have made their mark on the world. Indeed, when in 1995 my wife and I performed at Brown University in New England I received a phone call. 'It's Geoffrey Ribbans here – we used to be classmates at the Monoux. Do you remember me?' I did, but he remembered me better.

'You gave me some advice. I was taking German as a second language, and you said I was wasting my time, and should be taking Spanish as you were – so I did.'

'Great. What are you doing here?'

'I'm director of Hispanic studies', came the reply.

Life might well have gone smoothly at the Monoux, with the brighter among us cruising on to university scholarships or an easy slide into the business world, in either case leading to prosperity, security and a quiet life. Three terms every year, with the family summer holidays to Clacton on Sea, or Cromer in Norfolk, or Hastings or wherever coming predictably round each year. But such patterns were about to change – to my surprise, although quite predictably for those wise enough to see all the symptoms and draw their inevitable conclusion. The world was sliding towards war.

* * *

People can usually remember where they were when an item of world-changing news breaks, and I am no exception. We were on our annual family vacation at a holiday camp in Kent, near the symbolic white cliffs of Dover. While I and my sister were playing with our new-found holiday friends our parents were listening anxiously to BBC news bulletins assessing the likelihood of war.

People of our parents' age-group knew war from experience; some had even lived through air-raids on London by the German zeppelins during the 1914–18 conflict. Our prime minister, Neville Chamberlain, had thought he had made a deal with Adolf Hitler which would avoid war. It now became increasingly clear, as German troops crossed the border into Poland, that he had been mistaken. And on one bright morning towards the end of our blissful fortnight at the holiday camp I noticed people gathering round radios listening anxiously, and heard the fateful words: '. . . consequently this country is at war with Germany'. Fateful words which changed our lives. Immediately plans were made for us all to return home, which we did the following day. Gas masks which had been issued some time previously were got out and prepared for use, blackout curtains were rigged hastily to avoid tell-tale light patterns for navigational use by enemy bombers, air-raid wardens braced themselves to assist during raids, hospitals opened special casualty wards.

And nothing happened. The 'phoney war' – the period in which neither the British nor the German forces facing each other on the Franco-German border waged war in any way that affected basic life-styles in the British Isles – was on. Nevertheless, knowing what might happen, the government decreed that the plan for the evacuation of British schoolchildren from cities considered vulnerable to air attack should go ahead immediately. And that of course included London. And London of course included me.

And so on a duly appointed morning, with a small suitcase packed with the barest necessities and a gas mask in a cardboard box slung across my shoulder, I reported with hundreds of others to the railway station – for an unknown destination. My mother waved me a tearful farewell and we were off.

In London we changed trains, then streamed off anew in a different direction, stopping eventually in a small market town, Ampthill in rural Bedfordshire. Eventually we were distributed around the surrounding countryside and allotted accommodation in houses and cottages in a number of villages and their outskirts. I was in a little place called Lidlington, the guest of an elderly couple. Their five-year-old grandson lived with them – I never found out what had happened to the boy's parents – and for a while he and I were room-mates, in a cottage with one toilet (at the bottom of the garden) and one source of running water (the kitchen tap).

Our lessons continued sporadically and somewhat chaotically in the village hall, or the church, or anywhere that could be grabbed for use by our harassed teachers. But we were at the very most half-operational during those times, with no equipment and no proper school premises to work from. Moreover, nothing whatsoever was happening in London, other than food rationing, to upset normal everyday life. Yet the schools were empty.

It was not surprising then, that after a month or so many youngsters, including me, started to drift back to their London homes. The scheme had never been compulsory, and the lack of war activity made evacuation seem pointless. But hardly had I got accustomed to my own cosy bed (instead of the straw-filled mattress of my digs) and re-established myself as a member of the family when the war began in earnest. The Nazi war machine overran Holland, Belgium and finally France, the British army was driven into the sea and (what was left of it) back to England, and the enemy took up positions only twenty-odd miles away from Dover and began to shell our hitherto unassailable island.

And the air-raids on London started. Quickly we were redispatched to the safer areas, parting from our parents amid hasty and sometimes emotional farewells and leaving them to face the music in a beleaguered – and later badly battered – city.

The Battle of Britain and the severe bombing of London in 1940 and 1941 came and went, as did other attacks during the course of the war. I was sent first to Colchester, where the Monoux shared premises with the city's grammar school, an amazing choice for a refuge, since Colchester itself was a potential and indeed likely target – it was in fact a garrison city. We were eventually moved on to Leominster in Herefordshire, where we adopted a similar pattern of school-sharing with the grammar-school boys.

Life in Leominster had its interests. One of my hosts was a railway signalman, and we lived in a railway-owned cottage by the line itself at a place called Ford Bridge, just outside the town. I spent hours in the signal-box, helping to pull the enormous levers that manually operated the wires connected by hundreds of pulleys to the 'semaphore' signals themselves, as the express steam-trains roared through, belching their smoke in all directions. Occasionally I was allowed to pass on a bell signal to the next signal-box, or even to enter into the log-book (with a nibbed pen which was periodically dipped into an ancient inkwell) the time of a passing train.

But during the next lull in the London air attacks homesickness got the better of me once more, and I sent a telegram to my parents. 'Coming home on next available train', it read, and none of their pleas could persuade me to do otherwise. 'If you're going to be blown to bits I'd rather be blown to bits with you', was one of my first remarks as I presented myself on the doorstep. So from now on all of us Dankworths were in this together.

*   *   *

In the event, my return to the battle zone turned out to be a good move. Schools had been reorganised, and about one in three was open again. Monoux was not among them, though, and my educational activities were relocated to the nearby Leyton County High School for Boys – I was a 'school guest' yet again. It meant a long bike ride to school, but at least my daily life returned to one approaching peace-time normality. The war was not by any means over at this stage – and it was to have a sting in its tail that was to surprise us all – but the Germans were doing badly on the Russian front, and air-raids had virtually stopped. As for an invasion of Britain, that seemed almost impossible now, since Britain was jam-packed with US forces, armed to the teeth and preparing to invade Europe.

And then – joy of joys – the Monoux reopened, and all its evacuees, staff and pupils returned to the unscathed building and proceeded to establish anew all the school traditions of good education. I was by this time ready to join the sixth form, the five-year course having finished, and this I duly did.

Things started well enough, and without a doubt I had the best of intentions. When the war appeared all but over, however, a new factor came into our lives. First came the pilotless plane bombs known as V1s; they caused major disruption and considerable loss of property and life. Moreover, they were bad for morale, since those that got through the cordon to the inner-London area were extremely visible (during daylight anyway) and quite frightening at times. Much less effective in this respect were their successors the V2s, quite simply because nothing could be done about them at all. There was no way of predicting the arrival of these explosive rockets, with the result that the only possible course of action for us Londoners was to go about our business pretending that no such thing as a V2 existed. It was essential that you adopted a philosophy about the thing – if it had your name on it then it was going to get you, and if it got you you wouldn't know much about it anyway!

Such events led surprisingly to a feeling of normality in 1944 in London, which, in spite of the V1s and V2s, continued to function. At this point came the event that cast the die for my lifetime. I discovered jazz.

* * *

It had been all right when I left the house five minutes earlier, but now it was beginning to drop down quite thick and fast – I could hear the tell-tale sounds on the rooftops around me. I reluctantly realised that it was time to shelter in someone's front porch until things eased off a bit. I didn't want to be late for the jazz record night at the youth club, but such conditions didn't usually last too long. This current shower, and the thundery sounds that accompanied it, I knew from experience would be followed by a lull which would probably last long enough for me to reach my destination in comfort and without too much of a hurry.

The downpour was likely to inflict far more discomfort than a soaking, however. What was in progress was not a rainstorm but an air-raid. On nights like this one, when the sirens had wailed their baleful warning of an impending raid, life frequently went on as if nothing had happened. It never occurred to anybody of my age that there was any danger involved in walking the blackout streets of the eastern suburbs of London while the enemy planes prowled the skies immediately above. The tinkling of falling metal sounded deceptively harmless for something so lethal. Funnily enough, it wasn't the Nazis that were causing the shower of unpleasant materials to descend from the clouds; it was the shrapnel from our own anti-aircraft guns that forced me to take shelter.

But the object of the journey – to compare notes with other young jazz buffs on the merits of Louis Armstrong's *Weatherbird* or Duke Ellington's *Harlem Airshaft* – was uppermost in my mind. There was absolutely no question about the wisdom of the whole expedition: the risk involved in getting there was well worth it.

Being a jazz fan during World War II wasn't exactly easy. Yet on reflection, considering that the future of the free world was at stake (and with it, according to the philosophies of the Hitler regime, the future of jazz as well), the music was surprisingly easy to obtain. True, the new jazz releases amounted to just two or three double-sided 78 rpm records a month (just, say, half a dozen three-minute morsels of jazz), but since we were living on an island under siege and fighting for its very existence that tiny ration of jazz (by today's standards) didn't seem too bad, especially as the sum total monthly issue of discs of all types of music amounted to only twenty or so. Looking back, it was a very fair percentage for a musical style that had already outlived its 'popular' period and was fast becoming considered an 'art' music.

It nevertheless amounted to precious little evidence of what was happening at that time in the birthplace of jazz across the submarine-infested Atlantic. In those circumstances every bar, every note, every nuance became the object of close scrutiny and endless discussion. Access to our music might have been severely limited, but it was certainly an assurance that what we did get was studied – and then studied, and then studied over and over again.

The result was a collection of records bearing the scars and scratches of continual replay, with numerous grey areas, caused by overplaying of a special passage in an effort to dislodge its secrets, and plenty of craters which created the illusion of unscheduled drumbeats. Even the use of needles made from thorns to minimise wear didn't help much – they required such frequent sharpening that the puny sound they made wasn't worth the effort. Steel needles at sixpence a box were still the only real choice, in spite of their lethal effect on the discs.

And the wind-up portable gramophone which activated my pitiful assembly of scratchy sound-bytes was primitive, even for those days. It frequently needed a boost to its clockwork mechanism from the handle on the side to make it last the whole record, otherwise Ella Fitzgerald would in mid-phrase start a gradual but inevitable sliding metamorphosis into Paul Robeson. And, as it had no volume control, the only way to avoid waking up the whole household and incurring parental wrath was to stuff a rolled-up pair of football socks in the mouth of the speaker horn! By using this admittedly unscientific but vaguely effective bit of 'noise reduction' I was able to extend my hours of jazz study well into the time when all decent God-fearing people were asleep – or in the air-raid shelters.

Thus began my jazz education. Although it wasn't quite as simple as that. I had, after all, been brought up in a classically inclined household, where all other kinds of music were regarded with an air of benign superiority. There was no real embargo on any specific style of music, but the general parental message was that the only 'quality' music was of the classical variety. This was the edict tacitly understood and until now rigidly observed by all.

Except for my Aunt Nell, an independent-minded schoolteacher who lived with us for a while during the war. She was a very active lady in the local music world. She played the viola in an amateur orchestra, but, much more surprisingly, also at times performed on the french horn, the trumpet and the cornet, the last in an otherwise entirely male marching band. It was to Aunt Nell that I initially confided my interest in jazz – the true jazz, that is, not the dance music which generally had the label 'jazz' attached to it at that time. I had of course discovered this music for myself, as young people do, but I had no idea of how to get more deeply involved in the study – and perhaps eventually the performance – of this exciting music. Neither had I heard from other lips any encouraging or supportive words to lead me to believe that my quest was worth while, and not just a teenage phase which I would pass through and eventually abandon. And even as I told Aunt Nell of my jazz interest I felt sure that she would disapprove, and so started to refer to it in a slightly deprecating way.

When we were chatting together one afternoon at home, some-thing must have caused her to detect my insecurity. 'Well', she said, 'there's certainly such a thing as good jazz, but it's often confused with dance music and the Tin Pan Alley stuff you hear such a lot of on the radio.' I felt I had already realised this, but to hear Aunt Nell's endorsement was music to my ears. 'Louis Armstrong, for instance', she went on, 'he's wonderful.' Her eyes twinkled. 'He's got lips like leather, y' know', she added with the air of someone who recognised that quality from personal experience. 'Benny Goodman, too', she went on, 'he's a virtuoso in any sense of the word – plays classical music as well!'

This was enough for me. My plan was formed then and there. If I took up an instrument that was used classically too, I just might get my mother on my side – and thus the wherewithal to get a clarinet.

I left my aunt sitting by the fireside looking slightly astonished at my sudden movement for the door, perhaps wondering what she had said to occasion this flurry of activity from Number One Nephew. I rushed through the kitchen, causing my mother, who had just removed a tray of newly baked cup-cakes from the oven, to side-step with the adroitness of a skilful matador. I ran through the lean-to garage at the side of our semi-detached abode, grabbed my bike, and hurtled down Hollywood Way to Hale End Road and on to the radio and record shop near the station. I dashed into the shop, straight to a rack containing dozens of jazz records (probably some job-lot of old stock that the current owner had inherited from a previous one), and grabbed hold of a disc I had often seen while browsing in this little store but had never before had the motivation to buy – *Tea for Two*, by the Benny Goodman Quartet!

In no time I had persuaded the startled salesman to defer payment till the next day and was back home again playing my prize on the Columbia portable. My mother was too dazed to react, but Aunt Nell beamed approvingly and even tapped her feet to the warm, beguiling Goodman sound. And I had made my big lifetime decision.

I was going to be a jazz clarinet player. Yet my decisive choice of an instrument had done nothing to finance my habit and, like any other addicted person, I felt I could stop at practically nothing to procure what financial assistance I needed. Money, even though I was still a schoolboy, became a pressing problem in my life as a jazz junkie. I knew of only one way to solve it.

*   *   *

Getting up in the wee small blacked-out hours of the morning in wartime London to do my newspaper round was not something I relished in the slightest, let alone enjoyed. Neither did my mother enjoy getting up at that time to stir her heavy-sleeping son for his task. I was amazed that she did so at all, since she had thoroughly disapproved of my taking the job in the first place.

But for me a paper round had one overriding advantage. It provided extra money for gramophone records, still virtually the only means at my disposal for hearing jazz at the time. And as a result I now found myself trudging through rain, hail and snow in order to raise the funds for an additional six or seven minutes of the music which had captured my life. There was one other by-product of my employment. A paper round was a good opportunity to whistle.

I had already started thinking like a jazz performer rather than a jazz fan, even though I was still the latter rather than the former. Jazz tunes were already presenting themselves to me as opportunities for improvisation. As I still had no instrument to improvise on, the answer was – whistling! I whistled my way round the streets – softly to myself, of course, since the town was still sleeping – and imagined myself as one of my new-found idols. Benny Goodman, Bix Beiderbecke and Johnny Hodges all unknowingly helped me get through my task on those dark mornings in the war-torn city.

Despite my income from the noble task of paper delivery the exchequer still didn't run to an instrument. I had, during my stay in Leominster, acquired a penny-whistle and managed to get some sounds vaguely like jazz out of it. But by now I was becoming ever keener to get myself something more acceptable in jazz circles. My mother's antennae seemed to pick this up, and within weeks her Townswomen's Guild bush telegraph had located a clarinet, for sale by the friend of a friend. This was a breakthrough indeed, and we lost no time in making a pilgrimage to view the merchandise.

The history of this particular instrument was vague, and since neither Mother nor I knew the first thing about clarinets we relied heavily on the vendor, who knew precious little about them either. The only thing about it that we knew was exactly right for us was the price. It was to cost just 35 shillings – in today's parlance just under two pounds (or five dollars)! We didn't bother to bargain – in those circles it was hardly the right thing to do anyway.

The instrument was brought home in triumph, viewed with circumspection by my father, and at the insistence of my mother, passed over the garden fence for a close inspection by our neighbour Mrs Turner. 'Ooh, it's a really nice one!' she cooed, fingering the instrument nervously. 'Is it a trombone?' she added. She must have found it hard to know exactly what to say.

Next day, with the help of a friend, I found a local musician and persuaded him to pop round and view my treasure. He eyed it with the air of an expert. 'Very nice. And what sort of lamp did you say it was going to be?'

'Lamp? What do you mean?'

'Oh, I thought you were going to make it into the base for a reading-lamp – you know, run the wire up through the middle with a bulb and a shade on top. People often do that with these old things. They look very classy, too.'

I told him that my needs for it were musical and not electrical. With eyes glazed from the sheer boredom being inflicted on him by this clarinet ignoramus, he patiently enlightened me. Not only was the system of key layout an obsolete one, but the pitch of the instrument would not be compatible with anything else in any band – or even with our beloved domestic piano! I thanked him warmly for this blissfully welcome bit of enlightenment and retired hurt.

Before he departed, leaving this endless trail of bad news, the man had nevertheless (out of pity I suppose) got the instrument into a state of playability, with a reed in place on the mouthpiece, ready to blow. The thing still looked wonderful to my eyes – just like Benny Goodman's. Too bad it had turned out to be a sort of woodwind leper, from a practical point of view.

Not to be completely defeated I got out the tutor book which I'd bought for this very moment. I placed my fingers gingerly over the holes as instructed, wrapped my hands round the beautiful African blackwood body, drew the slender instrument to my lips, and breathed gently into the mouthpiece. Nothing.

I tried blowing a little harder. Still nothing.

I unlearned the advice of the manual and reverted to brute force. A stark, searing squawk escaped from the reluctant instrument, provoking a chorus of barking from the neighbours' dogs and rattling the crystal glassware on the sideboard.

Frustrated, depressed and angry, I was about to hurl the thing across the room when somehow I managed to persuade myself to have one more try. I forgot all the book's advice, and blew. This time a sound emerged, a luscious low murmur in the chalumeau register. Within seconds I was finding the other three notes needed to satisfy my immediate desires. Ten minutes later I was beside the Columbia wind-up portable fulfilling my dream.

My career had begun at the top: I was playing *Tea for Two* with the Benny Goodman Quartet, and from that moment on I was unstoppable by the proverbial wild horses – or anything else – in my intention to become a jazz musician.

2

Beginning to see the light

But what exactly was it that jazz possessed, of all the types of music available to me, that captured my musical heart?

Quite recently I found myself in front of a television set with no particular plan in mind as to what to watch – a dangerous time-waster indeed. I channel-flipped until I came across a special performance by the folk group Peter, Paul and Mary. It was a kind of reunion, a retrospective look. Present in the audience – and frequently participating – were other folk performers: Tom Paxton, Odette, John Sebastian and others were popping onto the platform and joining the main artistes, or sometimes staying where they were and joining in the choruses.

As I watched and listened, two things became apparent to me. One was that the camaraderie between them was similar to that in the world of jazz – the easy-going and modest way of displaying their considerable skills, the sharing of repertoire, the mutual respect among talented performers, the ability to merge into each other's routines with minimal difficulty – it all mirrored very closely the working style of the jazz fraternity. I felt that if I had been invited to step through the TV screen and join them all on the podium it would have presented no problem for either them or me.

So I began to ask myself, why did I choose to join the jazz world and not the Peters, Pauls and Marys of my day? The answer lies in the second conclusion I reached that night. What I was listening to consisted of music and words skilfully fashioned into social comment, and often social protest. But often – indeed almost always – the message and the words overshadowed and indeed outshone the music. While the verbal content was subtle and rich with argument, innuendo and satire, the musical content was virtually bereft of any new departures or specific points of interest. This is not a criticism – far from it, since the music was almost always just the right type of enhancement for the message. But it made it obvious that folk music attracts devotees whose priorities lean towards the words, and particularly the message, rather than the music, and thus it holds less interest for the especially gifted musician.

Jazz started on a similar course, with the early protest blues – whose words carried perhaps an even more poignant story than did the folk singers of the fifties and sixties. Stories of toil, sweat and injustice, stories of discrimination and hopelessness, stories of floods, natural disasters and lynchings. But as jazz developed its musical structure, through some alchemy of fate about which we will theorise forever and never quite be able to explain, it became beguilingly attractive to musicians and composers of special ability – a sort of school for exceptionally talented students if you like. And as its sophistication increased, the meaning of lyrics – and indeed the lyrics themselves – dropped further down the list of priorities in a musical scene ever more concerned with the instrumental side of things.

The result has been that, ever since the midthirties – and perhaps before – jazz music has tended to attract the cream of musical talent available in the geographical areas in which it has gained a foothold. This is true even today. The standard of ability present in the best jazz performers – the musical IQ if you wish, but really much more than that – far surpasses that of their counterparts in any other area of musical expression. This is vividly demonstrated by the way in which jazz musicians are avidly incorporated into rock, pop, folk, country and similar groups, and by the way in which classical composers from Debussy onwards, lacking the ability to involve actual jazz performers, have striven (sometimes with limited success) to reflect or sometimes incorporate the subtleties of jazz in their own work.

So, in short, if you are musically bright and happen to get yourself exposed to jazz in your formative years, the chances are that you'll land up a jazz musician. And I suppose, with only a half-hearted attempt at modesty, I can confess that I was considered musically bright at the tender age of sixteen and a bit. I suspect that the judgement came solely from my family and close relatives, since I had never at the time publicly demonstrated any musical prowess. Nevertheless, I think it is something you are aware of within yourself if you are lucky enough to be equipped with above-average ability; this in turn gives you more confidence to pursue your goals with a single-mindedness that others find hard to understand.

And pursue my goals is what I did – with a vengeance. I bought music and tuition books for my clarinet. I continued to keep in touch with the latest in jazz via the radio, records and specialist magazines. I practised the clarinet daily, and often all day. Within a week or so the word had somehow got around the Sir George Monoux Grammar School that Dankworth was playing the clarinet. I had not taken music as a subject – wartime movement between various places had somehow contrived to preclude that – but my musical skills were well known in the school, and indeed I often assisted the music students with any homework that they found difficult. And so it was not long before I received a request from the leader of the unofficial school dance band to attend an informal jam session. The prospect of playing with other musicians meant a change of instrument and I managed to buy (with a combination of paper-round wages, pocket money and parental benevolence) my first really usable clarinet. On reflection I realise that it was in fact an audition, to ascertain my suitability to join them on a regular basis, but it all must have been rather premature – because I accepted their invitation, and didn't hear from them again.

Undeterred, I formed my own band, the first of several small groups for which I managed to get occasional jobs. The first one to achieve any sort of cohesion, or indeed any success for that matter, was a quintet. I have forgotten how I came across these fellow aspirants for jazz immortality: Jack Davenport, Ken Moule, Cliff Dunn and Peter Huggett. Somehow the bush telegraph of suburbia puts like-minded souls in touch with each other.

Jack was about my age, the son of a local drummer who played with a quartet at the Majestic Ballroom in Woodford, a few miles from my home. Once we got to know each other he would take me to the Majestic, where I would be allowed to sit in with the band on quiet nights – a great source of experience for me. Later, when we got started with my own group, Jack acquired a discarded milk-float – the kind you pushed – to transport his drum kit, and we would think nothing of propelling this strange vehicle three or four miles through the blacked-out streets of east London in the early hours of the morning after a gig.

Jack was at that time somewhat slow at reading music but later went to the Royal Academy of Music to correct this shortcoming. By contrast, pianist Ken Moule was a good sight-reader and indeed an accomplished musician for his age. Early childhood illness, which he barely survived, left him with a cadaverous look which went well with his ridiculous sense of humour. He was tall and bony, with a long face which switched easily from intransigence into a twinkling grin, and with arm movements so comic that they would have been perfect companion pieces to – and just as side-splitting as – the silly walks of John Cleese. The Moule delivery of words was also quite distinctive: a lugubrious drone with long, semi-nasal vowel sounds, which were further exaggerated when he assumed character parts.

Ken had another, more serious side, which constantly found itself at loggerheads with much of the world outside. Indeed later in his career he was frequently to come to verbal blows with those working with him. He seemed (as I suppose do so many of us) unable to call on his highly developed knack of laughing at life to get him through any current problem, which he inevitably took very seriously. Yet after such incidents, recounting his altercations with this misguided BBC producer or that excitable TV choreographer, his sense of humour returned and he would have us convulsed with mirth. That was apparently enough to mollify the outrage that still lingered in him.

I met Ken when I heard him playing at the Rhythm Club (as jazz appreciation societies were then known in Britain) in Woodford, and our mutual musical needs brought us together in what was to become a lifelong friendship. His confident piano style proved a sheet-anchor for our little group, and his ability to arrange music – later to become a great asset in his career in the days of BBC resident orchestras – was a great help. Ken and I found out early in our relationship our common tendency to compose alternative lyrics to well-known tunes.

One night, during one of our frequent late foregatherings at one of our homes (usually mine) where we sipped cocoa and listened to jazz records, I burst into song to the tune of the then well-known ballad *I love the moon*, whose lyric predictably ended with the line 'I love you – I love you'. My somewhat less romantic version went:

> I love balloons, I love cream buns
> I love Jamaica and ferret-runs
> I love red lamp-posts
> Frog-spawn and pancakes
> But best of all
> I love snakes
> Big green snakes.

As my last note died over the kitchen table, so Ken's first note took over and blended in, like a medley of hits. He droned in his doleful voice, to the tune of *I'm in the mood for love*, something close to:

> I'm in the mood for whales
> Give me a piece of blubber
> I want it for my supper
> I'm in the mood for whales.
>
> Can't sleep for dreaming of them
> Black bodies floating past me
> Plenty of rubber dinghies
> I'm in the mood for whales.

(Then there was a bridge section which I can't recall but included the line: 'They keep on shouting "Grandma"', – then:)

> I'm in the mood for whales
> (But) can't seem to find one nowhere
> But there are sharks, so – do I care?
> I'm in the mood for sharks.

Later we were to hone our skills, improving on these first puerile efforts and producing better – if more surreal – creations. The catalyst for our latest improved versions was seated at that very kitchen table that night. His name was Cliff Dunn.

Cliff lived, like Ken, in nearby Chingford with his mother, a vivacious lady named Doddie, and was the only child in a single-parent household. He showed all the signs of emergent talent on his instrument, and was one of the few guitarists at that time to be in possession of an amplifier, amazing though that may seem today. Cliff also had a ready sense of quirky humour, but rather more surreal in nature than Ken's.

The quintet was usually completed by bassist Peter Huggett. Peter lived with his parents in a semi-detached suburban-style villa in an acacia-lined avenue a little nearer to the centre of London's sprawl than the rest of us, and his front parlour was always available as an alternative rehearsal room – a not uncourageous act on the part of his mother, who was only too aware of the din (by the standards of those days) we were capable of creating. Peter was the one among us with the gift of the gab, and was well equipped to take over the job of haggling with prospective clients. And so my group was complete, with all the requirements of a small dance band of the day. Except engagements.

The king of the suppliers of dance bands for casual engagements in the east London area at that time was Will de Barr. I had seen the name 'Will de Barr and his Band' emblazoned on poster after poster announcing this or that dance in this or that church hall or such and such a municipal baths. He was obviously the man to woo. And I had seen his name every day, cycling home from school, outside a tiny social club near Wadham bridge, a short hop from my home, which advertised a regular Friday night dance featuring the Will de Barr Band. I decided to target him the following Friday. I would go there and sit in, like they did in the films I had been seeing, and in the books and articles I had read. That was the way to do it.

I planned my assault with the precision of a military commander: 'It starts at 7.30, right? OK, at 7.22 I'll arrive, introduce myself to Will and ask if I can sit in, and once he hears me he'll offer me dozens of gigs – couldn't be simpler.'

*　　*　　*

It is Friday night. I get out my bike, make sure front and rear lamps are both working, and pedal off to the dance hall. Not much sign of life, but a few chinks of light through the blackout curtains. I padlock the bike and enter the hall. It is drab, dusty and as yet deserted, except that at the far end a small band seems to be in the process of setting up. A pianist is tinkling, a drummer assembling his kit and a bass player taking the canvas cover off his instrument. I approach the pianist, clutching my clarinet nervously. 'Are you Mr de Barr?'

'Not guilty, sonny. Will doesn't come to this gig – just puts the band in. What d' you want him for, anyway?' He began to look suspicious.

'Thought I might sit in', I venture casually.

His hitherto helpful attitude now changed completely. 'Will doesn't like people sittin' in.' But something in him took pity on this obviously nervous youth, clutching an instrument case as if his life depended on it. 'But – er, what d' you play, son?'

'Clarinet.'

'Well, Dave the tenor player is leader tonight, and he's late – motorbike broke down. We'll let you play a number before he gets here.'

He must have seen my eyes light up. I ripped open my clarinet case, and within two minutes we were into *I got rhythm* at quickstep tempo. During its progress Dave the Sax strode up the centre of the dance floor. There were still no customers. He manoeuvred himself onto the stage, peeled off an enormous leather coat, opened a case with his motorbike-begreased hands and produced a couple of saxophones and a clarinet together with a metal-framed contraption on which to stand them all, then proceeded to join in.

It soon became obvious that I had passed my audition, as not another word was said about the 'no sitters-in' policy of the Will de Barr regime. I shared the rest of the evening happily with those seasoned gigsters, as well as with the intrigued patrons now thronging the dance floor and eyeing my youthful appearance with some amusement, until we brought things to a close with *God Save the King*.

Next morning my mum woke me up excitedly, earlier than usual. 'Quick, Will de Barr's on the phone.' Her voice insinuated that it might as well have been Winston Churchill. I leapt down the stairs three at a time instead of my usual two. The great voice echoed down the line into my ears. I could hardly believe what I heard. 'I hear we've got a budding Benny Goodman living in Highams Park.'

'Oh, thanks, Mr de Barr, but I'm not really that good.'

'Good enough to do the gig for money next Friday – if you're free?' I made a pathetic attempt to shuffle the pages of my diary near the mouthpiece of the phone to make him think I was really checking, but I don't think I fooled him.

I did the gig at the Roberts Social Club the following Friday. For money. At the end of the evening, from the hand of Dave the sax, I received, predictably begrimed with motor-cycle grease, a ten-shilling note.

*   *   *

Meanwhile the quintet continued to exist, even – in our terms – to thrive. Apart from local gigs we had somehow managed to land a three-nights-a-week gig at a tiny watering-hole called the Mozart Club in Stoke Newington, an inner London suburb several miles up the commuter line. It presented a transport problem – it was much too far to wheel a milk-float – but it was far too important a career step to turn down. It meant a twenty-minute train ride, and then a journey on foot of about a mile to and from Hackney Downs station, carrying everything we needed in the way of instruments from drums downwards – every Thursday, Friday and Saturday. No wonder my schoolwork started to suffer.

Things were developing fast at the Mozart Club too. We had scored a hit there, and the word spread quickly around the neighbourhood. Not far away lived a family which boasted three sisters, whose close-harmony singing had already begun to attract local attention. Their family name was Chinnery, but they called themselves the Beverley Sisters. The twin girls, Teddy and Babs, had an elder sister, Joy, as a sort of spiritual leader, and they somehow got invited (or invited themselves – I fail to remember) to appear at the Mozart Club. Naturally our quintet was asked to accompany them, since none of the girls played anything and there was no one else to provide a backing. It seemed to be at that time a constraining factor on their career.

It was also just up our street: Ken's sure-footed reading and accompanying together with my fast-developing arranging skills filled the bill perfectly. So well, in fact, that the girls asked us to appear with them at Stage Door Canteen in Piccadilly, where they had been booked to perform in a show for the American forces, thousands of whom were either stationed or on leave in London in those days. It was heady stuff for us lads, a sort of catapulting to stardom (or so it seemed) that we had hardly dared dream of. We did that show with the Bevs, and if I remember rightly a couple of others, before their career inevitably took off and our ways parted.

But the connection made with the US forces entertainment machine led us to other things, including a regular gig at Rainbow Corner – a booking in our own right and on our own merits. And so our local commuter train (drawn in those days by an old and grimy steam tank engine) now started to puff and heave us not just a few stops to Hackney Downs, but right to the end of the line – the London terminus at Liverpool Street.

Those were exciting times, which I still think of with practically undivided pleasure, and it is indeed hard even to remember that London was at war. Though for many it must have been a worrying period – for the soldiers whom we entertained, who were enjoying short respites from risking their lives, for their families back in the States, and indeed for the millions of Londoners who went to bed every night in fear of their lives – for us teenage would-be stars it was joy undiluted.

We played requests for nostalgic GIs, one of them a version I had concocted of Artie Shaw's *Concerto for Clarinet*, a jazz piece with a bravura introduction, a boogie-woogie main section and a cadenza-style coda ending on an altissimo C, an extremely high note which I, a clarinet player with months rather than years of experience behind me, was singularly ill-equipped to pull off. I did it by a lightning change of reed during a few bars' rest near the climax, which made the elusive note attainable for me. Deservedly or otherwise, it managed to bring the place down on most of the occasions I played it. And, moreover, I seemed in my innocence able to handle the unexpected with calmness and efficiency. On one occasion the child star Petula Clark popped in to entertain the GIs and required accompanying. We did the job as effectively as seasoned pros, and earned the plaudits of all concerned.

* * *

Meanwhile, back in Walthamstow, Will de Barr, concerned that many of his gigs demanded a saxophone player who doubled on clarinet rather than a clarinet player who didn't double on anything, had offered to lend me a saxophone on which to learn to increase my versatility. I jumped at the offer. The only reason I had not already taken this step was a lack of the necessary finances.

I found my way to Will's house near the Crooked Billet in Walthamstow, and as I approached met a rather shady-looking character coming out of the front door. Those were the days of the black market, and dance-band leaders, or at least some of them, did not allow themselves to be left out of that side of commerce.

'Wanna buy a pair of hot scissors?' was my greeting as I entered the dark front hallway of the terraced Edwardian house. I responded with nothing more than a grin, but I think the question was a test rather than a genuine enquiry. Will knew, and I found out, that – with the acquisition of that saxophone and my consequent full-blooded entry to the business of wartime gigging – I was entering a somewhat shadowy and illegal world. We would sometimes drive to gigs in an unlicensed car running on illicit petrol, and containing in the back seat a musician with dyed hair and a bushy moustache who, it was whispered, was an army deserter. We would meet in dark side streets to avoid attracting attention, and take circuitous routes to our destinations rather than risk encountering a checkpoint on a main road.

It all made gigging with dance bands seem to me an unexpectedly risky business. But there was no other way to learn and progress. After all, it seemed pretty small beer compared with the exploits of jazz bands in Chicago during Prohibition that I'd read about, who dodged machine-gun bullets as they played for the likes of the Al Capone gang.

* * *

By contrast, the lifestyle of the Dankworth quintet was about as innocuous as anyone could possibly imagine. None of us drank alcohol seriously, and the word 'drugs' meant pharmaceutical preparations as far as we were concerned. Any money earned was religiously divided equally between the five of us. Girls, or sex for that matter, played little or no part in our world at that time. We lived only for laughs and the music, for our playing, our listening and our learning.

Our evenings were nearly all spent with music in some shape or form. One of my personal favourite haunts was the Feldman Swing Club (later called the 100 Club) in Oxford Street, and it was in this simple basement that I kept in touch with what was happening in the London jazz world. The partially sighted drummer Carlo Krahmer was a sort of musical and artistic director. He also ran (and played in) the jam sessions there, in which most of the prominent players of the time, many of them in uniform, appeared periodically – among them trumpet player Kenny Baker, drummer Jack Parnell, pianists Ralph Sharon, George Shearing and Dick Katz, and saxists Aubrey Frank and Jimmy Skidmore. It was also occasionally the scene of a visit by American musicians. On one memorable night a group from the Glenn Miller Band treated us to an hour or so of wonderful music, and I was able to savour the delights of pianist Mel Powell, clarinettist Peanuts Hucko and drummer Ray McKinley. It was an experience that made a deep impression on me, and it became my ambition to play at the Feldman Club one day – hopefully with a spellbound audience hanging on my every note, as they were for those Americans that night.

One evening around that time an unfamiliar face appeared on the stand. A young Scottish tenor sax player, who had reached London playing with some touring band or other, had asked Carlo if he could sit in. Carlo, whose ears were ever open for a new talent on the scene, assented, and the young man started to play. It was wonderful: I was transported by the unique way he was able to marry force with finesse and produce such effective results. I was in fact listening to Tommy Whittle at the very beginning of his brilliant career, and I made a mental note to utilise his talents if ever I was in a position to do so – although that last thought seemed most emphatically theoretical rather than realistic at the time. 'The audacity of it', I said to myself. 'You're thinking about giving other people work when you can barely get enough of your own!'

But often events in life don't proceed in the expected order. The next morning I heard my mother pick up the phone. Moments later she called up the stairs. 'John – it's for you . . . Will de Barr.' She had shed most of the reverence in her voice that had been present the first time Will had phoned. His frequent requests for my services seemed to my parents to be undermining my schoolwork, and they feared the worst: that this musical interest which had started as a sort of hobby – and as such had received their support, or at least acquiescence – was now turning into a monster which would ruin their son's chances of a regular wage-earning, pension-producing occupation.

I picked up the phone. 'Hello, Will. What can I do for you?'

'Would you like to do a couple of weeks at the Paramount in Tottenham Court Road with your little band? The relief group there has got a couple of weeks' leave, and they need someone to fill in.'

It all seemed like a script for a movie. But the realist part of my mind raced through the pros and cons of such an enormous step into the professional world – while I was still at school. Heaven knows, the V1 buzz bombs had just begun to rain on London, and whatever time we older boys didn't spend on the school roof to watch out for the missiles was spent in the air-raid shelters doing no work at all. True, the Paramount was in central London where all the darned things were being aimed, but the ballroom itself was below ground level, with several storeys of apartments above it – certainly as safe to my mind as the school shelters. I wouldn't be missing a thing academically; in fact, I was pretty sure they wouldn't miss me.

'Just one thing', added Will. 'You'll need to make it a sextet. Another sax player would do nicely.'

'We'll do it', I heard myself say. Ten minutes later I had extracted Tommy Whittle's phone number from the Feldman Club office. To my astonishment he was free and willing to do the gig, and in another thirty seconds I had booked him.

The die was cast, and the patrons of a major London ballroom were going to get a taste of our kind of music – whether they liked us or not.

3

Spread a little happiness

It all seemed so impossible, yet there was no denying it was real. I had spent evening after evening rewriting all the quintet's arrangements to include Tommy Whittle's tenor sax. We had rehearsed all the new stuff time and again until we felt confident that we would have enough suitable material. Since my very first efforts on the family piano at the age of about five I had experimented with writing music down, and later with arranging it and indeed composing pieces for the quintet. Now my experiences were proving to be very useful in fleshing out the band's repertoire.

And so I found myself standing in front of my five faithful cohorts in the artificial semi-darkness (it was mid-afternoon outside) of this sweetly odorised Mecca ballroom in the heart of the besieged capital, watching the male dancers (many of them in uniform) propelling their partners around the French-chalked dance floor while we provided them with – a plaintive slow fox-trot. The multicoloured follow-spots swirled, the crystal ball cast its countless pinpoint reflections indiscriminately upon humans and inanimates alike – and all was right with the world.

Our sessions soon had a routine feel about them – as did our daily journeys to and from the suburbs on the old commuter steam-train, and on the connecting underground trip from Liverpool Street to

Tottenham Court Road. To a group of high-spirited teenagers such as us it could all easily have become boring. But in fact nothing approaching boredom ever set in – thanks to our guitarist Cliff Dunn. In the cause of amusement Cliff would commit acts that were totally beyond the pale for the rest of us.

Every night Cliff, with his deadpan look, would enliven the return journey to Chingford with something extraordinary. Perhaps for the entire journey, in a carriage shared by other passengers, he would read a newspaper upside down, and then proceed to eat the middle page. Or wear his jacket inside out, continually brushing and preening himself, the while with the air of a dandy. Or mumble to himself in a bogus foreign tongue, occasionally bursting into folk-like ditties in that same language.

As the two weeks progressed he got more outrageous. One night he wore a fez and a bath gown and carried a lighted candle, declaiming nonsense from a large, ancient leather-bound tome. The rest of us as usual pretended we had nothing to do with Cliff – until Jack Davenport nonchalantly went up to him and lit his cigarette from the candle.

Soon we all caught the disease. Who first thought of it I can't remember, but once we dreamt up a campaign called 'Bones for the Austrians'. We would stand on street corners carrying placards and solicit passers-by for the spare bones from their meagre meat rations. We even had leaflets printed to hand to those who stopped, wondering what on earth it was all about. 'What do we want to give them our bones for? They're on the other side', said one indignant woman.

'Ain't yer got no compassion, mum?' I countered.

'How would they get them there?' asked another inquisitive old girl, anxious to help yet rather mystified by it all.

'Specially converted Wellington bombers, lady', said Ken, with the air of an expert. 'Drops yer bones over Vienna and Salzburg every Tuesday afternoon, reg'lar as clockwork.' The old dear sounded satisfied, and went away mumbling a promise to bring some bones along next day.

On another memorable occasion we were approached to play on a regular basis at a small club in Walthamstow. The money and conditions were good, but somehow during the audition, which was on the way to clinching the deal, we all simultaneously began to realise that it was not the sort of gig that we would enjoy, or even want to do at all. So we began to play badly to cause the club owner – whom none of us had taken to – to change his mind. However, our ruse didn't work – we had obviously been too subtle. The man was delighted with what he had heard. 'So it's all settled then – you can start next Monday?'

I was lost for words, but Ken was not. 'John, have you told Mr Gross about *Armadillos?*' Before I could reply he went on. 'You see, sir, by tradition we always open each show with *Armadillos* – it's a kind of cabaret turn. We'll just run it for you – ready, Cliff?'

Cliff needed no further cue – this was right up his street. Without a second's hesitation he launched himself onto his stomach and slithered to the centre of the tiny club dance floor. Ken played some atonal arpeggios at the bottom of the piano, while I produced a series of ear-splitting screeches in the clarinet's least pleasant register. Add a few gong crashes from Jack and some sinuous scrapes from Peter's bowed bass, and the sum total was pretty obnoxious by any standards.

But the club owner's eyes were on Cliffy. He was lying on his side and simultaneously performing a kind of horizontal convulsive cake-walk around the floor. I have never seen an armadillo under stress, but I have always pictured a rather mild-mannered animal. In contrast Cliff was baring his teeth, foaming at the mouth and snarling in a most disconcerting way, and from time to time emitting a banshee-style wail. It all went on for an unpleasantly long time.

After the conclusion of *Armadillos* we packed our instruments and said our good-byes. Mr Gross promised to phone me over the weekend. We never heard from him again.

* * *

The season at the Paramount Ballroom did not catapult us to stardom – in fact it seemed to have precious little impact either on the great metropolis or on us. Tommy Whittle left for other pursuits and the rest of us resumed our casual gigs, both as a quintet and as individuals.

On the other hand, my absence from school – and from my home every evening – did indeed have an impact, one which was to affect

my future. My parents were extremely worried that their son, hitherto bright as a button at school, was now frittering his life away in
dance halls and pubs, while his school reports were getting pro-
gressively worse. It was surely time to put a stop to this nonsense and
get the boy back on course – a course which to them meant security,
success and happiness.

The headmaster was called into the picture. My father had phoned
him and complained about my lack of progress academically, and I
was consequently summoned to the head's study for interrogation
and a dressing-down. The proceedings of the meeting were summed
up by the headmaster at the time in a memo which was discovered
over forty years later, and it succinctly relates the happenings from
one point of view:

Sir George Monoux Grammar School, Walthamstow

DANKWORTH   John Philip William   Age 16
                Date of admission   13.9.1938
Came from Leyton Centre September '43 into VI form (Matric)
Intending teacher
Plays clarinet (self-taught)
Feb '44 Father rang up. Worried about boy – little interest in work,
and intends to take up a job and do dance-band work in evenings.
Father (an educated man) dislikes the idea.
Interviewed boy and talked it over at length, but without much
obvious success. Boy had genuine (if perverted) interest in 'swing'
music. Already, to my horror, plays for dance bands in ('high-class')
pubs one or two nights a week, from 7 till 11. Pointed out that this
was not reconcilable with VI form work.
Later had telephone conversation with father; decided to let it hold
for a bit.

Sept '44 Left to take a course at the Royal Academy of Music.

The last sentence was appended some time later, and recorded the
outcome of a showdown with my parents when it became apparent
that my meeting with the head had not had the effect they desired.

I explained to Mum and Dad that I had made up my mind: I wanted to be a jazz musician. I pointed out to my classically trained mother that this did not mean that I would never play classical music. Benny Goodman was the living, breathing proof of that. I did, however, want to devote all my available time to music, and not to the other subjects which were then part of my curriculum.

My parents were stunned. But they were intelligent enough to take me seriously – they could see that I would not be deterred. 'Well, if you must play this type of music, you should certainly go somewhere to learn your instrument properly', said my mother. 'We'd better see about applying for a place at the Royal Academy'.

The argument was over. A prospectus was sent for and perused, and in due course I embarked for an audition in the foreboding building near Madame Tussaud's wax museum in the Marylebone Road – the Royal Academy of Music. My sister Avril accompanied me at the piano for a couple of clarinet pieces, and then I played one of my own compositions at the keyboard.

I was accepted to begin studies that autumn. It couldn't have been a difficult decision for the authorities there, since the air-raids were still from time to time plaguing London. Many would-be academicians were away in the armed services, so there must have been more vacancies than applicants for male student places; since I wore long trousers they could not bring themselves to refuse me.

Life at the academy was a completely new world for me. The self-discipline required to work and practise unsupervised meant a whole new outlook on life, quite different from the enforced drudgery of schoolwork. It also paradoxically gave me more free time in central London to meet, talk to and play with other jazz musicians.

My clarinet teacher at the academy was an elderly retired symphony player, who helped me with some groundwork on the instrument but frankly did little to inspire me. My inspiration came from a fellow student named Edward Planas. Ted later became a leading authority on the anatomy of the clarinet, and masterminded several important improvements in the construction and mechanism of the instrument. At that time, however, he was an enthusiastic aspiring symphony clarinettist, and I found myself sitting next to him (as his assistant principal) in the academy's second orchestra, as well as on occasional paid gigs at small orchestral concerts in the home counties. He was my guiding light and my mentor.

The second orchestra was at that time conducted by Ernest Read, whose fame endures as an organiser of children's symphony concerts. The experience of ploughing our way through the classical repertoire was invaluable to me – participating in the thrilling sound of a symphony orchestra in full cry was the part of my studies that I enjoyed the most.

One day at rehearsal, the suite *L'Arlésienne* by Georges Bizet appeared in our folders. Flicking through the pages, I noticed that at one point my part had a cue on it marked 'alto sax'. I wondered what would happen when we got to that cue. By now I owned an alto sax, but rarely had the courage to bring it within a mile of the academy. When I did, and students enquired about the contents of the longish case, I used to tell them it held a bassoon.

Mr Read started to rehearse the piece. When we got to the sax bit he stopped. 'Does anyone in the woodwind play the . . . er . . . saxophone?' he enquired. I froze. I had never heard the word uttered inside the hallowed walls of the institution until this moment.

'Go on, Danky!' whispered Ted, who knew all my secrets. 'Now's your chance. Tell him.'

I cleared my throat. 'Sir, I'd . . . I'd like to have a go.' I faltered. 'I can borrow a sax.' It would be going too far to admit that I actually possessed one.

'Splendid. Bring it to next week's rehearsal', the conductor replied.

I did, and played the piece in classical clarinet style on the larger and somewhat beefier instrument. I was petrified, but luckily got through it without any mistakes. As the last note of my ordeal died away Mr Read quietly put his baton down and addressed the orchestra in his cultured tones: 'The saxophone is a much-maligned instrument. But this is because it is so often unpleasantly played by dance-band and jazz players, who give it a somewhat undeserved bad name. But you have just heard it used by someone who is quite untainted by such undesirable influences, and in consequence has produced the true beauty of which the saxophone is capable.'

He gently led with soft applause, and the orchestra followed, the string players tapping their bows delicately on their music-stands and beaming at me in appreciation. Mr Read had made me the hero of the rehearsal and I loved him for it. Perhaps I should have invited him to the little jam session in a Windmill Street rehearsal studios I was planning to attend that night. But I'm glad I didn't. Sometimes it's best just to let well alone.

Unfortunately life at the academy had very few memorable moments such as that. My time there was during one of its low points, which was not surprising, since the war must have severely limited its activities and removed many of its most talented personnel. It has become much more alive, broad-minded and forward-looking in more recent years. It now even boasts a jazz course, which I was able to instigate in the early seventies, later to be developed by Graham Collier. But in those days my lessons and classes on clarinet, piano, harmony, musical history and aural training all seemed to lack the ingredient needed to fire me up and cause me to progress. It was almost certainly my fault: I should have been more prepared to adapt to the academic way of thinking, rather than expect it all to work on my terms.

But something came up which did in fact generate some excitement and attracted a little attention. I had played in a pub on a couple of occasions with an accomplished and naturally gifted trumpet player, Freddie Randall. Freddie led his own group, but also worked for a bandleader named Freddie Mirfield, who led a band known as the Garbage Men. Randall had informed Mirfield of my abilities, and I was recruited into the band just in time to compete with them in the National Dance Band Championships organised by the music journal *Melody Maker*. After a couple of successes in the eliminatory heats we found ourselves in the grand final at Belle Vue in Manchester. We were eventually placed second as a band. This was a disappointment, since we had hoped to win, but the press reported that ' consider able credit goes to the youthful clarinet player, who thought out an original solo for himself instead of using the conventional one of Barney Bigard's, and played it with a taste and technique that would have been a credit to a professional instrumentalist'.

As a result of that performance, I received at Belle Vue the individual award for best clarinettist. It was a useful way of creating a bit of public limelight for me. And the press coverage, in the main popular music paper of the day, meant that it didn't go unnoticed in the profession of which I was about to become a part.

After that moment of triumph life went on at the academy, where an increasingly busy schedule meant that I had to leave the Garbage Men who, basking in the glory of their *Melody Maker* successes, turned professional. But one morning almost a year later I picked up the ever-ringing phone at home and recognised the voice immediately – Freddie Mirfield.

'Why, hello, Freddie. How's life on the road?' I enquired cheerily.

'Well, that's just it – we're off the road for a bit. We've got a week playing variety, at Clapham Grand.' He referred to an ageing London theatre which was a 'number three' house on the variety circuit, one of those places whose top of the bill was often a relatively little-known act such as the Garbage Men. 'And we need a clarinet player. Two shows a night, Monday to Saturday. Twenty quid for the week.'

This sort of mouth-watering financial bait had the desired effect on me, and I duly found my way to Clapham. What I didn't know was that the Garbage Men, in order to earn a living, had changed status, from a Dixieland jazz band into a comedy team aimed at the same market as bands such as Spike Jones and his City Slickers or, in Britain, Sid Millward and the Nitwits. No soulful, poetic solo on *Mood Indigo* for me this time. The clarinet player was required for a very different role.

The featured music was the overture *Poet and Peasant*. My job was to play a very obvious goof, an extra couple of solo notes when the rest of the band had stopped. My punishment: a prop violin smashed over my head. The whole phrase was then repeated, and again I goofed. This time a guitar came crashing round my ears. We enacted this identical routine twice each night. A harassed Mirfield, poor man, spent the entire time between shows repairing the shattered instruments in preparation for their second decimation, although a shred of sympathy should also perhaps be saved for the youthful clarinettist, who, despite a padded wig, saw more than a few stars on a couple of occasions. Sad to say, my Academy course did not include instruction on injury avoidance when assailed by a musical instrument. I have since suggested that this serious omission be corrected for the well-being of future students.

One afternoon during this edifying week I happened to be travelling on a bus near my alma mater, the Monoux Grammar School, when who should board that very vehicle but that institution's head of music, Mr Bellchambers. My main recollection of this gentleman was his choice of a song entitled *My mother bids me bind my hair (in bands of rosy hue)* as a suitable piece to be taught to a class of pubescent schoolboys. The fellow also tended to be an incorrigible musical snob, and frowned on almost any other music than the strictly classical. However, he had heard of my move to the Royal Academy, and was thus able to greet me with a smile. 'Well, Dankworth, how are you enjoying your serious musical work at the academy? Making good progress, I hope.'

'Getting on reasonably well up to now, thank you, sir', I replied.

'And who are you working with?' his enquiry continued.

I realised afterwards that he was referring to the identities of my professors. But too late I found myself blurting out automatically, 'Well, just this week I'm working at Clapham Grand with Freddie Mirfield's Garbage Men.' I followed this statement quickly with a correction, but the damage was done. I saw his face assume a look of pain and contempt – there was after all no hope whatsoever for this young moron. We parted company at the bus stop near the Crooked Billet and never met again.

*　　*　　*

My life, which used to centre around the eastern suburbs, was now finding its focal point in the centre of London, where jazz flourished and jazz musicians met. The main meeting place for professional musicians was Archer Street, a backwater behind two theatres off Shaftesbury Avenue, just a stone's throw from Piccadilly Circus. Archer Street was a kind of open-air labour exchange where bandleaders booked musicians in the days before the telephone became a household commodity in Britain. Monday was the special day there, but if you needed a drummer or a sax player in a hurry to replace Charlie Farnsbarn who had just gone down with the flu or Joe Bloggs who broke his ankle last night, you were more likely to find a replacement in Archer Street – or a cafe nearby – than in any other part of the city.

It was there that I met, directly or indirectly, such contemporaries who, like me, were in love with jazz and determined to make a livelihood out of it. There was Ronnie Scott, the son of a well-known sax player, who himself played the tenor sax with great promise – as indeed did Don Rendell, who was later to become a close friend, and Leon Calvert, whose fluent trumpet playing attracted my attention. Pianist Tommy Pollard, drummers Laurie Morgan, Cecil 'Flash' Winstone and Tony Crombie, bassist Lennie Bush and trombonist Ed Harvey were all typical of the youngsters who went to the 'street' in search of work and communion with fellow musicians. Of course there were plenty of the lower echelons of the dance-band profession there too – some fine musicians, others who found it hard to get work because of their limited abilities. It soon became easy to spot the bandleaders from which the best offers of interesting work were liable to come.

Archer Street sometimes seemed to be mainly a social centre, but no young musician could afford not to show his face there from time to time.

One shadow constantly threatened to appear on the horizon and interfere with young musicians' careers in those days: conscription into the armed forces. My student status meant that my national service would be deferred until my course was finished. In my final term I was examined for my performer's diploma (Licentiate of the Royal Academy of Music) under the eye of one of my heroes, the famous clarinettist Reginald Kell, and I was naturally delighted when I opened the letter which informed me that I had passed. 'Johnny Dankworth, LRAM' looked good on my new business cards.

But of course the bad news was that I was now eligible for call-up. In the summer of 1946 I reported to Maidstone Barracks in Kent. The first six weeks consisted of basic training – marching and drilling, firing rifles and machine-guns, sticking bayonets into sacks of hay and so on – as well as being required to polish boots until they glistened, for no creative reason at all.

Then we were moved to various units. Since my interview about my future in the army bore so little fruit (my lack of interest in things military must have shone through like a beacon) I was dispatched to join a Royal Army Service Corps wing just outside the little market town of Cirencester in Gloucestershire. The posting seemed to indicate that I had been judged as lacking in any outstanding brain-power, so I was certainly not expecting much musical or intellectual stimulus there. But to my surprise I found that the unit boasted a ten-piece band, unofficial in status but strong in musical quality, who by the rarest of coincidences needed an alto sax player. The band was expected to provide the music for camp dances, but we were paid a fee for each of these – a totally admirable arrangement which sometimes tripled our meagre service pay. Moreover, we sometimes climbed in the back of a bone-shaking army lorry and were wafted off to a neighbouring camp to provide a similar service, and sometimes even to civilian dance halls.

The whole set-up was so agreeable that it hardly seemed like being in His Majesty's forces at all. True, RASC Cirencester was a transit unit, and any of the band could theoretically be posted overseas at any moment. But in fact the camp commander, a captain with a liking for swing music, bent all sorts of rules to ensure that useful band personnel were given 'special duties' so that they would be retained on the base as long as possible.

One of the other sax players was Al Gay, a fine young musician who was later featured prominently in traditional jazz in Britain. Our 'cover' job was the caretaking and well-being of the camp entertainment centre. In case this conjures up a picture of a Las Vegas-like structure festooned with lights and teeming with amusement facilities within, let me assure you that this was in fact a rusty pair of corrugated-iron Nissen huts located in a lonely position in the middle of a field, a long way from the nerve-centre of the camp. Here Al and I lived, far from early-morning wakey-wakey and roll calls, a life of ease and comparative luxury, using the only piece of amusement equipment in the place – a full-sized snooker table – with great regularity and ever-increasing skill. We even used some canary-yellow and royal-blue paint, requisitioned for brightening up the band musicstands in regimental colours, to adorn our bedroom. Three electric fires consumed such large quantities of army electricity – and this during one of the coldest winters on record – that the place often became uncomfortably stuffy.

My state of euphoria was threatened when I saw on the camp

notice board an order requiring S/1900221 Dankworth J. P. W. to report to the headquarters of the RASC band in Aldershot, Surrey, for an audition. My Academy credentials had apparently come through the system and to the notice of the bandmaster, and I obviously seemed a natural candidate for the official corps band, a move I did not contemplate with any enthusiasm whatsoever. Indeed I resolved to do everything in my power to see that it didn't happen.

I arrived for the audition and went into the bandmaster's office. Just as he began to talk to me he was called away to another office for some reason. My file was left open on the desk. One quick glance was enough for me to realise that the man had no information about me at all in that file, and certainly not a word about my LRAM – merely the recommendation that I be auditioned.

The officer returned, and proceeded to ask me to play certain scales. I was playing a not-very-good clarinet he had lent me for the occasion, so it was consequently very easy indeed to sound incompetent, which is exactly what I did. He then brought out a book of studies and opened it at a piece which looked very familiar indeed – it was one of the set-pieces for my diploma examination. So I knew precisely the most likely points at which to falter, and I think I made a grand job of it. The man was clearly embarrassed that someone actually thought that this mediocre player should be considered for his prize band. He had to say something. 'You haven't much sense of rhythm, have you?' was his first – and last – comment on my performance.

'No, sir. It's always been my weak point.'

I was bundled out, put on the next train back to Cirencester and never heard from the bandmaster again. I often wonder whether this bit of malingering was a mistake, since there is a lot to be learned in military music circles, and I may well have lost myself some worthwhile musical experiences. I will never know.

However, my charmed life at Cirencester was not to last. Our sympathetic camp commander was himself posted, and his replacement had little interest in preserving the band – or the entertainment centre for that matter. I soon found myself on a train bound for my new posting, back in Aldershot as it happened. Something somewhere was telling me that perhaps I shouldn't have fluffed that audition, especially as my new posting brought home to me the time-wasting doldrums that I was floundering in as a result of my call-up – for a war that was already over.

*   *   *

My period of army conscription eventually came to an end. I was given eight weeks' demob leave and an outfit of clothing including, I remember, a pork-pie hat. I donned the lot and made for Archer Street at the very first opportunity. The first person I saw was Ronnie Scott. 'Just the bloke we were looking for', said Ronnie. 'I hear you're out of the army. Are you interested in a job on the *Queen Mary?* It sails for New York in July – first time since the war ended – and they're auditioning bands. Not much money in it . . . but then, we'd be able to hear Bird . . .'

4

Transatlantic lullaby

Bird . . . the name sent waves that transported my imagination across that great divide, the Atlantic Ocean, into some imaginary sleazy dive, listening to and hanging on every note emanating from the horn of the great jazz idol of the era. The horn, the alto saxophone – the man, Charlie 'Yardbird' Parker. But to any jazzman it was enough to say just 'Bird'.

Although at this stage of his career Bird was virtually unknown to the general public (a stage which more or less persisted throughout his curtailed life), his arrival in New York from Kansas City a mere two or so years previously had quickly convinced his peers that his abilities were not only prodigious but utterly original. Here was a man with a new perspective on jazz who, in collusion with a tiny group of like minds, was to revolutionise the music over the next two decades. Not unsurprisingly these unique qualities, together with a virtuoso command of the instrument itself, had sent the name 'Bird' resounding through the entire jazz world – and Britain, in the initial stages of its long haul back to postwar normality, was no exception.

However, the first thing to do was to get the job on the *Queen Mary*. And how on earth was a disparate conglomeration of young and dedicated jazz musicians going to be booked, in preference to older and more experienced opposition, for the responsible task of providing music for the world's largest passenger liner? Ronnie Scott, the son of a dance-band musician (and thus probably a bit more street-wise than most of us), became our leader for this project, and it was he who put into words what we all knew in our hearts to be true. 'We'll have to be commercial.'

Every jazz musician knows just what that means. It meant in this case that we'd have to play tuneful, simple music that was easy to dance to although often boring to play, and included popular songs of the day and Broadway show hits, as well as waltzes and novelty dances which were definitely no part whatsoever of the jazz repertoire. So very soon my arranging talents were put to their very first major test, as I rolled out scores for our seven-piece band – tunes of the day such as *Time after Time*, standards such as *Stardust* and waltzes such as *I'll see you again*. Whether it was the arrangements that did the trick, whether it was our individual ability to ape the current dance-band styles, whether it was our youthful innocent air, or whether it was sheer luck we shall never know – but we got the job.

And soon afterwards we found ourselves in the middle of the North Sea getting our sea-legs and rehearsing our arrangements, while our new home from home, the RMS *Queen Mary*, cavorted around the ocean in zigzags and circles like a demented water-beetle on a duck-pond, being put through its final sea trials before proceeding across the Atlantic for the first time since the war with fare-paying passengers. Resplendent in her new refit after five years as a troop-carrier, the *Queen Mary* was the very epitome of sheer unadulterated splendour, and we were conscious and proud of the honour bestowed on us.

*　　*　　*

Our departure from Southampton was watched by thousands of sightseers and a press corps nearly as large. This was big news in those drab times – a return to prewar luxury travel, with its destination the nation now deemed the new world champion of peace, democracy and freedom. A memorable moment indeed.

But it was not as memorable as the event some four days afterwards – our arrival in New York. From the first sighting of the Ambrose lightship – the final landmark (or, I suppose, seamark) before the Hudson river, Pier 92 and Manhattan – things began to simmer. First the pilot boarded the huge ship from a small cutter, then a bevy of journalists, who immediately swarmed everywhere and stole a march on the main body of the press, who were to arrive much later. Then, as we drew nearer and into the Hudson, a chorus of hoots, whoops, water-belching fire hoses and flag displays from the other ships; and from the distant shores groups of waving onlookers, which turned into crowds and then throngs as we approached the Cunard dock. The now augmented press contingent, movie-news teams and radio brigades were already interviewing, flash-snapping and filming the VIPs, stars and celebrities. And as the gigantic vessel – now completely in the control of several bustling little tugs – edged slowly towards the quay, the promenade deck of the liner became as crowded as the quay itself, which had for some hours now been packed solid with our welcoming committee of countless well-wishers and sight-seers.

If this sounds to you a thrilling scene, you can easily imagine what an impact it and the ensuing days had on us youngsters. We had in the space of about four days travelled from a continent still dazed and shattered by an orgy of unprecedented destruction and killing, a continent in dire need of just about everything. Large parts of the city of our birth, London, still lay in ruins, and its population was still desperately short of food, fuel, clothing and other essentials of life.

And here we were, walking down a ship's gangway into a dream world: a land physically untouched by war, with every imaginable kind of creature comfort for the taking; a land jam-packed with seemingly endless quantities of consumer goods, clothes, food and luxuries unheard of (or long unobtainable) in the stricken continent we had just left. While the homeless, stateless millions wandered aimlessly across the European continent, thousands of Americans flocked through the shopping streets and the department stores of their skyscraper cities and bought, bought, bought. Few shortages, and certainly no rationing here – just as much of practically everything as you wanted, provided you had the money.

We rambled through the back streets and the main shopping thoroughfares – Broadway, Fifth Avenue, Times Square – and quickly learned the simple midtown grid-pattern geography. We got out our hard-earned dollars and spent them everywhere, from Macy's, Gimbals' and Abraham & Strauss's to the tiny family-run back-street grocery shops, buying everything from zoot suits to canned butter, the former to flaunt back in Archer Street on our return, the latter to help augment the family larders in our homes. But our main targets were the record stores such as Sam Goody's (later a national multiple but then a solitary store with Mr Goody personally in control), where we browsed for hours, grabbing anything unavailable in Britain which featured our jazz heroes – until the cash ran out.

We were careful to set aside enough dollars to buy an occasional thirst quencher at a soda-fountain or drugstore, since the intense heat in Manhattan that summer was overwhelming, especially as most stores lacked the air-conditioning taken for granted these days. But we also conserved our precious greenbacks for another important reason – the night-time, and 52nd Street

The section of 52nd Street between Broadway and Seventh Avenue has at the end of the twentieth century become a boring, featureless street in midtown New York, where rows of forbidding, impersonal tower-block offices line the way. But in 1947 the same area consisted largely of once-residential brownstone townhouses whose basements had been converted to little night-club premises. These tiny establishments became the musical showplaces for the jazz attractions of the time, and many of the names featured therein were well known to at least the jazz fraternity; indeed, some names, such as Ella Fitzgerald, were familiar to the great unwashed as well. However, a few of the smaller clubs, unable to afford established names, featured newer arrivals on the scene, and were of constant interest to the student of jazz seeking to sample the more recent developments in the music.

So as the daylight faded and our shopping sprees came to an end, we would return to the bowels of the ship to dump our booty, change clothes, and wend our way to 52nd Street. Since the *Queen Mary* was docked virtually at the end of this street, which ran across the entire width of Manhattan, all we had to do to reach the jazz club area was walk the length of four or five long city blocks. This journey told us everything about New York. The first block or so was a far cry from the glamour of our destination – it consisted almost entirely of poor, run-down tenement buildings, with shabbily dressed children playing in the potholed streets. Clearly this section of town had no part in the American dream.

But then the picture would gradually and even dramatically change, and soon we would be on the approaches of the Great White Way – the same Broadway that we had seen since our childhood days on the silver screen, at the movies back in England. And there it was before our eyes, with all the familiar ingredients. The continual honking of impatient motor horns, the never-ending stream of sleek, streamlined, pastel-coloured automobiles and yellow taxicabs, the occasional urgent wail of the siren from a police car, an ambulance or a fire truck, against a counterpoint of loudspeakers outside record shops belching out the latest hit-parade numbers, the gleaming lights, the flashing neon signs, the pungent smell of sizzling hamburgers and frankfurters pervading the warm night air – it all seemed as if the movies we had seen all our lives had crystallised in front of us, in glorious Technicolor.

We crossed the famous thoroughfare for the last stage of our pilgrimage, our pace unconsciously quickening. A few strides further and there it was – the vision we had so long imagined and longed to see – spread before us: the jazz clubs of 52nd Street.

Our first-ever visit to this our dream world. Exhilarating, fulfilling, breath-taking, magical – call it what you will. But it posed a problem: how on earth were we to choose which place to try first? We were bombarded with tempting messages from the various club doormen as we passed each establishment – 'Come on in, guys – no cover charge. Coleman Hawkins just going on the stand', 'Hi, folks. No minimum tonight – Miss Billie Holiday just about to perform', and so on. Wherever we passed, by incredible good fortune the artistes concerned were just about to start their performance. (We later found that the artistes concerned presumably took up to an hour to make their last preparations before finally stepping on stage, so long did we have to wait between the doorman's promise and the artiste's actual appearance. We put it down to the former's exaggeration and the latter's procrastination, but in fact nobody really knew for sure when, or even if, anyone was about to perform in this slightly chaotic world.)

However, before we had gone many paces on that first trip along 52nd Street our choice of entertainment was made by events beyond our control. We bumped into our British drummer friend Laurie Morgan, who actually appeared to have been waiting for us. Laurie, who was not part of the *Queen Mary* contingent, had managed to cross the Atlantic by some other means, and was now positioned outside the Downbeat Club in front of a huge placard which proclaimed 'Tonight – the Dizzy Gillespie Big Band!'.

A picture flashed across my mind – the famous trumpet player in this very building, just a few feet away, probably in his star dressing-room, with his hairdresser putting the finishing touches to his coiffure, his manicurist tending his hands, his valet brushing his suit, and all his other aides preparing for his oncoming show. They do things that way at a club like this – we had seen it all in the movies.

I was awakened from my reverie. 'Come and meet Dizzy', said Laurie. We knew Laurie to be a man not devoid of the necessary chutzpah when needed, and he had obviously made contact with the great man or his staff. He shepherded us to the entrance of the place, and I straightened my tie in preparation for a walk through the club to the backstage area where the dressing-rooms were no doubt located.

I walked past the doorman. 'Dizzy, this is John', I heard Laurie say – and I found myself gazing at the outstretched hand of a man leaning against the wall in the tiny porch-way of the club. He wore thick-rimmed sunglasses, a beret on the back of his head, and a warm, natural, welcoming smile on his jovial face – and I realised I was about to shake hands with Dizzy Gillespie.

I gulped. 'How do, Diz?' was in its crass stupidity the only thing my tongue would come up with when I finally got it untied. We were all then whisked into the club, and in what seemed no time were listening speechless to the wild, reckless, yet magnificently disciplined sounds of Dizzy's full seventeen-piece orchestra. Milt Jackson played the vibraphone. Dizzy sang as well as played, and we – a dazed and quite overwhelmed little group of limeys – finally emerged, ostensibly to go on to another club to hear something else. But we were by this time both physically and emotionally exhausted, and could barely summon the energy to crawl into a cab to take us back to the ship and our bunks. It was almost too much for one day.

* * *

The weeks and the months went by, and our trips to New York came and went about every two weeks. The scenario on 52nd Street changed considerably on each of our visits, and each time we were able to sample the work of different artistes. And of course visits to other parts of Manhattan – Harlem and Greenwich Village, for instance – found us in different surroundings listening to yet more music. Furthermore, the cinemas and ballrooms of the city frequently featured jazz groups we wished to hear (films would in those days often be interspersed with a set from a famous band – Tommy Dorsey or Gene Krupa, for instance), while a band such as Count Basie's or Ray Anthony's could be heard in a place such as the Roseland Ballroom. Cafe Society Downtown could showcase anyone from pianist Teddy Wilson to drummer Buddy Rich – and so on. We journeyed to and fro over the city, listening and imbibing new sounds, many as yet too new to be available on record.

But our main activities were around 52nd Street. Here we would seek out Bird wherever and with whomsoever he might be playing. At that time the trumpet player with the Parker combo (since Dizzy Gillespie's departure) was a youth named Miles Davis. Max Roach was still the drummer, and pianist Duke Jordan and bassist Tommy Potter completed the quintet. More than once our little group of Cunarders would stay in the club, nursing our drinks to make them last as long as possible (to the disgust of the predatory waiters), and far outstay our welcome. After all, in a tiny night-club in the wee small hours, when business has virtually come to a standstill, the overwhelming desire common to musicians, waiters, bartenders and owners is to close – and our presence was the fly in the ointment. We were obviously a nuisance, but we were completely oblivious of the fact, and sat there with eager looks on our faces, obviously prepared to nurse our 75-cent beers for hours if possible – it must have been very disconcerting to those who wanted to go home. One night in such circumstances, with only us *Queen Mary*-ites, a drunk and a hooker in attendance, Bird asked the depleted gathering for a request. '*Donna Lee?*' I ventured (choosing a now well-known Parker tune which was then brand new). Bird counted the band in, and *Donna Lee* was performed faster than anyone has heard it before or since. We took the hint, and as it finished we left and they began thankfully packing their instruments.

But such places provided excellent opportunities to study the music, and to make findings that were difficult to deduce from records. For instance, one feature of the new music was the use of quasi double tempo, which meant that pieces of a moderate speed were suddenly invaded by cascades of notes, for short and often unpredictable periods. Musicians are often good imitators, and many were quick to employ this feature but not to understand its motivation. One night I was lucky enough to be able to find out first-hand.

Bird was playing a standard, *Just Friends*, at a medium tempo in the crowded club. In the middle of his second chorus two rather blowsy blondes, both wearing sweaters which tended to showcase their anatomical features betwixt the throat and the midriff, edged past the bandstand on their way to the ladies' powder room. Indeed space was so tight that one of the said parts of the anatomy must have done everything but brush the bell of Bird's saxophone. Anyway the whole incident caused an explosion of a thousand or so double-tempo notes from Bird's horn, their creator following the women's progress along the front of the bandstand in time with their walk. Of course it brought howls of laughter and a round of satirical applause from the audience, and a look of embarrassed bewilderment from the blondes. From then on I knew something that the record students didn't – Bird had a lively sense of humour, and sometimes incorporated it in his music.

The only limitation that these listening sessions had was our own mental capacity. Try as we did to imbibe everything the musicians did during these sets, it was inevitable that sooner or later concentration would falter. On occasions we even found ourselves drooping towards sleep, an action we would never have thought possible in the presence of such greatness – rather like a devout follower of Christ nodding off during the Sermon on the Mount. But the human brain, still (thank God) light years ahead of the most sophisticated thing that Apple or

IBM or even Bill Gates can come up with, nevertheless has a finite capacity which cannot be stretched. And as a result there must have been many, many musical things that eluded us – not because they were ungraspable, but because our brains were just plain too over-loaded with goodies to grasp them. However, there were many that didn't escape us, and at every opportunity on our periodical returns to London we hired rehearsal rooms and went to jam sessions with a dual purpose uppermost in our minds – to practise using the knowledge we had gleaned, and to pass as much of it on to others as we possibly could.

In the end our fortnightly trips to America became routine, and in lots of ways rather boring routine, since our work on the ship, which mainly involved playing for dancing, held few musical kicks for us. True, we met passengers and formed friendships, most of them short-lived, but in general we were not very fulfilled people, and as a result we got into some mild mischief. Stupid mischief, I realise in retrospect, but then twenty-year-olds are quite often stupid, even today.

Three of us – my close friend Ken Moule, vibraphone player Tommy Pollard (who was also pianist) and me – started practical joking. The targets were usually the members of the other dance band (there were three bands on board altogether), who played a later work-pattern than us, and consequently slept longer in the mornings. We took breakfast at the first sitting, while theirs was the second, around an hour later – we would wake them on our return. One night a storm was expected, and the metal porthole-covers were closed. When we were sure that they were all asleep after work one night we waited till about 4 am and then, ourselves fully dressed, woke them all up as if we had just finished breakfast. Since the portholes were battened they could only assume that it was daylight – we had also changed the clock on the wall – and they arrived at the dining-room to find it dark and deserted.

This of course could only be a one-off prank, but we continually searched for other annoying silliness, which gradually got more serious – collapsing bunks, for instance, and locking victims in or out of cabins and so forth. One further episode involved blacking someone's brown shoes, which resulted in a serious scuffle between Tommy (whose drinking habits sometimes tended to make him aggressive) and another musician, who made a complaint. The result was that Ken, Tommy and I were all quite rightly fired, and our music-appreciation crusades abruptly ended. It was no more than we thoroughly deserved. It was also the only time I have ever been ignominiously sacked, and I learned a valuable lesson from it – I think.

My career in Geraldo's Navy, as the job was known in the profession (the agency belonging to a bandleader of that name who booked the gig), was over, and it was time to look for a job.

Perspective I

My career was on the cusp – between two eras of jazz.

Successive phases in jazz history have seen marked and sometimes quite sudden and startling changes in style and emphasis. To a working jazzman such as myself, a simple pattern seems to fall into place.

Since the end of World War I, in 1918 – which is about the time we begin to have recorded musical evidence to back our theories – jazz has appeared to regroup itself about every decade, very roughly speaking. The period up to the end of the twenties – say 1928 for convenience – saw the first emergence of a jazz style to which we can relate, when guitars took over from banjos, the tuba gave way to the string bass and the saxophones began to play a significant role in the proceedings. Similarly, the music itself began to wear the hallmarks of sophistication, with simple blues and blues-related tunes being augmented with more complex material.

1928 was a milestone for the emergence of the larger organised bands such as Luis Russell, Fletcher Henderson, McKinney's Cotton Pickers and Duke Ellington, on the one hand, and of smaller groups such as the Louis Armstrong Hot Five and Hot Seven and Frankie Trumbauer's band, featuring the legendary Leon 'Bix' Beiderbecke. It also hailed the beginnings of the instrumental soloist; much of the earlier jazz had been largely ensemble work. During this phase jazz duly progressed and evolved further, the skills of both the players and the writers speeding its development at an ever-increasing rate.

And one more factor had begun to influence the evolutionary process – the extraordinary commercial appeal of the music. In the eyes and the ears of the masses all over the world jazz had arrived, which is why this period is sometimes referred to as the Golden Age. But it was golden in another sense: writers and critics in the world of 'serious' music began to draw attention to the quality of content in jazz. The British conductor Constant Lambert, himself a bit of a musical trail-blazer, drew attention in a book to the extraordinary talents of Duke Ellington and his significance as a major force in twentieth-century music. Moreover, classical composers were clearly interested in what jazz had to offer, many making serious attempts to capture the sounds of the music in their work. Maurice Ravel, William Walton and Igor Stravinsky were just a few who showed more than a passing musical reference to jazz during this period, and they were to be followed later by hundreds of others, including Béla Bartók and Aaron Copland. So jazz could arguably be cited as a rare instance of a 'naturally evolved' music (I could say folk music, but the word implies rural rather than urban origins) whose actual texture was taken seriously and incorporated in some instances into the structure of Western symphonic music.

By the middle to late thirties, let us say 1938 for neatness' sake, even more sophistication (some might say glitz) had been added, and jazz became frequently referred to as 'swing' (the first widely used alias for jazz music, unless one counts the onomatopoetic title 'boogie-woogie', the name given to a percussive style employed by saloon pianists at one period). In any event, the 'swing' epithet was adopted to describe, and particularly to market, the new phase.

At this point big bands really came into the spotlight. Clarinettists Benny Goodman and Artie Shaw each had their own band and, together with Jimmie Lunceford, Count Basie, Chick Webb (featuring a teenage singer called Ella Fitzgerald) and many others, joined the ranks of existing bands such as Duke Ellington on the never-ending tour circuit. They all had a hand in the popularisation of swing – but so did the musicians using smaller combinations, such as vibraphonist Lionel Hampton, pianist Teddy Wilson and the great tenor saxist Coleman Hawkins. With increasing lay public interest, players such as Armstrong and pianist Thomas 'Fats'

Waller developed their showbiz gifts as well as their music; both used their vocal chords to augment instrumental prowess. Jazz, under both its original and its new name, had arrived. It even, in September 1938, invaded the hallowed precincts of New York's prestigious and hitherto strictly classical Carnegie Hall.

But, applying my ten-year yardstick, something exciting was due to happen around 1948. It did. In fact in New York a major musical revolution had started two or three years earlier. By 1948 it was at its height.

This time the changing of the guard was to be the most drastic so far. New names — trumpeter Dizzy Gillespie, alto saxist Charlie 'Yardbird' Parker, pianist Thelonious Monk and drummer Kenny Clarke — had taken the city, then the nation and eventually the entire jazz world by storm. Their whole outlook, rhythmically and harmonically as well as stylistically, shook the music by its roots. Someone called it 'bebop', and the name stuck.

To say that jazz was divided on the validity and the desirability of bebop would be seriously understating the case. It would be like saying that the Americans were a tiny bit cross with Japan after Pearl Harbor, or that Hitler was unkind to the Jews.

This was not just a division; the jazz world was at war, a fratricidal war every jot as bitter as its geographical counterpart – World War II – that had so recently ravaged the globe. Many of the most prominent jazz stars debunked the new music, among them Louis Armstrong, who publicly pronounced against it; only much later did he agree to share the same stage as Dizzy Gillespie, the father of bebop trumpet playing. Others, recognising that bebop made great demands on a player's musical skills, were more guarded in their statements and actions, but hostilities continued unabated nevertheless.

Indeed, in Britain the advent of the new style coincided with a return to basics, a revival of New Orleans-style traditional jazz, and the result was that every British jazz exponent was categorised as a 'trad' or a 'mod' – nothing in between was ever even considered.

But all these extreme reactions, however unreasonable, were certainly understandable. Jazz had leapt in one fell swoop from one of its most accessible periods to a new phase which, although ordered and logical to qualified musicians – or those with young enough ears, anyway – sounded like abstract and disordered cacophony to the less tutored perception of the general public. It would indeed be difficult, perhaps the work of a genius, to *fashion the newly emerged sounds into something the 'fringe' jazz lovers would accept.*

Then there was another snag. Hitherto most jazz had been suitable for dancing. In the United States, as well as in Britain and many parts of the English-speaking world, jazz-orientated big bands toured the dance-hall circuits. Their musical appeal attracted a minority of enthusiasts, but they were able to survive (and sometimes thrive) because their presence was in effect subsidised by a much larger crowd – those who came to practise their version of the terpsichorean art in the process of finding a mate – lifelong or just for the evening, as the case may be.

However, there was one fact about bebop about which there was no dis-agreement between the 'pros' and the 'antis': it was not dance music. So in fact in one Olympic-sized jump jazz had propelled itself over the edge of the fertile plateau of swingdom into a canyon with far leaner pickings at the bottom – and in the freefall waved good-bye to nine-tenths of its support group. It was not exactly a businessman's idea of a good move, but then cre-ative artistes have never been inclined to put practicalities and financial stability before creativity – otherwise Mozart would have amassed an array of wealth and power in excess of Andrew Lloyd Webber's, and Vincent Van Gogh would have made a fortune endorsing oil-painting courses.

5

April in Paris

So here was I in no man's land – I was an in-between. I with a passionate love for the alto sax whether played by Charlie Holmes or Charlie Parker, I who waxed lyrical about Bix Beiderbecke's and Miles Davis's trumpet styles, I whose favourite clarinettists were Jimmie Noone and Benny Goodman. Such a being did not exist in the eyes of the 'us-or-them' brigade, and their philosophy ruled the British jazz fraternity for I suppose at least ten years, after which the musicians (or most of them), and later the jazz public (or the large majority of them), slowly came round to a more broad-minded point of view.

Not surprisingly, then, I was concerned only with musical topics at this time, such was my total absorption in the anatomy of the new musical development in jazz. I was blissfully unaware that I had entered the jazz profession at a time when, however lofty its new ideals might be, it offered pretty grim prospects for a breadwinner. It is also almost superfluous to say that, had I thought it through and discovered this for myself, or had some older, wiser and more experienced musician taken me gently to one side and explained it all to me – it would not have made the slightest shred of difference.

I had read about Buddy Bolden, whose horn could be heard across the Mississippi as he toiled in a Storyville bordello for 50 cents a night. How they found Bunk Johnson working as a janitor in Memphis, bought him a new trumpet and got him back to make a recording which proved the catalyst for his career comeback. How Benny Goodman, in short pants in a Chicago ghetto, sneaked out at nights to listen to Johnny Dodds. How Bunny Berigan and Bix Beiderbecke had both succumbed to drink at the height of their powers and in the flower of their youth. So, given that youth never devotes a moment's thought to practical matters, where would I ever have got the idea that there was any money to be made in playing jazz in the first place?

It was all so romantic; who cared whether there was money to live on or not? From my avid ingestion of articles in the jazz connoisseurs' magazines, the only way to make money from jazz was to 'go commercial' – and that would be a fate worse than death, the most despicable thing an honest jazzman could ever perpetrate on his fellow musicians and his public. Yet I was worldly-wise enough to realise that the story-book side of jazz would not last long in the real world.

To put it into terms that made more sense to me at the time, I knew I had to find a foothold in the profession to achieve my immediate goals. I felt that I had a message to spread. A message to my musician pals in England who had no opportunity to hear the bebop greats in the flesh. A message to the British jazz fans who had heard nothing of this music save for a few pathetic three-minute 78s. And eventually, perhaps, a message to the world – who could tell?

In other words, I needed a job. So the next step was – back to Archer Street, the open-air employment exchange where we youngsters met and got to know each other. Soon little groups of us banded together for informal jam sessions at each other's houses in the suburbs or, when we could afford it, in rehearsal rooms in central London.

We were an interesting but perhaps motley crew. There was Denis Rose, just about the first trumpet player in London to adopt the bebop style using the methods and chord structures of Dizzy Gillespie. Denis, whose rather swarthy exterior concealed a gentle nature, seemed always to be at the centre of any activity; even though his instrumental technique was not the best around at the time, he became a kind of guru who represented the new musical thinking we had all adopted.

Ronnie Scott, Tommy Pollard, Leon Calvert (the first man I heard who was able to capture the sound of the then little-known Miles

Davis) and I represented the Geraldo's Navy bebop apostles; then there was Don Rendell, whose attempts to re-create the sounds of his idol Lester Young resulted in a highly individual style; and Johnny Rogers, who like me had been inspired by Bird and had chosen the alto sax. In the rhythm section department was Laurie Morgan, our link with Dizzy in New York a short time earlier, and one of several drummers; another was Tony Crombie, whose grasp of the new music enabled him to oblige occasionally as a keyboard player when no such specialist was available. The position of bass player was at times discharged by Lennie Bush, who was for the ensuing half-century to occupy the throne as Britain's senior bebop bassist; on other occasions it was Joe Mudele, later to concentrate more on non-jazz studio work. Another of our entourage had already spent some time in the commercial world of dance music – Bernie Fenton, whose work as pianist-arranger with Oscar Rabin's dance band was already well known in the profession. There were many others, lots of them excellent jazzmen worthy of mention, but the few I have just referred to chanced to play an especially significant role in the evolution of British jazz at that time.

If by now you have come to imagine Archer Street as a busy backwater of London's city centre, thronged with hundreds of work-hungry musicians at certain times, you have assimilated an important part of the picture. But only a part. Archer Street is a stone's throw from the very heart of the metropolis – Piccadilly Circus – and on the fringe of the colourful area known as Soho, with its mixture of clubs of all sorts (savoury and otherwise), betting offices, snooker halls, restaurants, shops, studios and businesses of every kind, legal and illicit. As a result, many human types other than musicians were to be seen in the neighbourhood – especially in this postwar era. There were street merchants, black-market operators (rationing and severe shortages still existed), hookers and their pimps, petty criminals and drug dealers as well as every kind of Soho inhabitant with more usual occupations. Moreover, wherever there are musicians there have always been agents, managers and entrepreneurs, some with years of experience and some as new and as green as we were. Certain of these were there out of a genuine interest in music – and others simply to make a quick buck.

So it was no surprise when after a few months of these experimental informal jam sessions a dapper young man, whom we all knew by sight, struck up an acquaintance with us with a view to doing some business. His name was Harry Morris, and his carefully cut zoot suit and clip-on bow tie gave him a certain business-like air that made us listen to him. His eyes twinkled attractively as he stirred his tea slowly, meticulously and meaningfully in a café on the corner of Windmill Street. He eyed a handful of us knowingly over the overflowing ashtray which adorned the centre of the Formica-topped table. 'You guys are crazy shelling out that bread for rehearsal rooms.' His jargon, laced with the latest American vernacular, was nevertheless couched in the sounds of cockney. 'People should be paying you! Listen. All you have to do is to organise yourselves into a couple of bands and take it in turns to play. I'll get some posters and a press ad done to spread the word around. Then on the night I'll be on the door and collect the loot while you cats shoot the bop. At the end of the night we pay off Mac the owner – and split the rest between us.'

We winced a little at the use of the word 'cats' and the phrase 'shoot the bop'; it was all slightly over the top, but we were even prepared to take that from our newly found marketing man. It all sounded disarmingly simple, the more so because one of the places we rented for our private sessions was Mac's rehearsal rooms in that very street – Windmill Street, opposite the famous Windmill Theatre – where the posters advertising their mildly naughty strip-shows always added 'We Never Closed' – proudly boasting of their wartime record. Mac's had been a club in a previous life, and its main room was still intact, complete with gaudy, trite murals of gondolas in Venice, rickshaws in Shanghai and so on. It had a bandstand (in fact it had two), hundreds of chairs, a few tables and even a small dance floor. It seemed a perfect starting point for Harry's brainchild.

Somehow the musical side of the plan got itself organised. The two bands were to be a sextet and a quartet. The six-piece outfit was to be led by Ronnie and included Denis Rose on trumpet, Rogers on alto sax and a rhythm section comprising Tommy Pollard on piano, Lennie Bush on bass and Tony Crombie on drums. I was elected leader of the quartet, and my partners were to be pianist Bernie Fenton, bassist Joe Mudele and drummer Laurie Morgan.

The ten of us took over Mac's one Saturday evening in 1949 and began the music, while Harry sat expectantly at the door behind a card table with a roll of pink tickets. It was an anxious time for all eleven partners. We had launched the Club Eleven. It was no small deal for us: we had invested heavily in the project – £25 for the rental, £10 for the posters, £10 for the press ads, and £2 for the roll of tickets. There was no going back.

It worked. By the time we reached the second number a steady trickle of people were sauntering in and taking their places, some near the bandstand, some leaning on the counter of the coffee-bar in the far corner, some striding purposefully onto the dance floor. But there was no doubt that the majority had come to listen, and there was plenty to listen to. As the evening went on it became obvious that young London had thronged to hear us, and during the ensuing months our once-weekly appearances were doubled and then tripled to satisfy the burgeoning demand. News of Club Eleven spread rapidly, first to the music papers, then to the record companies. We were persuaded to make excursions out of our dowdy surroundings into London concert halls. Later came a memorable invitation to the Astoria ballroom in Manchester, and for some reason this proposal – readily accepted without much thought about its logistical difficulties – seemed to convey to us more forcefully than anything else that we were now a national phenomenon. It had us searching for one more positive step to sweep us indisputably into the big time.

The answer was – uniforms. In those days band uniforms spelled out stability, quality and trust, and no musical group worth its salt was without them. We discussed the matter after the club finished one night and delegated the power of negotiating a deal to Harry Morris. The next night he came in beaming, adjusted his bow tie and brushed his palms together in a gesture that indicated the conclusion of a job well done. 'We collect the suits from Cecil Gee's at ten tomorrow morning on the way to Manchester', he announced. 'Coach leaves Archer Street 9.30 sharp!'

Well, of course, no jazz band bus ever left anywhere sharp. The inevitable lateness of some is allowed for by the experienced manager by a built-in time allowance – in other words, a call-time which is earlier than necessary. So in the absence of such an experienced manager we left Archer Street not so sharp – just about an hour and a quarter late, to be exact. By this time we had assembled not only all the musicians, but also an entourage of about a dozen or so friends, hangers-on, travel opportunists – call them what you will – all eagerly anticipating a cost-free outing to Manchester.

At long last we departed. We had not long to wait for our first stop, however. It came after roughly three hundred yards up Shaftesbury Avenue and a left turn into Charing Cross Road. We drew up regally outside Cecil Gee's men's outfitting emporium to pick up our suits. The bus disgorged its entire occupancy into the store – a rag-tag army of musicians and allied tradesfolk. We emerged about half an hour later after a chaotic and hurried fitting, and sped on our way towards the Great North Road. Only when we were bowling along at a terrifying fifty miles an hour and the vehicle began to warm up were top-coats shed by some of our supporters' club members, to reveal a collection of Cecil Gee garments which, stylish as they were, had somehow left the store quite independently of the deal Harry had made. Whether their disappearance was noted, or maybe abetted, by any of the Cecil Gee staff I have no idea to this day.

Had the Great North Road been the motorway which later linked London with Manchester we might conceivably have just made our gig on time. But it was not, and we finally arrived at our place of work halfway through the evening. On looking back, the miracle was that we got there at all. By this time many of our fans were already leaving, yet we did our show and Harry managed to get our money from a none-too-pleased ballroom owner.

Over the months and indeed years that followed the Club Eleven became synonymous with progressive jazz thinking in Britain – a sort of jazz Bauhaus. Visiting musicians and critics from overseas dropped in to listen or jam. Saxophonist Spike Robinson, then resplendent in a US navy uniform complete with bell-bottoms, was one. Another was legendary pianist-composer Tadd Dameron, whom I remember vividly as he gamely battled with the beat-up grand piano allotted to my quartet. Much later, with only a handful of the originals left, the Club Eleven moved to premises in Carnaby Street, then a deserted back alley behind the stately stores of Regent Street, later to become the centre-piece of the swinging sixties fashion boom in Britain.

Club Eleven in its heyday epitomised the emergent cerebral element which had become part of the jazz equation, at the same time proved that such music can be performed with virility and charisma. Many of the players who performed there over the years, both on a regular basis and otherwise, went on to make great individual contributions to jazz. Even in its heyday, however, the club was by no means our whole musical life, and our search for more inspiration and more fulfilment in our own playing continued in other directions simultaneously. One of the main problems for British jazzmen at that time was the difficulty in hearing live jazz played by top performers from other countries. During the war this was paradoxically much less of a problem – it had been easy for US armed services bands and their entertainment units, including many well-known jazzmen, to come and go. But now hostilities were over some long-standing prewar differences between the British and US musicians' unions re-emerged, with the result that American musicians, free to roam continental Europe, were not allowed to appear in Britain. So the only way we ex-habitués of 52nd Street could hear the sources of our inspiration again was to wait for them to come to Brussels or Dublin or wherever else they might be invited – and take an educational trip.

Thus when the 1949 Paris Jazz Festival was announced several of us decided to go, and a few of us – Ronnie Scott and drummer Allan Ganley among them – trekked off to the French capital to catch Charlie Parker, Miles Davis and a number of other top jazz artistes, including a Swedish contingent led by the superb alto saxist Arne Domnérus, in concert at the Salle Pleyel. Although none of us Brits had been invited to perform, Ronnie and I both took our instruments with us (it seemed as natural when going abroad as taking a toothbrush at the time), and in fact soon after our arrival we found a little jazz club on the *rive gauche*, the Club St Germain, where sitters-in were welcome. Thus we gravitated there to play each night after the concerts. We were not the only ones – I remember the American tenor saxist Don Byas was sometimes a visitor – and our sessions there began to settle into a sort of routine.

One night, however, things were different. I had just finished a solo in *Groovin' High* when the manager of the club edged his way to the tiny bandstand and stepped towards me. At the same time I could see across the crowded room that some sort of excitement was focused at the entrance, and the buzz was permeating rapidly through the club. The manager was obviously elated about something, but his countenance nevertheless had a look of concern. He directed his attentions specifically to me. 'Meester Charlie Parkeur', he accented the last syllable, "ees in the club. But 'e 'as no saxophone. Would you please give 'im your saxo to play?'

I said I would be delighted. I knew my own saxophone was exactly similar to a Conn underslung octave model I had seen Bird using in photos, so I felt that he might take to it quickly. Before I could consider the matter further, however, Bird was standing beside me. I handed him my instrument and prepared to withdraw as gracefully as I could, but he grabbed my arm and motioned me to sit down in front of the bandstand – neither of us actually able to get on the podium itself.

He started to play the theme of *Anthropology*, and was soon launching into an improvisation which bore all the hallmarks of classic Parker at his best, in spite of the fact that the foremost of the fans now mobbing the bandstand were just about standing on his feet. The solo came to its conclusion amid wild applause, and as the other participants, mainly French musicians keen to share the limelight with Bird, continued with further solos, I sat entranced in this dream world – had he really been playing my saxophone?

I was awoken from my reverie by an aftermath even more surprising. Bird handed the alto back to me, yet showed no signs of leaving. When my turn came around to solo he listened carefully. As I finished I handed the Conn back to the master. Then there began a series of badminton-like exchanges, with my alto as the shuttlecock, as we each contributed in turn to the sixteen-bar (and later eight-bar) mini-solos which are characteristic of this type of jazz. We both chuckled as it turned into what must have looked like a sort of parlour game.

At the end the crowd roared. Bird surrendered my now-sanctified Conn back to me, gave me a handshake accompanied by a reassuring wink, and disappeared into the throng of besieging admirers. I never saw him again, but to this day possess with pride my precious Conn alto, suitably engraved on the bell to mark the occasion.

The incident had an interesting aftermath, perhaps almost as

memorable in its own way as that unforgettable Paris experience. A
short time after, back in England, I received an invitation from the
Swedish promoter Nils Hilstrom to perform in a couple of concerts
with Arne Domnérus and the American soprano sax wizard Sidney
Bechet. Arne and I were to share the first half of the events, Bechet
doing the entire second half, joined for the finale by us two youngsters
– I was twenty-two at the time, Domnérus perhaps slightly older.

As I was not yet well known even in my own country, let alone
Sweden, I was quite honoured by my inclusion. Yet I was also a little
bit puzzled. However, on my arrival at the venue in Stockholm a
poster, in Swedish of course, caught my eye, and did something to
explain my presence. It seemed to say something like:

THE BATTLE OF THE SAXES
ARNE DOMNÉRUS

('The best European alto saxist', say Paris Jazzfest critics)

versus

JOHNNY DANKWORTH
('The best European alto saxist', says Charlie Parker)

YOU DECIDE!

I have never seen the poster since, nor any evidence of it or confirma-
tion of what I deduced to be its message. But what it purported to say
may conceivably be true for two reasons. Firstly, the Paris critics
reviewed the festival participants only and had no way of knowing
about unannounced appearances in small jazz clubs by unannounced participants. So I almost certainly would not have figured in
their assessments. Secondly, since performers at a jazz festival are
more often than not unable to get to hear the other artistes on the bill,
I may well have been the only European alto player Bird heard on his
Paris visit.

In any event the concerts went ahead, and soon I found myself
rehearsing with my second jazz legend, just a few months after an ad
lib performance with my first. Bechet soon established his ascen-

dancy over us greenhorns (in the nicest possible way) and took charge of the situation. He told us exactly how the last three choruses of the finale would proceed and what we were to do in support – nothing would be left to chance. It was an important object lesson for me early in my career, and it was also a bit of a shock. I had imagined all the early New Orleans musicians – and Bechet was one of the earliest – were rather inarticulate, both musically and verbally.

Bechet was neither, by a long chalk. His musical mind and his ability to impart his ideas was a surprise to me. But through his personality came shining all the hallmarks of an intelligent old man whose second Golden Age was upon him (he had just become the hero of the French Nouvelle Orléans revival movement of the late forties and fifties), and he intended to make no mistakes in handling it successfully.

The concerts went well. On reflection I suspect that Arne won the sax battle. He was the more experienced player and he was on his home ground with hosts of local supporters. I on the other hand was the one who was required to prove something, or perhaps just felt I was. I was also, unlike Arne, working with unfamiliar musicians and in consequence couldn't raise my playing to its best level. Not an excuse, not even a good reason for not playing well – just perhaps a mitigating circumstance. In any case it was the finale, devised and choreographed by Bechet, which sent the crowds home satisfied – the results of the canny tactics of a revered name in jazz who in addition revealed himself – like many other jazz greats – as a consummate showbiz performer.

The opportunity to perform with two such all-time giants of jazz at such an early stage of my career made this period of my working life an exceptional one. Yet it was made even more so by one more remarkable stroke of fate, an event that came my way which brought to full circle my very earliest musical ambitions. Indeed it seemed that my initial choice of instrument was in a sense prophetic of one phase of my future in the world of jazz.

It was an invitation to play with the man who first inspired me to be a jazz musician – Benny Goodman.

*   *   *

I cursed to myself almost audibly as I jumped from the still-moving train onto the platform, gripping my saxophone case in one hand and steadying the clarinet bag, slung over my shoulder, with the other. I landed with an ease borne of practice and was soon joined by dozens and then hundreds of commuters who, like me, lived in an outer suburb of London, but unlike me did this routine journey by steam-train to grimy Liverpool Street Station every day of their working lives.

Why was I with them? Because on this particular day I had my first rehearsal at the London Palladium with Benny Goodman. And why was I cursing? Because I was late. I had rejected my mother's sugges-tion that I catch the train before this one (what a stupid waste of time!) and had allowed my usual nine minutes to sprint to Highams Park station, where the train was invariably in the act of grinding to its temporary halt just as I streaked into view. This morning, however, the train was early. It must have been early, because I missed it, and had to wait ten precious minutes for the next one. Once on terra firma at Liverpool Street I stampeded to the ticket office and then down the escalator to board the underground train bound for Oxford Circus. Finally at the Palladium stage door, I almost literally flew towards the backstage area, and then heard one of the most dreaded sounds a musician can hear – a band rehearsing without him.

I assembled my instruments as quickly and unobtrusively as I could and slid as inconspicuously as possible into the unoccupied second alto chair in the sax section at the front of the band. As the number ended I looked anxiously at Benny in the hope of a smile of recogni-tion as a cue for me to offer my apologies.

Nothing. Not even from the band, all of them London musicians, some of whom I knew quite well by then. They were all only too aware of the famous Goodman 'death-ray' look, and dreaded the possibility of being the first Briton to receive it. I then realised that I had beaten them all to it – I had been its first recipient by virtue of my spectacu-lar late arrival.

'Let's try *Let's Dance*, folks', said Benny. I turned the music over in its well-worn folder until I came to an age-begrimed sheet of music. It was Benny's signature tune, and our counterparts in the States had certainly played it so many times that they no longer needed the worn-out and barely legible manuscript parts. We played it through once. Some of the parts had repeat passages marked, some did not. Most of them offered a choice of two notes to play, one inscribed by an ancient hand in ink, the other in rough pencil by a subsequent user. The pencilled note was more often than not the one required, but it took one run-through to discover this information. The result was that the first read-through of *Let's Dance* sounded – well, just terrible.

The first words I heard Benny Goodman – my boyhood hero – utter were indeed memorable. 'Jesus Christ!' he mumbled to himself. He must have wondered how a hand-picked band of London's best musicians could possibly sound so bad, and had obviously forgotten that life on the road (which was the lot of virtually all big bands in those days) tended to erode and eventually cause the disintegration of the music used by musicians under such circumstances.

The band gradually got into the swing of things, however, and after a couple of hours Benny gave us all a break while he went on to rehearse the sextet, a splinter group in the tradition of the famous Goodman small combinations of the past. The other musicians thankfully made a beeline for the canteen and a much-needed cup of tea, but I was interested to hear Benny play in a small-group context. I had not yet heard in the main rehearsal more than a tiny snippet of the magic I knew was still within his capabilities. I stood in the wings unobserved.

Pretty soon, as the small-group rehearsal got under way, it became obvious that the magic was still there – in abundance. Benny raced through *The World is Waiting for the Sunrise* and *Air Mail Special* – two of the musts of any Goodman performance at that time – and I was spellbound – captivated by the incredible technique, stupefied by the cascades of brilliant invention, beguiled by the warmth of expression. When the short session ended I sauntered back to my seat in the section ready for the resumption of rehearsals, scarcely able to believe my luck in being privy to such superlative clarinet playing and such great music-making.

I absent-mindedly turned towards my instrument stand, intent on fingering my own clarinet and maybe to work out just how one or two bits of the finger wizardry I had heard were actually done – after all, one clarinet is more or less just like another – and reached for my instrument. It wasn't there.

I puzzled for a moment. Then it all came – in a flash. Benny had been having a bit of trouble with his own instrument during the early part of the morning – perhaps that, as well as our first reading of *Let's Dance*, contributed to his air of slight grouchiness – and, being Benny, had developed a habit of borrowing instruments on such occasions from willing donors without difficulty, and certainly without having to seek permission. So in picking up my clarinet, and indeed continuing to use it for the rest of the day, he had done something which was to him completely normal.

The wonder of it all was that, whereas Benny had the pick of the world's finest clarinets at his beck and call, my own instrument, a lowly student model, whose failing mechanism had been shored up by at least half a dozen rubber bands, was about the lowest in the league of playable instruments. Yet in Goodman's hands it became, to my ears anyway, indistinguishable from a virtuoso's tool.

The Goodman fortnight at the Palladium went as planned and was well supported by the London public. Two interesting people who became friends through being guests on Benny's show remain in my memory. Benny had invited Toots Thielemans, the great – but then practically undiscovered – jazz harmonica player, and Toots and I struck up a relationship which has endured to this day. I can still see in my mind's eye a picture of Toots sitting beside me on top of a London double-decker bus, getting his harmonica from his jacket pocket and playing two wonderful choruses of *Body and Soul*, with only me and a handful of startled travellers as his audience.

The other friend I found was Frances Taylor, then a dancer in a small choreographed sequence in the Goodman show. Frances and I went out together during the show's run, but we lost touch when she departed for her native America. The next time I heard of her she had become Mrs Miles Davis – in fact Miles recorded a tune, *Fran Dance*, dedicated to my former friend.

Benny Goodman was a great virtuoso, but like some great people he was a trifle odd, and not at all worldly at times. At the end of the run he came up to me and handed me a gold-plated propelling pencil. 'Here's a thank-you present for your contribution to the show', he said. God knows I'd contributed precious little. 'I didn't have time to get these engraved. You should have it done yourself – y' know, "From

BG to JD", sump'n' like that.' He smiled and disappeared from my working life for about ten years – in fact until I started working in the United States. I have since lost the pencil – I never did get it engraved. But I will forgive Benny Goodman for almost anything, certainly for his terrestrial shortcomings. His genius is something that has never yet quite been replaced in the jazz world.

*   *   *

The Benny Goodman engagement was not to be the end of my association with the Palladium by any means. Nor indeed was it the beginning. One of my very first concert appearances had been there when, some years before, I stepped in at the last minute to fill a vacancy left by an indisposed guest star in the Ted Heath Swing Session series. Ted Heath, undisputed then as the man leading the top British swing band of the day, heard about me through the grapevine and, presumably since no one else could oblige at the few hours' notice available, I was booked. This began a longish association with the Ted Heath Band. I declined an invitation to work with them but made occasional guest appearances on the band's radio show and contributed one or two arrangements to the Heath repertoire.

Arranging and composing had always been at the very forefront of my interests, even more than playing in some ways, and I welcomed any opportunity to indulge my love of writing music as well as playing it. In fact the one drawback of Club Eleven was that, enjoyable though extended improvisation has always been, there was practically no opportunity for the skills of writers to shine. This became particularly galling when we heard on record the first sounds of an American band which featured extremely sophisticated scoring and composing tactics in an entirely new way. The salt was rubbed in the wound when we learned that the band consisted almost entirely of prominent jazz soloists of the time, many of whom we had never heard in such organised musical surroundings before – Miles Davis (the instigator of the group), Gerry Mulligan, Lee Konitz, John Lewis and so on.

The whole phenomenon became known as the Birth of the Cool, and its inspirational effect on me was electric. Why had I not thought of assembling a few friends the same way that Miles had? Heaven knows, they were always popping in and jamming at the club – why not have some music for them to read next time? I nailed Don Rendell one night as he put his tenor away after a jam. He agreed to come to a rehearsal, as did Ed Harvey, a trombonist who had made his first mark in jazz with George Webb's Dixielanders, but had been seduced away from the New Orleans style by the exciting new musical territory to be explored just by crossing the floor of the house, so to speak. I now had three blowers at my disposal – tenor, trombone and alto (me). Almost enough, but what was still needed was a trumpet player. I was on the point of deciding to ask either Leon Calvert or Denis Rose, our regulars, when something happened to settle my dilemma. A young Scot came into the club and asked to sit in. Within seconds of the first notes issuing from his somewhat dowdy-looking trumpet we all realised that here was something exceptional – an extremely young but already mature and gifted player. When he finally left the stand that night I offered him the job in my non-existent band, and Jimmy Deuchar accepted the offer – no payment unless we got some work. How the rhythm section came together I'm not really sure. It featured Joe Mudele, the Club Eleven bass player, drummer Tony Kinsey, already by then regarded as one of our top bebop exponents, and pianist Bill Le Sage, a talented keyboard player (later to add the vibraphone to his armoury) who always swore that he was never asked, but learned of his appointment in the music press.

Before long we had met for a rehearsal and fashioned a small repertoire consisting of a couple of tunes I had put on paper, plus one or two head arrangements – pieces where all the things usually scored by an orchestrator – ensemble passages, modulations, introductions and so on – are in fact worked out and memorised by the players themselves. We were a musical cannonball, just waiting for a cannon to fire us.

The cannon came from the unlikely direction of the Ted Heath office. I met the bandleader there in response to his request. 'Why don't you start a band, John? The timing seems right – you're the young musician of the moment. If you do, I'll launch your career with a spot at the Palladium.' I told him that one of his suggestions came too late – I had already formed a group – but that I would be delighted to take him up on the second.

Whether a Ted Heath concert was the ideal place for the debut of (by the standards of the times) a pretty far-out jazz septet is debatable. The Heath followers could be fairly described as of Glenn Miller rather than Miles Davis persuasion. Anyway we made our debut there and seemed to do alright without bringing the place down. I think any warmth generated in the audience was by the way we looked rather than the way we sounded. The *Melody Maker* critic sensed this, and his article boasted the headline 'FANS BAFFLED BY DANKWORTH MASTERPIECES '. Fortunately the first three words were directly above the last two, and we were thus able, for the purposes of publicity, to doctor the press-cutting so that the headline merely proclaimed 'DANKWORTH MASTERPIECES '.

Not that publicity assisted our cause in any tangible way. After such an auspicious debut at one of London's top entertainment centres we found ourselves facing the prospect of an empty date book. It was all part of the traumatic birth of the Johnny Dankworth Seven – and as things stood at that time it looked as though the new-born babe might never reach maturity.

6

Seven not out

The Seven's London Palladium debut in March 1950 led into an offer from the Wilcox Brothers' organisation, a successful promotion team in the world of traditional jazz. When they planned to sell us they delegated a young member of their staff, Jim Godbolt, to shape our destinies. Godbolt later migrated to another field, and became a respected writer on jazz topics. Our public relations were to be the duty of Les Perrin, a flamboyant character with an infectious grin and an approach to publicity which would take him to the top of his class – he was later to represent the Rolling Stones. He was one of the old school despite his youth, and his technique – to go down to Fleet Street (where every journalist with any clout was inevitably found in those days) and swap stories and beers with the journalists in their favourite watering-holes – paid off handsomely.

But the talents of the Wilcoxes, Godbolt and Perrin combined did little or nothing to alleviate the present problem – how to face the immediate future. The gigs barely trickled in, and indeed those that did were ill-suited to the style of music we had to offer. After about three weeks, having paid the musicians' salaries as well as the initial expenses of uniforms, music-stands and so on, my meagre resources were exhausted.

I called the band together after the last gig, a miserable affair at a

dance hall in a tiny Yorkshire town, with the patrons struggling hopelessly to dance quicksteps and fox-trots to our avant-garde sounds.
'Well, that's it, I'm afraid', I told them. 'We won't be the first band to
go under because our music is too good for the punters, or the last
either, for that matter. But I'm skint, and I know you blokes can't live
on hot air.'

'Well, maybe not, but at least we should try.' The voice came from
pianist Bill Le Sage. 'If we went co-operative we might make it. We're
jazz musicians, so we all know how to live on a shoe-string.'

There was a general murmur of approval – and the real Johnny
Dankworth Seven was born. Joe Mudele was already a family man
with a mortgage and thus had to withdraw to earn enough from his
London bass-playing connections. But the rest of us then and there
formed a profit-sharing alliance which operated with growing
success over the next three years – without a written document or
a signature from any one of us. Seldom since the famous partnership between Mr Rolls and Mr Royce has such a state of affairs
caused other than grief, but for all of us it lasted for over three years,
until we all felt that perhaps we should be moving on to other
things. Like any human relationship it was not devoid of minor
falling-outs and temporary upsets, but in the main it was a period of
excellent music-making, happy experiences – and lots and lots of
laughs.

Bill Le Sage, the driving force behind the co-operative idea, became
the manager. Bill was from the start a mainstay of our group. He fitted
perfectly into our social pattern, and was always a sobering influence
on us when any among us had a foolish or impracticable idea in mind.
He was also a fine musician. I was to continue leading and writing
arrangements and new material, a task shared by trombonist Ed
Harvey. Ed was a deserter from the trad-jazz camp, and an articulate
musician whose writings were always full of interest.

Don Rendell, from London's outer suburbs, was a fluent and spirited tenor saxist. He was married and thus, we all felt, qualified for a
'rent allowance', meaning that when business was bad and the
financial pickings were meagre Don's rent was taken out of the kitty
before the split. This rule, also unwritten, always applied when
anyone with extenuating circumstances needed a bit of assistance.

Our rhythm section featured drummer Tony Kinsey, whose brilliant drumming was already in demand in London jazz circles. He helped congeal the Seven's style in its formative days. Eric Dawson was the new bassist. He had been a late starter on his instrument, but his drafting into the coal mines as an alternative to military service during World War II had left him with time in his off-duty hours to study his instrument further. He thus became a bass fanatic and a welcome addition to our fold.

The pattern was completed by two singers. Marion Williams, a tall attractive girl of African/English parentage, was our original choice, but even though we placed her on a salary far higher than our own weekly drawings in our co-op scheme it proved not to be enough to keep her, and we were soon on the lookout for another female singer.

Our male vocal department was in good hands, and was to be for years to come. Frank Holder, from Guyana, was not only a singer with great stage presence and tremendous energy, but a consummate and potentially show-stopping performer on the bongos, the conga drum and indeed practically all of the enormous family of Latin-American percussion instruments. He was one of the enduring assets to the showbiz aspect of our performances.

Our co-op era didn't start with any tumultuous success. One of the early experiences was the 400 Ballroom in Torquay. Once a thriving business, it had seen a decline in its fortunes with the changes in style, and it was desperately seeking a solution to its problems. To us the offer of 90 per cent of the box-office takings for a week sounded like riches indeed – until our opening night attracted about a dozen customers. At the end of the week the paltry total barely paid our lodgings bill.

Yet somehow we survived. We dealt with early complaints from dance promoters – that it was impossible to dance to our music – by producing a clutch of versions of popular tunes and standards arranged with reference to the style of the Victor Sylvester Orchestra (the leading ballroom-dance band of the day), placing these at strategic points in the programmes to wean the unsuspecting dancers on to the more far-out items of our own repertoire. We added showmanship – waving of instruments in unison, lighting effects concealed inside the drums, marches through the audience, long spectacular

Latin-American epics with all of us on percussion instruments – and even comedy routines.

Thus over its first year of existence the Seven developed the style for which it was becoming famous not only by means of our increasingly frequent appearances all over Britain, the Irish Republic and indeed in continental Europe, but by our radio broadcasts, our recordings, and eventually our appearances on that up-and-coming medium – television.

Our collective musical brightness made us develop the art of the head arrangement. In the complexities of the new bebop departures in jazz, most music was initially written down for the musicians, even if it was only a unison single line to be shared by the blowing players, plus a chord-symbol sheet for the rhythm section. Anything more complex than that – the 1949 Miles Davis Birth of the Cool band, perhaps the Dankworth Seven's strongest influence, was a case in point – was carefully committed to paper, and the new wave of jazz musicians, unlike their 'trad' counterparters, came usually with a built-in general musical literacy which enabled them to read such music fairly fluently.

However, we acquired a knack of concocting some quite involved musical routines without written music by conceiving them at rehearsal by committee, so to speak, and memorising them on the spot. It had a big impact not only on our style but on the visual effect of our show, making our low-slung gleaming white music-stands, adorned with a gold crown and a figure 7 (a Les Perrin suggestion, implying royal anonymity), more a decoration than a necessity.

Our image grew, and from time to time, with the help of Les Perrin, the national press and broadcasting facilities (it was too soon to call them the media) noted our progress. One of the earliest assignments was an evening gig in Birmingham after a BBC lunch-time broadcast An ancient coach was hired to transport us from London to Birmingham. A few miles past Dunstable on the old A5 one of us noticed a small dirt-begrimed hole at the base of one of the windows – it looked vaguely like a bullet-hole in the toughened safety glass. It became a minor topic of conversation and a few jokes at the back of the coach. The laughter reached the ears of Les Perrin, sitting at the front. He took one look at it, and soon the vehicle came to a screeching halt by a wayside telephone box. We watched Les jump out, enter the box and talk with an urgent look on his face. He eventually came back with the urgency replaced by his usual grin.

Next morning, on our return from the Midlands, my mother seemed both concerned and relieved. 'I've been so worried, but as long as you're all right . . .' She ended my puzzlement by showing me the previous day's *Evening Standard*. 'SNIPER TARGETS BBC BAND', shouted the headline. A brief account of an apparent attempt on our lives by some unknown gun-crazed killer followed. It was a typical Perrin stunt – but it did get our name, spelt correctly, in the paper. To Les that meant 'mission accomplished'.

We went on becoming both better and better known. But one thing was still troubling us, a problem to which we seemed unable to find the right solution – the absence of a female singer. Marion Williams had been followed by a young singer, Linda Ellington, who was at that stage of her career a touch unprepared for both the unforgivingly high musical standards of the band and the rather unkind environment which most girl singers with an all-male band in those days were forced to suffer almost by tradition. After a while Linda had understandably had enough.

We started to audition girl singers. There were obviously going to be some duds applying for such a job, and indeed we had our quota. But there were also some extremely talented performers. They included Lilian, a young Londoner who quite clearly had tremendous talent – but not in our collective opinion the right style for the task of singing with the Seven. Consequently we didn't offer her the job. Later Lilian changed her name to Georgia Brown, and became a leading performer on the British and US musical theatre scene. Perhaps on reflection we were being just a little too choosy. In fact I'm sure we were very choosy indeed, because more than fifty girls came and went during our auditions – and we ended up deciding we would have to do without a girl singer.

Then, in the summer of 1951, came a special day for us all. We had agreed to be the resident attraction at a new club in Great Newport Street, near Leicester Square. It was appropriately enough called the '51 Club.

I was at the club that morning sorting out some business with Bill, who was now deeply involved with managing the Seven. The phone rang. 'John, it's Harold.' Harold Davison, our agent, was on the line. (We had parted amicably with the Wilcoxes and Jim Godbolt during our first gig famine, and Harold was part of our burgeoning success story.) 'I've got a guy in the office who's brought in a girl who wants to audition as band singer. I've told them that the only band looking for one on my books is yours. Can I send her round?'

'Oh, well – I suppose so. We may as well try one more', I replied, a little wearily. I could hear Harold's sigh of relief – he was obviously pleased to have an excuse to get these two out of his office.

Presently the girl arrived with her escort. Nothing about her heralded anything other than – well, just one more person to be polite to after having heard a chorus or so, then explain that we really weren't actually looking for a singer very seriously, and perhaps she should try Joe Loss, or Billy Cotton, or . . . whatever. 'What would you like to sing, love?' I enquired.

Stormy Weather was the answer.

'Brought any music?'

Sorry, no.

'What key would you like Bill to busk it in?'

Sorry, no idea.

'Give her an introduction in C and E flat as a starting note in, Bill.'

Bill eased his way into the song, coaxing a few gentle bars out of the keyboard to prepare the girl for her first note.

> *Don't know why*
> *There's no sun up in the sky . . .*

The first lines floated across the dusty, low-lit club towards me – and I knew that something out of the ordinary was happening. The throaty, slightly husky tones were already giving a new meaning, a fresh individuality, to the well-known words. By the time the girl had reached the middle section and was a mere twenty or so bars into the classic standard it was all too apparent: here was a very unusual talent indeed. Obviously inexperienced, she nevertheless already had a presence to her delivery which conveyed both maturity and style.

I exchanged glances with Bill, and his reaction confirmed my thoughts – we were both listening to an exceptionally good singer. 'That's terrific', I said, after the final bars of the ballad died away. 'What about something faster?' She launched into *It was only a paper moon* in a rhythmic tempo which contrasted with the slow metre of the preceding tune. Good ballad singers are not always able to cope with rhythmic singing convincingly, and I was prepared for a disappointment.

It didn't come. The attractive sound, the attention to lyrics, the musical rounding of phrases was equally effective, in a very different way. I was now convinced that we had found our girl singer. We talked. I felt quite exhilarated and I'm sure it showed. The girl, on the other hand, appeared calm and controlled. Her eyes brightened a little when I congratulated her, but I detected a slight glazing when I began to explain that, as leader of a co-operative band, I couldn't offer her the job then and there. Same old story, she must have thought.

Clementine Langridge came from the western suburb of London known as Southall, where she lived with her husband George, a slater and tiler, together with their baby son Stuart. Although, like many girls of her age, she had dreamt of getting into show business, she had done little about it other than making an appearance now and then with a local dance band, by request of a bandleader who had happened to hear her sing. Then a bass-playing friend, Ossie Newman, who felt she had outstanding talent, persuaded her to go to auditions. She had done so, without success – until today.

She was a pleasant-looking, softly spoken woman with a quiet demeanour, and she carried very well an air of dignity, despite the excitement that our interest in her singing must have been creating. 'The other members of the band would need to hear you before we could make any decision', I told her. 'Could you come back tonight and sing a couple of numbers with the band?'

She could, and in due course, when the club was brimful of customers, I beckoned her to the bandstand. She sang the two tunes we had heard that afternoon, plus a couple of others. The audience reacted appreciatively – but it was the band's opinion that was going to count. We all retired to the tiny band room, where I addressed my business partners. 'What's the verdict? I think she's got something, don't you?' I gazed searchingly into their midst, waiting for some reaction.

It was Jimmy Deuchar who spoke first. 'Something? I think she's got everything', came the pronouncement. It seemed to encapsulate everyone's views, and the decision was made: Clementine Langridge was to be offered the job. It was time for a band break in the club, so our newly acquired vocalist was swept off to the corner pub, where a deal was struck – £6 a week and all found, came the offer. The quiet and acquiescent Clementine showed her other side for the first time: 'Make it seven', was her unexpected counter-attack – and so we did.

Thus began the career of a remarkable and significant personality on the British music scene. It is easy to write this with hindsight, yet somehow I feel that we all sensed it at the time. And now the die was cast it seemed a good moment to examine this woman with the unique voice more closely. Her mixed parentage – her mother from Wiltshire, her father from Jamaica – was not immediately apparent, to me at least, since her complexion was almost as light as mine and her hair controlled in a neat European style (Afro hair was definitely not the rage at that time). She was quietly dressed except for a fur coat, which it later transpired was borrowed from her sister-in-law. It was quite clear that she had suddenly found herself in a totally new world as a result of this new development in her life – yet was not one bit fazed by it.

Les Perrin was quickly told the news and came rushing to the scene. The introduction to Clementine Langridge was made, and a bemused look registered on the Perrin visage. 'Nice to meet you, ducky, but we'll have to do something about the name.' It certainly seemed a mouthful and needed shortening. Langridge shortened easily to Laine, but Clem or Clemmie didn't sound attractive enough. Then I thought of 'Cleo', having seen that name attached to a some-what obscure American singer in a record catalogue.

And so Cleo Laine was created. Perrin, with his flair for a new item with a difference, swore to the press that a number of first- and last-name suggestions were put into two hats, and Cleo Laine was what came out of the draw. Romantic-sounding, certainly, but I can assure you that such an important decision was not left to so haphazard a selection process.

Cleo was soon being rehearsed and dressed, and within days was with us on tour, helpfully assisted by the comparatively experienced Frank Holder. Within weeks she joined us on our live radio shows, and soon after that came into the recording studio for her first recording with the Esquire label. Not long after she figured quite prominently in the *Melody Maker* readers' poll. 'The only British singer who sings as if she's lived', was one critic's opinion.

It was by any standards a meteoric rise. I often observed in later years that Cleo started at the top – and worked her way sideways. The sideways movement in the space of the next few years took her into films, opera, the hit parade and public prominence, all of it rare for someone starting as a band vocalist.

But I am going too fast. I should return to that time in 1951. The Seven's difficulties in finding a niche in the broad spectrum of the British entertainment industry – the only way a jazz group could survive, particularly in those days – were gradually being overcome.

Our travels took us over almost every mile of the road network of the archipelago of the British Isles, playing for dances and concerts, with the occasional television or radio session thrown in from time to time. The Gaiety ballroom in Grimsby, the Belle Vue in Manchester, the Darlington Baths Hall, Leeds Town Hall, Cardiff Odeon, the Eldorado in Edinburgh, the Four Provinces in Dublin . . . all these and countless others were repeatedly visited by the Seven. We might not have been the ideal band for the strict-tempo dancers, but we obviously drew the crowds, otherwise we certainly would not have been booked for return visits as we so often were. Life on the road assumed something of a routine.

A rendezvous behind Baker Street station united us all at a given departure time in a ramshackle coach, and a journey would begin – sometimes southward, eastward or westward, but usually following the northern trail out of London, using the old A5, or Watling Street as it had been called since the Romans built it. This was of course long before the days of motorways, and any trip involved the penetration of some small town or other every twenty or so miles – only the biggest places were by-passed. The process was painfully slow, and thirty miles in each hour was a realistic average. Thus London to Manchester, a frequent recipient of our talents, meant, with a couple of journey breaks included, about nine hours of compulsory restriction inside an ageing vehicle. In a 1950s summer, when air-conditioned coaches were still a dream, the heat was sometimes debilitating. In winter we were occasionally driven to the extreme of bringing an oil-burning stove with us and standing it in the middle of the gangway, which proved an effective though hardly a safe way to keep our toes warm.

We were a social unit as well as a musical one, and spending leisure time together was almost a matter of course. As all of us were cricket fans, we were frequently part of the crowd in front of the Tavern at Lord's cricket ground north of our Baker Street coach departure point. We watched whatever match happened to be in progress, often involving the Middlesex team and batting stars Compton and Edrich.

Once, in the early Seven period, one of our frequent days off coincided with a crucial stage in a five-day test match between England, led by its first professional captain Len Hutton, and the then-mighty West Indies, including the 'three W's' with their prodigious combined batting powers – Weekes, Worrell and Walcott. We arrived at the ground in time to see the 'House Full' notice put up. Undeterred, Joe Mudele, our first bass player, singled out one of the many blocks of flats flanking the ground, marched us up several flights of stairs and knocked on a random door. 'Sorry to bother you, but we've come to see the cricket and the ground is full. Could we watch from your window?'

I marvelled with some embarrassment at Joe's impudence, but we didn't have to wait long for a result. 'But of course – come in, lads.' We all trooped in to a sea of welcoming faces, the crucial windows were cleared and equipped with chairs, and we spent the whole of that day – and the next – enjoying a grandstand view of the action. It was, I suppose, typical both of the trusting nature of the times and of cockney-style hospitality. I doubt very much if it would happen today.

Meanwhile our music was developing, and our original basic library was being augmented by new pieces, some in our familiar head-arranged style, others signalling greater sophistication. My own extended piece *The Conway Suite* showed, in retrospect, an Ellington influence and a wish to involve the Seven in concert-style jazz as well as the 'danceable' variety to which we were often restricted – dance-hall appearances being our staple diet in those days. I was not the only one seeking to explore that direction. Steve Race, then a working musician and later to become a prominent radio and TV figure, wrote an inspired *Suite for Seven*, using classical form to encase his jazz themes – the movements were called Chaconne, Rondo, Fugue and so on. We broadcast the piece but unfortunately never recorded it, and it has been lost in the sands of time so far as I know – more's the pity.

From then on our recording career flourished, with much of our repertoire being issued on the pioneer British jazz label Esquire, run by London drummer Carlo Krahmer from a primitive studio in the basement of his flat in Bedford Square, just off Tottenham Court Road. This unglamorous setting was the place for the first vocal recordings of both Frank Holder and our new girl singer. Cleo had begun her career with perhaps the top group of its style in Britain, and she continued her tradition of jumping off the deep end in her recording activities. One of her very first recordings was Billy Strayhorn's classic *Lush Life*. The song was then virtually unknown to even the jazz fraternity, but I had heard it on one of my frequent visits to Paris around the time of the 1949 Paris Jazz Festival. A small left bank club, Chez Inez, featured entertainment by the American singer Inez Cavanaugh, whose accompanist, also from the States, was Aaron Bridgers. The pianist was the lifelong friend of Billy Strayhorn, the great composer-arranger whose writings revitalised the Duke Ellington Orchestra from the forties up to the time of his death in 1967. Probably for this reason Cavanaugh included *Lush Life* in her repertoire, and I heard her sing it enough times to be able to jot it down for future use. Cleo was the first singer I had heard since who I felt could do it justice, and she did – in spite of an instrumental backing I wrote which I now feel had its shortcomings.

Soon we were tempted by bigger fish than Esquire, and found ourselves with a contract with EMI on the Parlophone label. This meant recording at London's Abbey Road studios – the place with the famous zebra pedestrian crossing in front of it – and under the guidance of our new A & R (artists and repertoire) manager George Martin.

George was then an ambitious youth, and was very much the 'new boy' in EMI. He produced our jazz recordings with sympathy and intelligence, although he was no jazz connoisseur himself. It was strange that the task of producing us fell to him of all people, since we were in a sense a phenomenon similar in impact to that of the Beatles about a decade later, although in a much smaller way. Perhaps George learned something from his dealings with us which helped him make Lennon, McCartney & Co. the tumultuous success that they eventually became.

Martin's success with the Beatles was at the time when multi-track recording and its techniques had just come into their own. But the dozen or so years before this, when we first frequented Abbey Road, the equipment was far more primitive. The records were literally cut onto a shellac disc relying for its motor power solely on a wheel driven by a piece of rope with a weight on the end. The disc could not be played back until it was processed some days later, and of course editing – the joining of parts of one performance with parts of another, which was to become so very easy when recording tape became the medium – was unknown at the time.

Touring was easily the most time-consuming – and in some ways the most essential – part of our work, and touring covered not only just about every corner of Britain, but the Irish Republic and continental Europe. Ireland was always a special treat for us. There was something about the place and the people that we found refreshing, although sometimes remarkably basic. Once we played for a dance in a place called Castlerea. The village hall boasted two respectable-looking upright pianos, but both proved to be tuned at a pitch that made them unusable with our instruments. A trip to the other side of town, however, on the recommendation of the hall keeper, produced a portable piano with a tiny keyboard which was at the correct pitch. We got it back to the hall on the back seat of a car and stood it on a couple of beer-crates on the stage. Somehow it got us through the night.

But only just – the citizens of Castlerea were not easy to persuade to dance. The women sat on one side of the hall, the men on the other, and nothing we played, including slow romantic waltzes, would get them on the floor. 'Give them a Viennese waltz', our hall-keeper friend who had solved the piano crisis advised from the side of the stage. We did, and they flocked onto the floor for the only dance they really enjoyed. We played several consecutively, then changed to our more familiar rhythms – and they deserted again. So we spent the interval wracking our brains and making a list of further Viennese waltzes, and played them throughout the night, only making a final change for *The Soldier's Song*, the Irish national anthem. The next night we played the Arcadia Ballroom, Cork, in the presence of the mayor. He congratulated us on our Viennese waltzes. Our Castlerea experience had made us past masters in the idiom – us, a modern-style bebop jazz band. I doubt if anything like it ever happened to Miles Davis.

An inevitable gesture to welcome the band in even the smallest Irish dance hall was a stack of crates of Guinness placed beside the bandstand. These were expected to be consumed by the performers during the course of the evening – and they usually were. After two weeks of such hospitality, and the resultant hangovers, some of us began to look a little green around the gills. On the last night of the tour an older musician from the local supporting band said to me,' If ya don't mind me sayin', Johnny, you look as if you need a pick-me-up – you're not lookin' too well at all. You should try a recipe I was given by an old lady who lives in the hills. Every morning, with breakfast, take a glass of Guinness. You feel better in no time.' I responded gracefully and promised to try it. I did quickly return to good health after we were back in England, but it was as a result of the absence of my daily Guinness intake rather than otherwise.

Those were the days when the border crossing between the Irish Republic and Northern Ireland was practically a formality. Even so, when we performed near the border the dance promoters were always extremely anxious that we played the correct national anthem at the end of the evening – *God Save the Queen* when north of the border and *The Soldier's Song* when south. The incorrect choice would no doubt have caused civil unrest, even in those relatively peaceful days. The difference, in that immediate postwar period, between life on either side of the border was quite startling. The south, not involved in the war, seemed to have plenty of everything; the north was still suffering from the gloomy results of rationing, austerity and indeed enemy action – Belfast was the recipient of air-raids, in common with most industrial cities in the United Kingdom.

But the consequences of war, still apparent in most of Britain in the 1950s, were much greater in defeated Germany, where the Seven was to undertake two extended tours. The first was a civilian-promoted visit to a dozen or so cities, all in the northern British zone. (Germany had of course been divided into four control zones at the time, governed by the Americans, the French, the Russians and the British.) The extent of the appalling wastage in the cities was very evident indeed at that time. Cologne Cathedral, for instance, had miraculously escaped major damage, but few of the prewar buildings still surrounded it. And in the port of Bremerhaven not a single hotel had been left in working order, and we, like all other visitors, were accommodated in 'boat hotels' anchored in the harbour.

Nevertheless, and quite extraordinarily, the German fans who came to see us and applaud us and wait at the stage door for autographs seemed to bear no malice whatsoever to us Britons, whose air force had been slaughtering them in their thousands less than five years before.

The civilian tour came out of the blue. What the promoters really expected us to deliver we shall never know, but we got there to find ourselves billed as 'Europe's jazzband No. 7 mit comedy team, JONNY DANKWORTH and his BOYS'. We played a mixture of pure jazz and semi-popular music, and even did a comedy routine on the Fritz Kreisler tune *Schön Rosmarin*. Looking back, I suspect that the audiences were a little puzzled by it all, especially the comedy, although the reception seemed warm enough at the time.

Incidentally, by this time the Seven had seen two changes of personnel. Tony Kinsey and Jimmy Deuchar both decided that touring was not for them, and their places on trumpet and drums were filled by two Eddies – Eddie Blair, a young Scot whose brilliant trumpet playing fitted perfectly with our style, and drummer Ed Taylor, from Chadderton in Lancashire, whose wry sense of humour was to keep us in fits, and whose excellent drumming was to become a cornerstone of our rhythm section.

It was felt necessary to have a German compere to open our concerts in Germany, and Heinz Heinrich was with us in this capacity throughout our stay. His concert openings were brilliant. He went on amid hissing and booing – the kids out front wanted to hear music, not be talked at by an older man. Yet Heinz continued to battle with them over several minutes. He gradually calmed the audience down and then started making them laugh, and came off eventually to rapturous applause. What he said to achieve this we never knew, but it seemed a minor miracle every night.

Heinz was abstinent throughout the tour and consistently declined alcohol, even after the show. So we were all surprised after our last concert to see him drinking in the bar, so heavily that he eventually had to be helped to his room in an almost senseless condition. It was then that we realised that he was an alcoholic who had successfully resisted his weakness throughout the tour, but had relapsed once the nightly strain of facing an audience rather hostile to him was over.

After the concerts, which usually finished early, we musicians would scour the town for a bar or club where we could wind down and enjoy ourselves, not an easy thing to achieve so soon after the war. In one small town, however, we managed to find one such place, a tiny and rather respectable club where the patrons were dancing to tangos and waltzes in a rather inhibited yet slightly teutonic style. Since we obviously could not sit in with the band, the only thing to do was dance. Bill Le Sage whisked Cleo onto the floor, and they danced happily for a few minutes until Ed Taylor walked onto the floor and tapped Bill on the shoulder – it was an 'excuse me' dance. The couple parted and Ed stepped in to claim his partner and raced off round the floor. The only unusual factor about it all was that he cavorted off with Bill in his arms, not Cleo, who was left standing there giggling.

The waiters looked concerned and the other customers either amused or just mystified. Eventually the maître d' took over the handling of the crisis. He approached the pair in the middle of the small dance floor. 'Excuse me, meinen Herren. In Germany, dancing for gentlemen mid lady – OK. In Germany, two ladies dancing – OK. But in Germany two gentlemen – no!' He smiled and the boys bowed gracefully to each other and left the floor. Our dancing patterns became more conventional for the rest of that night.

Our subsequent visits to Germany were to entertain the US forces in their sector in the south of the country. Here we performed only to American personnel, and often slept and ate on US army property.

My parents

An early bath

With my sister Avril and our dog

Schoolboy trio. *Left to right:* JD, Ken Moule, Jack Davenport

The Johnny Dankworth Seven
Top row from left to right: Eddie Harvey, Don Rendell. *Middle row:* Bill Le Sage, JD, Jim Deuchar
Bottom row: Eric Dawson, Tony Kinsey

Above left: Don Rendell
Above right: Ed Harvey (trombone), Eddie Blair (trumpe
Left: Les Perrin, our great publicist

When I was younger!

Days of the Big Band

Left to right: JD (alto sax), Dave Lee (piano), Eric Dawson (bass), Kenny Clare (drums)

Derrick Abbott, Colin Wright, Bob Carson, Stan Parker (trumpets)

Tony Russell, Danny Ellwood, Garry Brown (trombones), Ron Snyder (tuba)

Front row: Danny Moss (tenor sax), Dickie Hawdon (trumpet), Laurie Monk (trombone), Alex Leslie (baritone sax)

Left to right: Kenny Napper (bass), Johnny Butts (drums)
Back row: Kenny Wheeler, Ron Simmonds, Leon Calvert, Gus Galbraith (trumpets)
Middle row: Johnny Marshall, Tony Russell (trombones), Ron Snyder (tuba)
Front row: Vic Ash (clarinet), Art Ellefson, Danny Moss (tenor saxes)

A Dankworth Quintet
Left to right: Ronnie Stephenson (drums), Kenny Wheeler (trumpet), JD (alto sax), Kenny Napper (bass), Alan Branscombe (piano)

In exuberant mood

Moreover, we were not alone on such tours. We were put together as part of an integrated show featuring a comedian and four dancers, and part of our duties were to accompany the latter.

Working for the US military involved journeys to outlying bases, so it still meant seeing a lot of the real Germany. In addition we found ourselves with spare time in such interesting places as Munich, Frankfurt and Heidelberg, with plenty of places to go to, including an occasional jazz club, where we were able to keep our jazz skills honed. Our official appearances were more of an entertainment for the average GI than a treat for the jazz fans, so meeting with other jazzmen and women, both US and German, meant a lot to us.

Back in England the Seven continued to grow in popularity, and live radio broadcasts became more and more frequent. Our group's successes in the popularity polls run by the music papers became almost foregone conclusions, together with my own personal show-ings in the sections devoted to the clarinet, the alto sax, arranging and composing. Our visits throughout the four components of the United Kingdom meant that our knowledge of the geography of our native land became pretty close to unchallengeable. Even the small-est of places occasionally put on a special do for a factory in the immediate locality, or a miner's recreation centre, or a rugby club. This gave us a pretty good coverage among ordinary people, and our star continued in the ascendant. Most people came to dance to our music, but hundreds merely flocked round the stage to stand and listen, waiting for the special show section around the halfway mark of the evening.

Our progress was part of British jazz history. But the history of the nation and the world ran alongside our musical activities, and some-times that history affected us. On the morning of 6 February 1952 our coach left Baker Street for a place called Ellesmere Port in Cheshire, where we were to play at a dance. We eventually arrived, but the dance never took place. During our journey King George VI had died, and the whole of Britain was thrown into mourning. The dance was of course cancelled, and we spent a part of the evening rehearsing for a forthcoming London concert, our sounds echoing through an empty dance hall, until we decided to call a halt and returned to our hotel for an early night. The next day we woke to the dawn of a new monarch for Britain, as young Queen Elizabeth II began her reign.

Our solo performances on the Sunday concert circuit were also an important part of our weekly routine. These events were immensely popular with families events until the advent of television gradually dissipated the crowds. The concerts were usually built round a band, which meant that the duties of the resident band were to accompany other artistes as well as doing their own spot.

On one such occasion we were on the same bill as impressionist Victor Seaforth, who had his full orchestral needs prepared for us at a band rehearsal immediately before the show. Victor's grand finale was an impression of Quasimodo as the Hunchback of Notre Dame, and his orchestral arrangement to accompany the action on stage was an integral part of it all. Unfortunately the score relied heavily on strings, played tremolo to add to the suspense, plus a percussionist's tubular chime set to add the crucial toll of the cathedral bell – and we could provide neither. I managed to rewrite the parts to produce an effect vaguely similar to the original with a trumpet, two clarinets and a muted trombone. The best we could do for the bell was a cymbal crash, which definitely did not work, but it was all we had.

There were two shows that evening, one at 5 and one at 8. Victor did the early part of his act while we waited for the big Hunchback moment. We were well prepared for it and gazed down at our revised music with confidence. The moment approached as the impressionist began his monologue. As he did so, the lights changed to a green wash, a very effective adjunct to the spectacle. The only snag was that the light change rendered our music totally illegible, and we spluttered to a halt. The cymbal, responding to the famous line 'Can't you hear the bells?', only succeeded in invoking suppressed giggles from the audience.

After the first show Victor came to my dressing-room. 'What happened?' was his enquiry. I explained about the lighting problem, and he promised that he would see to it for the 8 pm show. The bell problem was addressed and discussed. 'Don't worry about it, Johnny', said Victor. 'I'll get the stage manager to find something and operate it from the wings.'

The second show arrived and the improved lighting enabled us to produce a good musical effect, only marred a little by the Hunchback's asides between his poignant lines: 'I am the lowly hunchback of the great House of God . . . *can you see boys?* . . . the keeper of this gigantic belfry . . . *are you all right, lads?*', and so on. But the tolling of the bells was yet to come. When the cue came – 'Can't you hear the bells?' – there was a miserable clanking sounding something like a drainpipe being whacked with a coal hammer. It was not one of the great theatrical moments of all time, but it was certainly something I never will forget.

Nevertheless, what with those lucrative Sunday concerts, plus our radio shows, our record-making and our dances, we were doing well, and things looked like going on forever. Consequently any thoughts of meddling with our now winning formula although admittedly from time to time such thoughts did occur – quickly receded into the backwaters of our minds. We were tops in our field as we were – and we knew it.

Perspective II

The advent of the bebop movement on the jazz scene of the late forties was bound to have some immediate effect on the status quo. Thus the next decade saw much jockeying for position, as the old guard appraised the situation. Some established stars, such as Coleman Hawkins, at that juncture probably the world's best-known tenor sax soloist (he practically invented a solo role for the instrument), were obviously deeply affected by the radical changes and incorporated them with some success into their existing styles. Others, such as Benny Goodman, left their own playing unaltered but took care to surround themselves with other players whose work represented the changes. Yet others, mainly big-band leaders such as Woody Herman and Stan Kenton, found that the problem was to a greater or lesser extent being solved for them by their arrangers and orchestrators; harmonies, rhythms and indeed whole phrases born in the Parker–Gillespie camp began to find their way into the everyday scores which were the stock-in-trade of the larger combinations.

The big-band world, fed by such new thinking, was in a quandary. Many bandleaders were left struggling with, and eventually succumbing to, a dichotomy of styles; others were able to continue to thrive, or at least survive, during a period when, for both social and economic reasons, big bands generally were in decline. The large combinations of Woody Herman, Count Basie and Stan Kenton were among those able to cope, while Duke

Ellington, always a law unto himself, practically ignored the whole phenomenon without apparent loss of inspiration.

In fact the big band, admittedly in demise as a popular touring attraction
in dance halls, was far from dead from the point of view of musical innovation. This was in part owing to the efforts of such arrangers as Gil Evans
and Gerry Mulligan, who were able to evolve a style of orchestration which
bore little resemblance to the big-band sounds of the past. Trumpeter Miles
Davis soon became involved with these new departures in jazz scoring, and
the resultant recordings, the Birth of the Cool, were influential in shaping
a new role for the big bands of the fifties and sixties.

During the same period Davis continued working with small bands with
an equally great influence on the jazz world. Never a player to feature cascades of notes in the style of Dizzy Gillespie or Charlie Parker, Davis was
wise enough to surround his own less spectacular playing with sounds from
other talented players – alto saxist Cannonball Adderley, tenor man John
Coltrane, pianists Bill Evans, Chick Corea and Victor Feldman, and
drummer Philly Joe Jones. Later he contributed, with Gil Evans in
command of the orchestral accompaniment, further style-setting recordings such as Sketches of Spain and Porgy and Bess.

Another great contribution to the continued existence of the big-band
sound was the Count Basie Band, whose scores by Neil Hefti and others
were transporting the band from its early successful Kansas City style into
the more complex realms of modern jazz.

Meanwhile, at the other end of the scale in group size, baritone saxist and
arranger Gerry Mulligan, always a most individual stylist in whatever form
his talents emerged, made a great impact on jazz with a very small sound, a
piano-less quartet – just adding trumpet (Chet Baker), bass and drums to
his own playing. At the same time Mulligan's fellow arranger on the Birth
of the Cool sessions, pianist John Lewis, added further to the history of jazz
'chamber music' by founding the Modern Jazz Quartet, where the frantic
nature of some bebop performances was discarded in favour of an ultra-cool,
carefully scored style involving just piano, vibraphone, bass and drums.

It was all evidence – Davis, Mulligan, the Modern Jazz Quartet and even
Basie – that controlled performances were an equally satisfactory way to
produce good and exciting jazz, and that extremes of volume and pyro-
technics are not always necessary. But the latter were admittedly sometimes extremely effective, as in the case of the giant Stan Kenton band,

whose large brass section captured the public imagination during this period. This was the other end of the scale, demonstrating the immense range of the music which was available to either the performer or the writer.

World War II had accelerated the influence of jazz worldwide. Whereas in the years before the war the occasional non-American jazz musician or group deservedly attracted attention – George Chisholm's trombone playing in Britain, guitarist Django Reinhardt and violinist Stephane Grappelli in France – most jazz born outside the United States was regarded as either imitative or just laughable. This was destined to change after the war, at first gradually by degrees and later quite radically, as Canadian, European, Asian, South American and Australasian musicians began to shine, both in their home countries and as migrants to America.

Until that time jazz had been almost exclusively the preserve of American artistes, but it was now fast becoming, like Western classical music, an art form with an international forum, a host of expert practitioners and a sizeable and enthusiastic audience all over the globe.

One other significant factor had, meanwhile, since its emergence in the early fifties, changed the perception of jazz – the introduction of the long-playing record. Although on first examination a technical change allowing longer uninterrupted performances from artists had little to do with the music itself, this proved not to be the case with jazz. Before its introduction the world heard three or four minutes of their chosen performer or group at each sitting; the tendency therefore was for the creative forces in jazz to opt for compositions and arrangements to be of around that length, to avoid the necessity of a 'stop–start' factor in the listening process. Not surprisingly, this discipline even often affected (somewhat unnecessarily) live performances, with the result that jazz improvisers recording in pre-LP days tended to be experts at short exposures of their talents. It had been, if you like, the era of the jazz sound-byte.

The short-solo age of jazz was to change as a result of the long-playing record, and this alteration in the basic concept of the improvised solo was to herald, during the sixties, a new generation of jazz soloists and writers who would exploit it to the full. It meant that some of my favourite players of the late forties and fifties – Benny Goodman, Coleman Hawkins, Lester Young and Teddy Wilson, for example – would decline in popularity and influence, while others whom I equally admired – Charlie Parker, Dizzy Gillespie, Miles Davis – would grow. There were obviously exciting times ahead.

7

Love walked in

'John, it's about time you started a big band.'

I had somehow prepared myself for these words for some time, yet they still came as something of a shock. But I had no reason to question their wisdom. Harold Davison, my agent, was not much older than my own twenty-five years, yet his worldly appearance and his already bald head gave him an air of authority I hardly ever dreamed of questioning – even inwardly, let alone out loud. Everything about Harold exuded knowledge and achievement, although in fact he had achieved relatively little by then. Projecting the right kind of image is what being a successful agent is all about, and Harold was already a past master at that. His office overlooking Shaftesbury Avenue and two of London's famous theatres, his large intimidating oak desk, his cigar – obligatory for agents at the time – and a face and bearing which could at any given moment convey gravity, humour, enthusiasm, distaste or a dozen other emotions according to the pronouncements he happened to be making, all played a large part in making Davison the internationally successful entrepreneur he was later to become.

Of course. Not the slightest doubt about it. It was about time I started a big band. Harold said so. And it wasn't exactly surprising to me when, after having headed the music papers' popularity polls in about six sections – alto sax, clarinet, arranger, composer, small band and 'musician of the year' – on and off for the previous three or four years, I was being gently guided – no, rather, pushed – into thoughts of expansion – a Dankworth big band. In one sense the Seven could have gone on for many more years than it did, but in another it was commercially the cause of its own demise by its very success. To an agent, the only way to translate achievements of these proportions was to go into the big-band scene. To Harold it was a natural, almost inevitable, next move for his young client. It meant a higher profile in the entertainment industry, a better chance of securing bookings in the larger theatres and dance halls, and higher artistes' fees – meaning of, course, a higher percentage for Harold Davison Ltd.

After three and a half years of the Seven we all had our own feelings for and against the notion of expansion, and how each of us might fit into such a scenario. For me it was a timely suggestion. Now that both the novelty and the first flush of musical enthusiasm was tending to wane, a change seemed a desirable way of regaining momentum. At the same time, though, I had by now experienced many of the headaches involved in running a small band, and I was only too aware that these would multiply out of all proportion with the advent of a big band. While I regretted the loss of intimacy and freedom which would no doubt accompany the disbanding of the Seven, I felt that I would welcome the chance for the development of my own arranging skills. For years I had taken my scores to other bands – Ted Heath, Jack Parnell and Cyril Stapleton's BBC Show Band were examples – and experienced the limited amount of time leaders are prepared to allot to the rehearsal of new arrangements. A band of one's own would be quite a temptation. 'Yes, Harold. It's a good idea', I found myself saying. 'And the sooner the better!' I added, just to make it sound a bit more like my decision and less his. And I went off to plan my big band – without having the foggiest idea of how to go about it.

* * *

So in October 1953 I gave birth. It was not exactly a planned event. There were very few provisions made for a change in lifestyle. Very little advice was sought. Very little financial back-up was in place –

although, unlike the birth of the Seven at the beginning of my career, my credit was worth something, since I already had a fair history of good box office, plus a considerable amount of public and media interest.

Perhaps my brain doesn't want to recall those weeks of pregnancy immediately prior to the event, when a thousand preparations were doubtless being made. Musicians contacted and fixed, music arrangers assembled and briefed, uniforms measured for and produced, publicists given the facts they needed for headline stories – to be augmented by those they manufactured themselves. Engagements, radio shows and recording contracts booked, tours routed and negotiated with travel operators. Rehearsal premises booked. Brochures printed, photos taken, biographies revised . . . only someone who has been through the birth of a big band can really relate the extent of the trauma of it all.

I went through all that – and I've forgotten every single detail. If I had to do it again it would be like starting completely from scratch.

But somehow, like magic, on 23 October 1953 at the Astoria Ballroom in Nottingham, my big band was born.

The *Melody Maker*, at that time still the journal devoted to our corner of the music profession (though in more recent times it would not be seen dead taking an interest in such matters), saw fit to devote an entire centre spread and the views of two major critics to the occasion.

There were twenty of us on the stand that night – four trumpets (Derrick Abbott, Bill Metcalfe, Bob Carson, George Boocock), four trombones (Maurice Pratt, Gib Wallace, Bill Geldard, Ed Harvey), five saxes (Lew Smith, Freddie Courtney, Alex Leslie, Rex Morris, Maurice Owen), three rhythm (Bill Le Sage, piano, Eric Dawson, bass, Allan Ganley, drums), myself, and three singers. The vocal trio – although they seldom operated as such – were all fine soloists. They were Frank Holder, Tony Mansell and Cleo Laine.

The band was innovative visually, in that the conventional uniforms were replaced by blazers of different colours for each section – cerise for trumpets, bottle green for trombones, fawn for saxophones and gray for the rhythm section. The use of bowler hat (derby) mutes for the trumpets made an impact on both eye and ear as the players waved them across the bells of the instruments with parade-ground-like precision. Indeed the whole band was well drilled in stand-ups, sit-downs and gyrations of instruments from right to left and from the floor to the heavens. We became known for these spectacular bits of showiness, and indeed years later added a finale number in which the whole band came to the front of the stage with foot-high letters hanging from the bells of the instruments spelling 'Thanks a mil-ion'. The missing letter was a problem created by the fact that we had only thirteen blowers on whom to append the said cards. We solved it by giving pianist Dave Lee a clarinet and a British learner-driver's 'L'-plate to hang on it, completing the message and underlining Dave's non-existent prowess on the horn he was holding. This sort of clap-trap helped amuse and impress our general audience, although of course it added nothing to our reputation in the eyes of the more po-faced critics and academic jazz fans, who are apt to frown on such things. But who cared – or cares? Keeping a band of that size alive to play any sort of music was a problem even in those days, and any-thing which helped sell it without affecting the notes we played in any way was to me fair game. The jazz purists might have sniggered (I hate the term 'jazz purist', because of course jazz is a hybrid music and therefore by nature highly impure). But in the next two decades the big band went on to play much worthwhile music with many jazz greats, and earned plaudits from musicians, critics and fans all over the world.

That first night, however, was just plain fun. And I, just past my twenty-sixth birthday, was enjoying every minute of it.

And now my thoughts race back over more than four decades, struggling to remember details of that group of music-makers and the activities that became a lifestyle for them as well as for me. They included every type of musician from reliable rank-and-file players to mercurial geniuses of jazz. Some of them are still performing in Britain, Australia, South Africa and North America; others have died from various causes, ranging from cancer and drug abuse to old age. Some went on to other things such as pub management, flying tuition, and indeed Hollywood stardom. Even some among our non-playing numbers prospered. A junior road-manager – known in those days as a band boy – later went on to mastermind a world-famous rock group; our onetime bass trombonist Gary Brown became the booking agent for the Cunard empire; another started a radio station.

But in those days the only thing that seemed to matter was the quality of the music. My big band differed from virtually all its predecessors in that the very successful British big band of the past was run primarily as a business. Its leader's aim was to present a product with the maximum appeal to its audience. My goal was never that. I did of course realise that commercial concessions had to be made to survive, but I played a kind of game with the popular music industry, and continually tried to stretch the boundaries of what was considered commercial in order to be able to cock a snook at the doubters, who would say with a sneer, 'Dankworth! He'll never make it with a big band – he's far too jazzy.'

The big band in its various forms lasted nearly a dozen years as a full-time source of employment for its members. We made hit records, did TV appearances galore, and were even featured in a couple of movies. We shared the concert platform with some of Britain's most celebrated symphony orchestras and several conductors of international status. We topped popularity polls with monotonous regularity, even sometimes dethroning our main market competition and arch-rival, the Ted Heath band. We travelled abroad to Europe and to the States, where we had a gigantic success at the world's greatest jazz festival, together with acclaim from the critics. We played the world's most renowned jazz club, and shared the bill in concerts with perhaps the most famous big band of all time.

Yet I find myself now trying to get into the detail of it all, to see if I can recall any unerring accuracy with which my career decisions were made, or perfect timing that made them effective, or any efficiency which characterised their enactment. And, to be brutally frank, I've decided that no special magic or even wisdom existed. It was all a result of a large slice of sheer luck coupled with a good deal of absolute bloody-mindedness. Nevertheless, one fact came leaping at me – calculation or luck, inspiration or folly, it mattered not which. I'd started something from which there was no going back.

On reflection, I ask myself if those big-band days were in fact the high point of my career. Some might say so, especially the age-group who passed their formative years listening to us – on the radio and TV, in Sunday concerts (perhaps with their mums and dads), at college dances (almost certainly not with their mums and dads), at their local palais de danse or town hall, or on record. Indeed, having been a jazz fan's delight for a few years, I was now becoming more generally famous. I wrote a column for the *Daily Express*, my life story (at twenty-six!) was serialised in the London *Evening Star*, and every concert or dance promoter in the British Isles was interested in booking the band.

In fact we seemed in retrospect to have been swimming against the tide. In North America the big-band phenomenon showed definite signs of waning, and bands were tending to cut down in size and activities. But not us. Our 21-piece team rode roughshod over the rule book and took to the road, playing all the major cities and many of the minor ones, with frequent deviations into the outback to visit smaller villages and mining or other industrial communities.

We played dances, which was appropriate, as much of the jazz material we played could be danced to in one style or another. But some ballrooms had a reputation of delivering music that was suitable to the ballroom-dancing purists personified by Victor Sylvester, the highly successful dancing guru of the era, who led a band which played metronomically correct music for his disciples. Here we would run into considerable trouble. Although we could at a pinch produce music to conform to these rules, such stuff would immediately antagonise the Dankworth fans, who had turned up to listen, not dance, and expected more exciting musical fare.

Worse still, if the fans did decide to dance they would do so in a style which was a negation of all that was right and proper in the Sylvester camp – and occupied the major part of the dance floor in doing so. This greatly upset the purists. While actual fisticuffs were rare as a result – the jitterbuggers usually looked like invaders from another planet to the ballroomers, and quite formidable – the purist dancers, always a very vocal minority, ended up threatening to absent themselves from our future visits – to the consternation of the promoter.

However, by and large we were accepted joyfully into the hearts of the British public throughout the land. The Gaiety Ballroom, Grimsby; Green's Playhouse, Glasgow; Belle Vue, Manchester; Cardiff Arms Park; the Four Provinces, Dublin; London's Hammersmith

Palais (here we followed the footsteps of the Original Dixieland Jazz Band in 1917), the Isle of Man's Villa Marina and countless other such venues came within our orbit during those halcyon years. Some patrons adored us, some hated us. But the majority of them did the most important thing of all. They remembered us.

*   *   *

As I mentioned the big band boasted three good singers – Frank Holder, Tony Mansell and Cleo. True, they occasionally made solo recordings of their own, but they felt left out of many of the band's most exciting engagements, and consequently they often found life boring.

Cleo and I were beginning to become close. I had always had tremendous admiration for the woman, so the fact that her disintegrating marriage had already caused her to separate from her husband George and make her home in central London indicated to me that perhaps our relationship was destined to become more permanent. She took a small flat in the Holland Park area, then later a share in a top-floor flat in Trinity Church Square, not far from London Bridge, whose principal tenant was my friend and colleague David Lindup. A later move took her to a small group of apartments in Kilburn, two of which were already occupied by musicians, pianist Stan Tracey and saxist Denis Ackerman.

Not long after that move Cleo's divorce was made absolute. Over this period we had seen more and more of each other outside of our working relationship. My fondness for this quiet, determined person had grown into love, and it was in this tiny flat over a shoe shop in Kilburn High Road that our love blossomed.

Cleo's exceptional artistry had already led to many engagements outside of her band-vocalist duties, and one such occasion, entailing a visit to a Manchester TV studio for a day or so, came shortly after the news of the official end of her marriage. Missing her, and given by her absence an interlude in which to examine my thoughts, I made a snap decision – and picked up the phone.

'Granada TV – can I help you?'

'Cleo Laine, please – it's urgent!' My voice must have made it sound so to the operator, since she located Cleo within half a minute. 'Darling, have you got anything in your diary for Tuesday morning? – yes, next Tuesday, the day after tomorrow.'

'No, I don't think so – why?'

'Because I've fixed Hampstead registry for 11.30.' The ensuing silence suggested confusion. Perhaps she thought it was a recording session. It all needed clarification. 'Oh, by the way, will you marry me?'

I nearly said, 'We're getting married', but felt that might sound a little too authoritarian. I was, after all, still her employer. I cannot remember in any detail the sequence of sounds and words that constituted Cleo's reaction, but I deemed it to be positive.

And indeed it was. On Tuesday 18 March 1958 the knot was tied, with just three close friends – David Lindup and pianists Pat Smythe and Ken Moule – to share our secret. With total and unforgiveable lack of consideration, I left my mother to learn of it only when the press phoned her to ask if it were true. Sorry, mum.

The union was not properly thought through, of course – by either of us. It was done simply on impulse and by instinct. And, as with so many instances where instinct overrules practicality, in my experience at least, it was a good decision. Great events with far-reaching effects on the future sometimes come about as a result of finding oneself in the right place at the right time. Cleo and I were both there. That simple fact changed both of our lives quite dramatically, and perhaps in consequence changed in some small but maybe significant way the course of the history of music.

*   *   *

Discerning from the bandstand the degree of acceptance by a given audience is, in common with psychology and acoustic architecture, an inexact science. A glowering figure with a homicidal air, pacing back and forth agitatedly at the back of an otherwise obviously supportive crowd surrounding the performers, probably turns out to be a lifelong Dankworth buff with a record collection of hundreds and a bibliographical bookshelf taking up a whole wall. Once, when we were playing at an ice rink in Kirkcaldy in Scotland, our customers listened and danced on one side of a huge screen while the game of curling (a sort of ice version of bowls) took place on the other side. We performed an identical programme to one which had raised the roof at the Beach Ballroom, Aberdeen, the previous night. The lack of any discernible applause for our efforts – or even recognition of our presence – left me so depressed by the interval that I decided to get a drink from the bar to alleviate my sorrows. I slipped on an old jacket to avoid being spotted and found a comparatively deserted corner of the bar to grab my drink. Two rough-looking characters were talking in their north-of-the-border twang as I passed them. 'Bloody guid bond!' was all I heard one say to the other.

But it can work both ways. On another occasion, during our third visit to the Irish Republic I believe, our itinerary included a small town somewhere in the hinterland. We were conscious of our successful image there and consequently perhaps loading the tolerant but discerning Irish public with too much esoteric and undanceable jazz. Nevertheless we interpreted the broad smiles after our quite impressive rendering of the Irish national anthem as an indication of general approval. So at its conclusion I bent down at the front of the stand to hear what a smiling, well-dressed, middle-aged fellow was trying to say to me. I extended my hand. He took it and shook it warmly, 'How d'you do, Mr Dankworth,' then added 'by the way, don't ever bring your band here again, will you?' We both smiled again and parted. Indeed we never did revisit that particular place; I know a piece of good advice when I hear it.

Continental Europe came into our orbit on a number of occasions. One instance was an invitation from a TV station in the Saar region of Germany to record two programmes. We were pretty experienced in television by then, and had no trouble putting together and taping a couple of hour-long shows in one afternoon at their (then) rather primitively equipped studios. To say that the management was impressed was an understatement. They had their own resident orchestra at the station, but this had been there so long and was so all-powerful (it was a state-run institution, and therefore highly unionised as well as being rather overmanned) that they insisted each programme be done in two stages, first sound and then vision. Doing it their way, the sound recording could easily take two or three days before the television part even began. This made our two shows in five hours impressive indeed.

The director approached me. 'We would like to do more shows with you', he said.

'Thank you', I replied. 'I know we're available later on in the year. When would you want us back?'

'Tomorrow', he said.

I think I concealed my surprise. 'Well', I said coolly, 'I don't see a problem in staying one more day, and we have plenty of material to make another programme or two. How many more were you think-ing of?'

'Twenty-six.'

They turned out to be 'filler' programmes of around ten minutes' duration apiece. With two good singers in Frank and Cleo at our dis-posal, the repertoire didn't constitute a difficulty. Apparently the German band had wanted to do one a day, so our counter-offer of the whole lot in an afternoon and evening was slightly more appealing to the cost-conscious management. We rattled them off with profes-sional fluency, rarely stopping for retakes. 'Yonny Dankvort: ein' quickly became 'Yonny Dankvort: zwei' for the man with the clapper-board, and by the time 'Yonny Dankvort: sechs-und-zwanzig' was reached we all felt a sense of achievement and the need for a beer – tempered by a slight feeling of guilt for having undercut the local musicians by – er – several thousand per cent.

Other images of European visits are equally vivid but less-flattering. On one occasion we were booked to play at a bullring in Majorca by a British businessman who felt that such arenas could be put to better use. The event was well publicised and organised, and the hospitality was great. Too great, unfortunately, for us ill-disciplined lot, who immediately took advantage if it – and the dirt-cheap liquor prices – to imbibe. Musicians of that era were expected and able to ingest a considerable amount of drink without too much adverse effect. But for one man – our bass player, who I think should remain anonymous, although he has since foresworn alcohol and remained drink-free for many years – it was all too much, and he arrived at the gig very much the worse for wear.

Sadly the crowd was sparse – the event was able neither to persuade the Spanish to try something different, nor to convince the Brits that they should spend their pesetas seeing something they could easily catch at home. But those present were watching and listening carefully, and we knew it. We shepherded our severely incapacitated bassist into the arena (we might have got away with it in a theatre behind curtains), but without any hope of avoiding giggles from the audience. We managed to prop him up into a position where it looked feasible that he might be able to pluck a few notes should he come around to it – literally.

How we got through that performance I shall never know. What we sounded like only someone listening could ever tell us. Perhaps by the grace of God it wasn't so bad. At least we weren't physically thrown off the island, as some of our compatriots have fared since. But I'm distinctly aware that we, normally a pretty smooth-running music machine in those days definitely weren't firing on all cylinders that night.

To whichever kindhearted, public-spirited Britisher booked us on that fateful night, may I offer by way of retribution for your patience and fortitude a complimentary copy of this book, or alternatively a pair of tickets to our next concert – where you may well notice the difference. Or perhaps a meal together at a London restaurant of your choice – preferably alcohol-free.

The big band played hundreds or even thousands of concerts with faultless behaviour and great professionalism during its career, so it seems a little unfair to single out one unfortunate occasion when it fell down. But such exceptions tend to be the ones that stay in the mind, rather than the times when everything went well, especially when they took place in a foreign setting as exotic as this one.

However, in 1954, just after the start of the big band, I deserted my new toy for a couple of weeks to undertake an overseas trip as a soloist. It turned out to be the most eye-opening experience of my life.

8

Black, brown and beige

The offer to visit three South African cities as a soloist and perform with a local group came early in 1954. This sounded interesting to me, then still only twenty-six, and keen to see more of the world. I was not aware of anything being wrong with race relations in South Africa. Occasionally one heard the term 'colour bar', but to a Londoner such a phrase was usually used in connection with a specific incident – a typical example being, say, that in deference to certain American clientele the Savoy hotel had refused accommodation to a black guest, which in turn had created a furore in the press. One imagined, naively, that something similar happened – rather more frequently, perhaps – in South Africa, and that was it. Anyway that seemed to be the picture to me – at that time a distinctly non-political animal. I was to receive a rude shock.

*   *   *

The plane to Johannesburg was several hours late, and we touched down at about the time the concert was scheduled to finish. However, I was met by the promoter and rushed to a waiting limousine, complete with a police motor-cycle escort. We finally got to City Hall. Clutching my sax case, I bounded up the imposing steps to meet hordes of fans, who had given me up for lost, coming down them. I entered the hall, walked down the aisle to the stage, and within minutes was jamming with the rhythm section. I can't imagine that I played well under such conditions, but it was certainly a memorable way to start a concert.

That event over, I began to take stock of things. My pianist for the tour was a Briton living and working in South Africa – Dave Lee. Dave was quick to point out the injustices of the South African system, the corruption in the police, the intransigence of most of the politicians and,most serious of all, the fact that the situation was not getting better, but rapidly worse. Dave was the first dissident I had met in my life. Had he not decided to return to his native Britain not long after my tour I'm certain he would have been in serious trouble with a regime that was growing more intolerant by the day.

On a free night before our next concert I was taken to a small, luxury theatre where Africans were allowed to perform to an all-white audience. Dave was keen for me to go to this event, as it always featured the cream of the crop of Bantu artistes. The bill opened with some glorious singing by a talented male–female group, followed by a solo pianist, Sol Klaster. Sol played a Chopin ballade quite beautifully, and received rapturous albeit patronising applause from a bejewelled, befurred audience.

Our next Johannesburg-based concert was at Witwatersrand University, where Sol was a music student. After our performance I was amazed to see him in a cleaner's dust coat, leaning on a broom in the wings. 'He came backstage to hear the concert and needed an alibi', explained Dave. 'He'd never have been allowed in otherwise.' And this was South Africa *before* apartheid officially began. It then began to dawn on me that my audiences were not representative of South Africa, merely of white South Africa, as of course was my accompanying group.

The Bantu contingent of jazz musicians was small at the time, and Dave was anxious that they should get a chance to jam with a more experienced player such as myself. The only way to do this was in a music store, where we got together round a piano and enjoyed each other's music. Later I had my photo taken with many of these musicians and enthusiasts, posed on the steps of the university auditorium just before a concert which they were not allowed to attend.

My fury with the whole system was coming to the boil. A few concerts, broadcasts and recording dates later, and my short stay in South Africa was over – yet the visit was to have long-term effects for me. Soon after my return to England a message came through from Johannesburg offering me a tour with my new band. £10,000 was the opening offer, and in those days such figures made headlines in the musical press.

But since my South African experience I had learned a lot more about the country. Father Trevor Huddleston, then regarded by non-whites in South Africa as almost a saint in view of his almost solitary campaign to defend their human rights, had appealed in the London *Observer* for a cultural boycott of the nation. It was an unfamiliar concept in those days, but I was in a position to be one of the first performing artists to respond. 'DANKWORTH TURNS DOWN £10,000 TOUR OF SOUTH AFRICA', screamed the front-page banner headline of the *Melody Maker*. I had made my decision, and explained it to the readers in a statement that followed: 'I believe that [racialism] is wrong. Under the circumstances it would be hypocritical for me to accept a tour that could be attended by only a section of the population.'

This decision led to a lengthy relationship with Father Huddleston, and to many concerts in Britain dedicated to fund-raising for Christian Aid, the organisation which assisted his work in helping the non-white majority in South Africa and usually arranged by Canon John Collins. Humphrey Lyttelton and Lionel Hampton were two of the many jazz artists to donate their services to the cause.

My refusal to play in South Africa and my participation in those concerts led to contacts with the 'dissident' society in London. Prominent among this faction was Sylvester Stein, who had once been editor of the magazine *Drum*, a white-owned publication with a wide Bantu circulation. When the black US tennis star Althea Gibson won Wimbledon in the early fifties, Sylvester selected a picture of the victor being embraced by her white opponent at the conclusion of the final – a harmless enough event one would have thought – for the front cover of the magazine. It was vetoed by the owners, which hardly surprised Sylvester; but for him it was the last straw, and he and his family packed their bags and left to reinstall themselves in London. From their home overlooking Primrose Hill he and his wife Jenny entertained like minds, and it was there that we met so many expatriate South Africans of all colours and their sympathisers.

Around this time I received a letter from Huddleston in Johannesburg. He brought to my attention the talents of a young trumpet player, Hugh Masekela, whom he somewhat quaintly described, if I remember correctly, as a 'budding Louis Armstrong'. He asked me to 'manufacture' the promise of a job in Britain, so that Hugh could get a passport. This I was able to do, and shortly afterwards I met my protégé on his arrival in Britain. Cleo and I contrived to assist him a little in establishing himself in his strange new surroundings, where there were no legal restraints on the movements and actions of non-whites. After a short stay in London he was able to move on to his eventual goal – the United States – where he quickly became something of a star.

Helping Hugh Masekela out of South Africa was a pleasant duty to perform and by no means onerous; Hugh was well able to look after himself once free of his shackles, so to speak. A more complex assignment, however, lay ahead. A phone call started it all. 'Mr Dankworth?'

'Speaking', I replied.

'Her Majesty's Prison, Winchester, here. We have a stowaway from South Africa in custody. Cameron Mokaleng. He says you know him well.'

It was true. Everywhere we went in Johannesburg during my visit I had been followed by a diminutive jazz-obsessed young African. His name was indeed the one announced by the prison officer, but the jazz fraternity in South Africa knew him by the name Pinocchio. Apparently my visit had inspired him to come to London, but not by the official route as Masekela had done. 'Er, yes – I do.'

'Mr Mokaleng told the magistrate in court this morning that you have agreed to vouch for and sponsor him, and that you have a job waiting for him – is this true?'

I knew that telling the truth would certainly mean an immediate return to the point of origin for Pinocchio, and I couldn't bear the thought. 'Well, yes – that's all perfectly true.'

'Then would you come and take him off our hands please, sir?'

I got in the car and about two hours later stepped through the fore-boding main gate of Winchester jail. Pinocchio was extricated, and I drove the delighted young man straight to a clothing store in Charing Cross Road, where he was kitted out, then to our Kilburn apartment, where he was installed until further notice. The next day I was able to persuade my good friend David Platz to find Pinocchio a job in the packaging department of his publishing firm.

Pinocchio didn't, however, manage to fit into London society very easily – he soon left the job and began to live on welfare. It occurred to us that maybe he was a frustrated musician, and so I loaned him (or I suppose you could say gave him, since I never got it back) a sax-ophone to master. He never did, and eventually disappeared from our lives. I rather expected that Pinocchio's arrival in Britain in this unorthodox way would herald the occurrence of many such occa-sions, but if it did we never knew about them.

My refusal to go to South Africa had other repercussions on my life apart from being considered a sort of 'safe house' for escapees from the regime. I had hitherto been totally non-political, in common with the majority of people in arts or entertainment – it was then the British tradition for such people to be seen as unaligned. But now the floodgates were opened – a stand on racial equality was, in the eyes of some, a show of support for the outlawing of blood sports, the aboli-tion of capital punishment, the power of the trade unions and so on. Every left-wing cause was thrown at my feet for assistance in some form or other – an invitation to speak at a meeting, to become a patron, or just to make a donation.

I did in fact espouse some of these causes (I spoke at the Royal Albert Hall against capital punishment), but I was somewhat irri-tated to find that, in the eyes of some, all issues proposing change to existing law or practice were the responsibility of the left. Some of the crusades I was asked to join I considered should be treated as cross-party matters, and felt strongly that racialism was one of them. To make it a party issue would alienate lots of would-be sympathisers.

So when there was racial trouble in the Notting Hill Gate district of London in 1958 a few showbiz people got together and formed what we called the Stars Campaign for Inter-racial Friendship, yet were careful to avoid party affiliations. Our main objective was to give prominence via the media to the fact that most celebrities had liberal views on race, thus setting an example. On one occasion Cleo and I were doing our bit for the cause by attending a televised discussion about race. Others there included a man named Colin Jordan, who was at that time pretty much the leader of the fascist movement in Britain. Jordan told the throng that his answer to the problem was simple – all non-whites should be transported back to the place of their birth. 'And where would you be sent back to, Cleo Laine?' asked the moderator.

'Southall, Middlesex', was the response in an intentionally broad cockney accent. Mr Jordan scowled – it was not what he had in mind.

SCIF didn't move mountains, but it must have done a little to decrease the tensions of those times. More important, in addition to performing artists, it brought out of the woodwork a number of well-known people from the press, the record industry and the literary world to show in public their support for racial justice. Later some ethnic minorities were able to gather their forces and campaign on their own behalf, although I thought (and still think, for that matter) that demands for racial equality were (and are) better made by a multicoloured lobbying group.

However, in those days the non-white showbiz presence in London amounted to a tiny handful of men and women of extremely varied backgrounds. As far as jazz and dance music was concerned, non-white musicians were usually treated pretty much on their merits, and integrated easily into work in bands with other British players. In the theatre and the film industry things were different. Non-whites were cast in non-white parts when they were available, but there the trouble often began. The parts were usually small ones – servants, maids and the like – and not very well written at that. Moreover, type-casting usually decreed that blacks had to be 'very-very-black'. Several times I met a black actor friend looking a good deal darker than usual. 'Been on holiday?' I asked on one occasion.

'No, just to an audition. A bit of Cherry Blossom boot polish makes a world of difference when it comes to getting the job!' my friend replied, with a wry chuckle. But it was no joke. Cleo had become involved in serious acting – in fact she impressed the drama world immensely in *Flesh to a Tiger*, a play by West Indian writer Barry Record – but several times in subsequent interviews for parts she was asked to black up.

I came back from my visit to South Africa convinced that there would have to be a bloodbath there one day costing millions of lives. It seemed the only possible resolution. I was happily proved wrong by the arrival of Nelson Mandela, the great African leader who emerged from twenty-seven years of incarceration to lead his country into a new way of life – his 'rainbow nation', as he called it. Mandela had not started his period of imprisonment when I first went to South Africa, but I never had the pleasure of meeting the man. Yet I suspect that he would have approved of my action in refusing to work there. I was and still am proud of my decision: by being perhaps the first prominent artiste to decide not to go I may have helped encourage others to make similar decisions.

Back from the exotic land and a southern hemisphere summer, it was time to reacclimatise to London's winter, and to concentrate anew on the welfare of my still fledgling band.

9

Band of gold

The big band had much the same travel routine in Britain as its predecessor the Seven, but a much more extensive one. Large and important venues, which had been rare visiting places for the Seven, were our regular ports of call. The tours got longer, the attention our visits attracted got much greater, and the financial side – if not yet really rewarding for me, with my huge payroll – became far more secure. Things were really looking up.

Long seasons of weekly live radio shows were now the order of the day, and on and off for years one midweek night a week we visited the Aeolian Hall, nestling rather incongruously among expensive shops in Bond Street, London's snootiest shopping area. This ex-recital hall, where countless legends of classical music had in the past performed – my hero Maurice Ravel was one – had become the home of BBC Light Music, a department of that august organisation that handled the affairs of everything from theatre organs to palm court orchestras, embracing brass bands and Dixieland jazz on the way. All day famous radio names could be spotted bustling in and out of its doors, saluted by uniformed gentlemen.

In those days it seemed that the BBC Light Music department had a supremo with almost dictatorial powers, and the impression in the world of popular music was that you needed to be on the list of that person's favourites – otherwise you didn't broadcast. To say that artistic merit, or at least professional proficiency, didn't come into this would I suppose be wrong; but if you were to become a regular radio performer a lot depended on how good a salesman you (or your agent) happened to be, rather than how good a musician you were or how appealing your music was.

There was Tawny Neilson, the woman who instigated the 'plug-list', a curious phenomenon which was an attempt to stop music publishers from bribing bandleaders in return for the broadcast of a certain song. Such actions had caused a scandal in the late forties, and to cure it the BBC issued a list of tunes – compiled by the publishers, of course – from which the bandleader *had* to select 60 per cent of his programme. Thus the publishers' goal was achieved without the necessity for bribes.

This infuriating rule obviously lowered the quality of a band's output, but nobody appeared to be able to come up with a better alternative. Moreover, it increased rather than diminished the activity of the 'song-pluggers', who hung round bandleaders and singers at Aeolian Hall like flies round excrement extolling the virtues of their latest tawdry batch of ditties. Now that financial bribery was out of the question, they had to resort to forcing their victims to acquiesce just to get such predators off their backs, with the result that the most objectionable song-pluggers often turned out to be the most successful!

Many were just a pain, but some were outrageous. One – I'll call him Max – would regularly assail me as I left Aeolian Hall to go to my car and, walking at my elbow, bring out three or four 'pro' copies of his latest assignments. Everything he ever had was, he assured me, just made for the Dankworth style, whether it be a cowboy song, a torch song (which he'd inevitably endorse as 'just right for the girl' – he could never recall Cleo's name), a lacklustre waltz (which he swore would transform into a great 'beat' number) or anything else. And when after all his blather he realised he had made no real case artistically for me to do any of his songs, he countered with: 'Well, mate, they may not be the greatest songs, but they're "commercial". You can't have it all ways. You know what I always say, Johnny – art for art's sake and money for Christ's sake!'

After Miss Neilson's departure a formidable Australian named Jim

Davidson ruled the roost at the Aeolian Hall; his edicts produced fear and despondency in the hearts of bandleaders and musicians alike. The BBC Show Band, led by Cyril Stapleton, was his baby, and his ambitions for it were well known. Also well circulated were his alleged off-the-cuff remarks to producers during policy meetings, such as: 'I'll get a British sound from the show band even if I have to change the embouchures of the brass players.'

Later the incumbent was Donald Maclean, a quietly spoken, cultured Scot who had worked his way up through the 'creative ranks' of the corporation, unlike certain of his predecessors. We got on well, since he was at least sympathetic to the cause of quality, but during one lunch together he talked of the need for 'press-button radio', inferring that sooner or later even the all-powerful BBC would have to phase out their long-established policies and go for the lowest common denominator. He meant, as I read it, that each wavelength should have clearly defined labels — popular, light music, classical and so on. And that of course meant that jazz – an ill-defined, hybrid music if ever there was one – would be struggling for a place under any of these labels.

The writing was on the wall. But we had many more years before the BBC reached its present stage, when live music is virtually disappearing from the airwaves. Our weekly broadcasts continued, often with guest artists to vary the diet. On one series we used a classical guest every week, such as violinist Alan Loveday, clarinettist Jack Brymer, violist Kenneth Essex and so on. (I use the word 'we' in these contexts to include my dear friend and co-arranger David Lindup, who was my constant aide not only in the planning of these radio shows, but in almost every facet of the band's activities.)

We decided to devote the spot one week to the tuba, and invited Gerard Hoffnung to perform with us. Although he was well known as a cartoonist, few people were aware of his ability on 'the bass of the brass', but he seemed quite flattered when we asked him to appear on the programme. We went to his house in Hampstead Garden Suburb, where we found him listening to Janacek's overture *Colas Breugnon*, which he had apparently just discovered. After we had convinced him that this work could not be arranged for tuba solo and jazz orchestra we started the quest for the ideal vehicle. *The Blue Danube, Alexander's*

Ragtime Band, Saint-Saëns's *Le Cygne* and *Don't Fence Me In* were all suggested and rejected. We settled for *Stardust*, worked out an appropriate routine and a suitable key, and said our good-byes, promising him a tuba part to study forthwith.

As we closed the wicket gate enclosing the little front garden, the front door reopened and Gerard emerged with his tuba. 'I've got it, I've got it!' he cried. 'What about . . .?' He played the opening bars of Richard Rodgers's *There's a Small Hotel* across the top of the gate.

Gerard played *Small Hotel* – quite beautifully – on the radio show later that week.

My band supplied the backing for numerous overseas visitors during its existence, but one I will remember above all the rest. The band was augmented with strings, the arrangements were by Nelson Riddle, and the lady singer – Ella Fitzgerald. Not all such visiting artistes behaved wonderfully but I was quite ready and willing to bear any sort of cross for this lady, so great was my respect for her. In the event she turned out to be one of the sweetest, kindest people I have worked with. Among her repertoire on that occasion was a Riddle arrangement of *Lady Be Good* – not the fast and furious treatment for which she is so famous, but a slow ballad version. The sounds that night in the BBC's 'Paris' studio in Lower Regent Street were ethereal. Many years later we were to perform together again with a much bigger orchestra – the San Francisco Symphony – but with equally enjoyable results.

Guest artistes, on radio, on TV or just on tour, came one after the other, some good, some not so good, but all of them pretty famous at the time – Al Martino, Sophie Tucker, Anita O'Day, Sarah Vaughan. But two of them provided special experiences for very different reasons.

One was Johnny Ray. He was a big name at the time of his tour with us, and our visits to the provinces provided full-time work for the respective constabularies of the towns we played. Towards the end of his performance a line of policemen was usually deployed along the edge of the stage to restrain the efforts of hundreds of young girls to clamber on, but generally a couple of them managed it. Johnny loved all that. Indeed if the police were too efficient he would get rather annoyed – it was a most effective part of his show to be mobbed!

Outside the stage door hundreds of fans waited for Johnny to emerge after the show, but he seldom did, as the police usually spirited him off through another exit. On occasions I became a sort of substitute, since when they couldn't get their hands on the star anyone would do. I always signed my name hundreds of times in these situations – on programmes, autograph books, records, shirts, forearms and even midriffs – to satisfy the demands of star-hungry fans.

Johnny Ray was possibly the worst singer we toured with. One of the best – certainly the best male – was Nat 'King' Cole. We toured with Cole more than once during his initial heyday in the fifties. He was a musician's dream to work with, a fine singer and a great pianist. He usually brought his own drummer with him – Lee Young, brother of the great saxophonist Lester – who drove our band along compellingly with the inborn skill of a great drummer. The arrangements Cole featured in his show were of high quality – many by Billy May and Nelson Riddle – and Nat loved our band and made a point of saying so to the audience.

The admiration was mutual. I had been a fan of his since my early days, even before I started playing. His group, the Nat 'King' Cole Trio, was well known in jazz circles long before he made the hit recordings as a singer which brought him to the notice of the general public. In the jazz context he had been equally recognised as a piano soloist, and I was disappointed that he played so little in the programme he had prepared for his British tour. 'Why don't you play more piano, Nat?' I asked him after the first concert.

'D'you think I should?' he replied.

'I'm sure the crowd would love it', I said. 'Why not give it a whirl?'

He did – that night. Without any warning, about halfway through the concert he played four bars' introduction into *How High the Moon* and motioned to me to join in. There followed a short jam session, and as I predicted the crowd lapped it up. Of course, at that time Nat Cole's popularity was such that he could have played the kazoo with one hand and the spoons with the other – not a bad combination if you think about it – and they would have loved that too. But the jam session stayed in the programme and everybody was happy.

Nat Cole was a family man, and on occasions brought his wife and children on tour with him. Years later, in the seventies, Cleo and I were on the Mike Douglas TV show which was being taped in Philadelphia. Natalie Cole was also on the programme. After the taping someone introduced us. 'I'm delighted to meet you', I said.

'Well, of course, we've met before', countered Natalie. Then she reminded me of a time in her dad's dressing room on tour in Britain when Nat had told a shy little girl, 'Say hello to Mr Dankworth, Natalie.' Kids remember things, and she had never forgotten the excitement of going touring with her dad to another country – and meeting a British bandleader. I felt extremely flattered.

Nat Cole struck me as an ideal star – talented, focused and possessing a highly definitive and individual style, yet modest, polite and untainted by the worst aspects of success (perhaps on account of his long career in the profession before stardom reached him). Being a black entertainer in this position was far from easy in those days, especially in the States, where the civil rights campaigners had yet to change the course of history in the Deep South, together with the lot of the African-American throughout the nation. He himself, by his own behaviour pattern on reaching the top, must have done a power of good to the cause.

One night at an important concert he surprised me by saying, 'Ladies and gentlemen, I'm having a great time performing with one of the best bands in the world.' I'm not sure if he really meant it, but by now I knew the man well enough to know his train of thought. He had probably realised that the audience tended to take us for granted since we were not transatlantic visitors. So he made his public aware that, like most American musicians, he judged his fellow performers by what he heard, and not by their origin. And, to be quite honest and immodest simultaneously, we were an extraordinarily good band at the time. If Nat thought so and said so I suppose that was fair enough.

Sarah Vaughan was another great person to work with and a great singer. Like many singers she was sensitive to tempos, and one night said after a show (after, as she never showed any sign of displeasure on the stage), 'John, the tempo to *Poor Butterfly* was a little slow tonight.' I knew it wasn't any slower than the night before. However, the previous song, *Just One of Those Things*, had gone a bit faster than usual, thus making the ensuing tune seem slower than normal. The next night I made sure that *Things* was a touch steadier, and played *Butterfly* at the identical pace that Sarah considered slow. 'How were the tempos tonight?' I enquired as we walked towards our dressing-rooms after the performance.

'Great – thanks for moving *Butterfly* along.' Years later, in the early seventies, Sarah was Cleo's guest on a BBC special, and I still treasure a video of the two girls singing a medley based on *Girl Talk*, each of them mixing snippets of good songs with cross-talk and conversation – about men.

*   *   *

In spite of all the excitement of touring with guest stars, however, the bread-and-butter work essential to a band's survival made more demands on my time. My orchestra needed not only to be good. It had to be distinguished – and, more important, distinguishable. Upsizing from small band to big band had given me an opportunity to put an individual stamp on the sound of my band, a musical identity which all bands sought to acquire but so few actually achieved. The Seven had an individual sound, but with such limited musical resources at its disposal there was always a danger of wearing out the magic. A big band, with its much wider range both musically and in terms of orchestral colour, presented in those days the ultimate challenge for its writers. I wanted to find a new sound for the band, a sound which would identify it as readily as Duke Ellington's or Count Basie's – or, for that matter, Glenn Miller's, although the last had little to do with my ambition, to make my own band closely allied to jazz. I was after a 'concept sound' that registered an instant identity.

The use of mutes for the brass was a comparatively easy but effective way of finding an identifiable sound. I was attracted by the bowler hat or derby mute, which had been used in big bands of the past but seemed in 1953 to be on the decline. I made them a prominent feature of the trumpet section and used the wa-wa effect they produced a great deal in the early arrangements. Not only did they sound good but the visual effect was quite exciting. (They were to have yet another use when, sometime later, touring in severe wintry conditions, the band coach got stuck on an ice-covered road ascending a hill. We found a pile of grit provided at the roadside to help the wheels grip the surface, but nothing to shovel it on with. The hat mutes provided the perfect answer.)

Another arranging ploy involved the saxes in using alternative fingerings to make an interesting sound, almost like the wa-wa effect available with brass mutes. The process is too involved to explain here, but it worked after a fashion, and the combination of these two factors, plus several others equally cumbersome to describe (plus some musical tricks like the use of consecutive fourths) set a sort of pattern for the style of the band. And so concerned was I about its control and its usage that I decided to do all the instrumental scores myself, leaving only vocal arrangements and the occasional speciality dance number to other writers. With hindsight I feel that this may have been a mistake; perhaps I should have started the library with a number of other points of view about how the new band should sound and let the identity of the group emerge organically. After all, the Miller sound was created not by Miller but by staff-arranger Jerry Gray, Basie's later sounds were dominated by Neil Hefti, and of course even the great Duke Ellington relied heavily on the contributions of Billy Strayhorn to maintain the special sound for which his band was famous.

One of the arrangers I then invited to join my team was a young saxophonist whose obvious future was in writing rather than playing. The aforementioned David Lindup became not only the staff arranger for the band, but my musical partner and friend for the next three decades, not only for my various big bands over the dozen years, but for a considerable amount of my entire output as a composer until his sudden death in 1994. He soon graduated from vocal arrangements to instrumental features, and the band found a new dimension to the sounds they were to produce for an ever-growing army of fans.

Our relationship changed gradually over the years from creator and éminence grise to an equal partnership. We wrote several suites for the band over the years, working together on a suitable main theme, and then separately on the component parts. They ranged from a commissioned piece for Lord Montagu's Beaulieu festival to a *Scrooge Suite* for a Christmas BBC Jazz Club broadcast. In addition David also orchestrated from my sketches for the great majority of my movie scores during the sixties and seventies, when this constituted a large portion of my work.

Sometimes we would share commissions as equals. For instance, after thirteen episodes of the Anglia Television series *Survival*, I felt I had written myself dry of new ideas for music accompanying soaring seagulls or galloping zebra. So I suggested to David that we split the task down the middle by agreeing on a common motif or short theme and each of us using this motif as a basis for independent portions of the required music. So successful was this way of working that we completed more than eighty further *Survival* scores.

We worked together so closely that we found ourselves merging our composing styles. When, several years later, soon after David's death, I was attempting to extract some of his best writing for a concert paying tribute to his work, I found myself quite uncertain about which pieces were his and which were mine. The handwriting usually gave the game away, but some of the scores had been lost and only the extracted parts remained, giving no clue.

Our working together meant that we had to be physically close on frequent occasions. I spent many hundreds of hours at David's flat in Trinity Church Square in Southwark, not far from London Bridge. One of my many failings is procrastination, and this meant that for some very important recording sessions we both worked throughout the night before. Occasionally I was able to catch a couple of hours' sleep, but David was seldom so lucky. As for our poor copyist, Ken Williams, who of course couldn't start his work until we were well on the way with ours, his sleepless night often carried on until about noon the next day, when he would find a space somewhere in the place of recording – often in the actual studio itself – and copy parts out in a race against time before we ran out of music to play. I must admit I occasionally malingered, taking more time than was strictly necessary over rehearsing a piece in order to give our copyist more time to complete the next set of parts.

Once when David and I were working together on an important item for the band, the only way to beat the clock and have it ready on time was for David to join me and the band on the tour. We decided to meet in Gloucester. On my arrival at the small hotel we had chosen I anxiously enquired whether David had arrived before me. He had, but was in a room a long way from mine. When I insisted he should be near me they offered a twin-bedded room for the two of us. I readily agreed to this, but not without causing a few raised eyebrows.

That night we elected to do our work in the resident's lounge, with the night porter navigating his vacuum cleaner around piles of our music spread all over the floor. At about five that morning I had finished my sketches, and went to bed while David soldiered on. He kept working through the whole night and didn't get to bed at all. So we eventually left the hotel that morning under an air of suspicion – word had quickly got around from the maids that only one of our two beds had been occupied. I fear that for a long time after that in Gloucester the nature of our sexuality – two married men – was in some doubt.

The nature of an orchestrator's work in relation to a composer's sketch is difficult to define. It depends a lot on the detail (or lack of it) in the sketch itself, as well as the amount of discussion (or lack of it) which takes place between the creator of the sketch and its orchestrator. As a result collaborations of this kind are often shrouded in mystery, and few people except those concerned know exactly who did what in certain of the many joint productions of, say, Duke Ellington and Billy Strayhorn, George Gershwin and Ferde Grofé, or Stephen Sondheim and Jonathan Tunick. The reason is that there is no overall answer: the extent of the orchestrator's work varies immensely from one occasion to another. In some instances my written instructions to David would be extremely brief, especially if time was short. I knew that he would flesh out the ideas I had passed on in a way quite similar to my own style. On other occasions I would be quite meticulous with my sketch and go into great detail of the role of each instrument, leaving my orchestrator little to do apart from the donkey work of spreading the information of three or four staves onto the twenty or even thirty required for a full orchestral score – a time-consuming but not an intellectually difficult task requiring immense skill. This is, anyhow, the way David and I worked over all those years – and all those many thousands of bars and probably hundreds of hours' worth of music. I was able to be much more prolific as a result of David's help, and felt quite lost for a while when our collaborations finally ceased with his death.

But the scores of mine which have given me the most satisfaction have been those in which the only person concerned was me. Writing music for a large group of musicians has something of the loneliness of a long-distance runner about it; you sit alone and devote your whole thinking process to that orchestra, and gradually it comes to life – in your mind. Each tiny note for every player, each touch of the bow on the string, each flourish of the woodwind, each brush on a cymbal, each whisper from a muted horn, each subtle glissando from the harp are crucial to the overall pattern. Working on a full orchestral score is something like I imagine a Renaissance painter adding gradually to the detail of a painting with painstaking care – until the crucial moment when he felt the scene was complete. Sometimes to go further than that point merely gilds the lily and perhaps confuses the basic simplicity of the original idea; it is surprising how often the most beautifully majestic sounds from an 85-piece symphony orchestra turn out to be, on consulting the score, just an arrangement of four or five well-chosen notes. The majesty comes from the sounds of the orchestra, not from any complicated harmonies or dextrous orchestral tricks.

Even though its role is limited, one of the greatest thrills for the music arranger is the sound of a fine string section playing well-written material. It has taken me years to feel that at last I can write for strings effectively and individually, and the few occasions on which I have managed to achieve something exceptional in the way of a string score have been among the proudest moments I can remember. Perhaps as a result of my early unproductive violin lessons I have remained all my life a frustrated string player.

All of my preoccupations about orchestration, however, served to reinforce my interest in what was still my main and favourite theatre of activity – my touring big band. I suppose that the band must have averaged anything up to 250 performances a year, most of them one-nighters. Some of them were important and challenging events; many others simply run-of-the-mill occasions. But there's no doubt in my mind as to which was the most exciting event in my big-band's career.

It was the American tour.

10

Drop me off in Harlem

A presence in the States is something every jazz musician knows is of paramount importance. To make your mark in American jazz is to go a long way down the road to becoming an internationally known star. So this was for me an opportunity to establish the band worldwide, and I knew it. But it was not just a visit to the States, it was a major appearance at what was at the time undoubtedly the world's major jazz festival – the famous event at Newport, Rhode Island.

Legendary names were to share the bill with us, and I wondered how on earth we would justify our inclusion. Count Basie, Duke Ellington – the big bands were out in force, and I just hoped, knowing full well that we couldn't outblow them in their own styles, that we had enough individuality to sound different and appealing to the transatlantic ear.

David Lindup and I worked hard to achieve this directly the news of our trip came through. I wrote a piece especially for the tour – named *Specs Yellow* after a rose dear to the heart of my lead trumpet player Derrick Abbott. Derrick was an experienced pilot and glider instructor as well as a gardening enthusiast, and a good friend during his many years with my band.

Together with several of my older pieces and David's excellent contributions we felt we had a good representative collection of material. The band was in good shape, and our ranks had been recently strengthened by the addition of a wonderful trumpet soloist, Kenny Wheeler, a Canadian living in Britain who was later hailed in international circles as one of the greats of his instrument. The band also included a number of other excellent jazz players, such as tenor saxist Danny Moss, trumpeter Dickie Hawdon, pianist Dave Lee and drummer Kenny Clare. Kenny, even before joining us in 1955, was a vastly experienced big-band drummer whose solos were works of art in their own right, and there was no doubt that he was one of the band's great assets. The singers – Frank, Tony and Cleo – weren't part of the package, as the invitation was for a strictly instrumental performance. Cleo came as a spectator.

It was July 1958 and we were off, all eighteen of us – seventeen musicians and our manager Don Read. A refuelling stop at Gander, Newfoundland, and before we knew it we had landed at what was then called Idlewild airport in New York. After the usual press photo call, with pictures of the whole band taken on the stairway down to the hot tarmac, the agency representative who met us whisked us into a bus and we were off. 'Off where?' I inquired.

'To the rehearsal studios', came the response. What on earth for, I thought to myself. We're in no need of rehearsal, and a sound check can't be done until we get to Newport tomorrow.

We arrived at a rehearsal place in midtown Manhattan, were welcomed warmly in that very American way, and settled down to play something or other – for reasons as yet unknown. Soon a music copyist appeared and handed out parts. What parts? Oh, they're the parts for Manny Album's arrangements. Manny then arrived with someone from Roulette Records. Then through the door came a lady whom I shall call Terri Winters, since in any case I can't remember her real name. 'What's the lady doing here?'

'Oh, she's a new Roulette Records artiste. She's singing with your band at Newport.'

Roulette Records. Perhaps I should explain. Since our inception in 1953 the band's representation on record in the US had undergone several changes. After a short and rather unproductive spell with the then new company Capitol Records we went on to Norman Granz's Verve label. Then shortly afterwards Maurice Levy launched Roulette

Records and bought us from Granz. Roulette immediately gave us complete freedom of repertoire choice, and the relationship seemed to be doing quite well up till now.

But slowly the real situation dawned on me. Knowing us to be artistes on his label, someone on the production side of the company who was involved in the launching of a singer had the brainwave of making our Newport debut a showcase for his new protégée. The fact that nothing was ever mentioned about it to me in England – I would obviously have said 'no', and they knew it – made it quite clear to me that this was a try on. And someone was hoping that the newly arrived greenhorn from Britain would let it slip by. I strode up to the man in charge with fire in my eyes. 'There would only be one singer sharing with us at Newport had they asked for one – and that's Cleo. But they haven't asked, so there's not going to be one – and that's the end of it!'

I surprised myself with my own belligerence. But it worked like a dream – the parts were gathered in, the record men disappeared as if by magic (probably saying among themselves, 'Oh well, it was worth a try') and an exhausted band packed their instruments and made for the hotel. I felt a little sorry for the singer; but she was a pawn in the game. And the whole episode taught me to stand up and be strong when you feel you are being taken for a ride.

The next morning we were up bright and early to make the four-hour trip to Newport. Some of the band were already out sightseeing. I lingered in my room – I knew Manhattan pretty well from my days working on the transatlantic liners, and walking around in July heat was not my idea of fun.

Don Read phoned, 'I've just had a call from the Glaser office. Do we mind giving Dizzy Gillespie a lift up to Newport? He has to be there about the same time as us – Junior Mance too.' I replied that it didn't seem too much of a chore to have the world's greatest jazz trumpet player and a great pianist riding with us.

On the way we stopped at a Howard Johnson's for a snack. The whole coach load trooped in, and Cleo, Dizzy and I were lucky to get a table. The waitress arrived for our order. 'What's the show?' she inquired.

'We're on our way to the Newport Jazz Festival. The band has come over from England specially, and I'm the bandleader.'

'Well, for heavens sakes. You must be famous – you'd better give me your autograph.'

I duly obliged. 'But I've got a surprise for you, ma'am. Do you realise' – I motioned towards my table-mate – 'that this is the great Dizzy Gillespie?'

The woman looked perplexed. 'Oh! You're a magician, aren't you?' She was obviously struggling, never having heard the name before. But Dizzy's appearance – African fez-style hat and robes – led her to believe that her guess might be a good one, and she dutifully collected his autograph. And of course in a sense she was right: Dizzy's music was indeed magic to all jazz lovers, as was the part he played in the formation of the musical language of bebop. But his work had still not reached the average American home and the ears of the likes of Dolly our waitress.

It taught me yet again that jazz is a music for the minority. It can only be truly understood and evaluated by people gifted with 'chordal ears' – in other words, those lucky folk who can listen to the improvisational skills of a soloist and still hear the underlying chord structure. So jazz music can only by luck become popular in the wider sense, and can rarely enjoy the financial security and mass acclaim which goes with that phenomenon. Thus most jazz musicians remain skilled, dedicated and poor, and even a jazz world-star name like Dizzy Gillespie's was – and still is for that matter – unfamiliar to most people in the country of his birth.

We arrived at Newport in a state of euphoria. This really couldn't be happening – it had to be a dream. The bus drew up at the artistes' entrance at the back of the playing area, but even from here we could sense the coliseum-like atmosphere and hear the roar of the huge crowd. We could hear the music perfectly as it was relayed backstage, and our ears quickly identified the tenor sax sound of Johnny Griffin. He was in the middle of a breathtaking, mind-boggling solo break in *Cherokee*, and at its conclusion the crowd gave him a roaring soccer stadium-style ovation. I would have joined in the applause, but someone grabbed my attention to introduce me to James Rushing, one of the great blues singers of all time.

Introductions galore followed, so many that it began to be hard to remember all the famous ones. But we were there to do a job, and it was soon our turn. Willis Conover, the great Voice of America jazz presenter, introduced us to the crowd – and we were off!

We played our hearts out on that midsummer evening in New England. We were nervous, of course, but by and large we gave of our best. The crowd seemed to love us and showed it by their applause. The critics were kind, too. 'This fine band from England', wrote John S. Wilson in the *New York Times*, 'displays an ability which seems to have been lost in many an American outfit – they are masters in the art of making the music swing.'

After the show that evening we ambled towards our bus in the fresh night air, mingling with the now thinning crowds and savouring the satisfaction of a job well done. Three more dates remained to be fulfilled in New York.

The first was in Palisades Park, on the New Jersey side of the Hudson river. On our arrival we realised that this was a sort of 'makeweight' date – a free concert in an open-air setting. We set up and started at the appointed time to an audience of a mere handful of people. We turned in a good performance and the audience applauded warmly, but frankly there were more of us than them.

After the concert the famous jazz critic Leonard Feather came backstage. 'I want you to come round and meet a few folks', he said. I followed him to a group of people. 'This is Bill Finegan.' I was dumb-struck – one of the jazz world's gifted arrangers listening to our charts. 'And I'm sure you know George', continued Leonard. I certainly did – by reputation. It was George Shearing. I was half a generation younger than George, and had only met him briefly at the beginning of my career in London – I doubt if he remembered. What he did remember was my introduction to *S'Wonderful*, which we recorded for our Capitol debut some years before. He proved it by singing it into my ear as we shook hands.

'And I'm sure you recognise Benny', Leonard went on. Oh, no! Benny Goodman was standing right there – my first jazz hero. When I was part of his band at the London Palladium in 1949 my role was that of an almost anonymous second alto player, and this was the first time he could have heard the real me. The very fact that he had been interested enough to come to New Jersey to hear my band – the equiv-alent of travelling from Rome to Cape Town in the eyes of a New

Yorker – was flattery indeed. It was also, incidentally, the first of a number of times when Benny attended our (that is Cleo's and my) concerts over the ensuing years – and as I often played clarinet on those occasions I was very glad I was informed of his presence after the event and not before. My nerves would never have stood it!

The second gig was at the Lewisohn Stadium – now no longer in existence – where we shared the bill with others, including saxophonist Gerry Mulligan, drummer Gene Krupa and trumpet player Wild Bill Davison, each with their own groups. Our set at the close of the first half was so successful that the promoters asked us to come on again to finish the show.

We did so with our traditional *Take the 'A' Train* finisher. As we reached the closing bars the master of ceremonies came on. 'Ladies and gentlemen', he said, 'you all must know that the great Louis Armstrong has recently been recovering from a serious bout of heart trouble. Well, the good news is that his recovery has been successful. And the great news is that Louis is here with us tonight and it's his birthday. Let's give Satchmo a great . . .' But the rest of his words were drowned in an eruption of noise and movement that would have put Vesuvius to shame.

To say that the crowd reacted favourably would be like saying that several people live in the Chinese Republic. The roar and the chanting went on for several minutes, and Louis had no option but to make his way onto the stage. And, once on the stage he had very little option but to perform – and being Louis he could never have resisted anyway.

Some versions of the story from eyewitnesses said that he borrowed a trumpet from Wild Bill Davison, others that the instrument belonged to Stan Palmer from our trumpet section. Be that as it may, there on the stage, with our band as collaborators, the great man led us into *When the Saints Go Marching In* to the ecstasy of the now delirious audience.

What a night! Hardly possible to follow, you might think. Still, our final night in New York was not to be sneezed at: an evening at Birdland, surely the most famous club in the history of jazz. This was an ideal venue for the band. Years of gigs at similarly laid-out London clubs meant that our players felt really at home in such surroundings, and their inspired playing reflected it. It was also a chance to bring

Cleo up informally to sing a couple of songs with the band. She did so, and perhaps the word got around beforehand, because there in the audience was Ella Fitzgerald. The two ladies exchanged greetings and began a lifelong friendship, manifested when Cleo received a jazz Grammy one day in 1986, and on the very next a bouquet from Ella saying, 'Congratulations, gal – and about time too!' But on that evening in 1958 Cleo was just a band singer. Birdland was unforgettable, and a great end to our work in New York. But now there was something that I looked forward to more than anything so far: we were booked to play for a whole week opposite the Duke Ellington band.

*   *   *

It was an obligatory hot summer's day in 1958 as our band bus drew into a parking lot near Lambertville, New Jersey. But looming in front of us, to our surprise, was not the usual concert hall or theatre with its loading dock and its artistes' entrance, but a large tent. St John Tyrell's Music Circus was in fact just what its title implied: we were to perform under the big top. Duke Ellington's band, our partners on the bill, had already arrived, installed themselves and departed to eat, leaving the bandstand resplendent with their smart music-stands, the Ellingtonian grand piano perched conspicuously in the front section of the stage. We made slight alterations to accommodate our special needs, played a few bars, checked the mikes and repaired to a nearby restaurant to dine before the show.

When we returned to the gig half an hour or so before show time we located the dressing-room area with no difficulty at all. The sounds of sixteen Ellingtonians warming up their instruments guided us in effectively. It was almost eerie to hear a certain alto sax being put through its paces in the next changing booth; my immediate reaction was the way the player had got the Johnny Hodges style off to a T. And then of course I realised that it *was* Johnny Hodges – one of my all-time heroes in jazz. In quick succession I underwent the same experience half a dozen times more as the unmistakable sounds of Clark Terry, Paul Gonsalves, Harry Carney, Ray Nance and Jimmy Hamilton floated across the band-room area. Few bands before or since can have boasted so many totally identifiable players, all of them masters of their particular craft.

As show time approached St John Tyrell, the impresario, came and welcomed us. He took me aside with a concerned look. 'John, I have a request from a well-known resident who wants to introduce the band from the stage. He's an ex-bandleader himself.'

'What's his name? Perhaps I know of him?'

'Paul Whiteman.'

I gulped. A man who had employed Bix Beiderbecke, Jack Teagarden, Tommy Dorsey and Glenn Miller and had conducted the world premiere of George Gershwin's *Rhapsody in Blue* at Carnegie Hall was, I felt, perfectly qualified to introduce an unknown band from Britain.

He did, and we tried hard to justify the terrific introduction he gave us. Somehow I think we succeeded, because the ovation was generous, and the praise we got from our Ellington counterparts was quite flattering. Many of us knew some of Duke's players from our meetings with them in Britain, but that week liaisons were strengthened and lifelong friendships were kindled with Hamilton, Terry, Hodges, Cat Anderson, Mercer Ellington and, of course, Duke himself.

One night, instead of our normal commute to Manhattan, Cat invited Cleo and me back to his Philadelphia apartment, where we were allotted the guest room. In the morning, as we sat down to breakfast, I was startled to hear our host say, 'John, would you bless our table?' I was totally taken aback, and heard myself saying, 'Cleo would be much better than me.' Cleo, lumbered in this despicable way, rose to the occasion with a 'for what we are about to receive', and saved the situation.

The Music Circus played like a theatre, augmenting the nightly performances with a Saturday matinee. We arrived for the afternoon to see Duke himself standing outside awaiting the arrival of our bus. He took me aside. 'Our drummer hasn't shown – he didn't know about the matinee.' Duke was using a temporary drummer at that time. 'Perhaps you could loan us Kenny.' He of course meant Kenny Clare, who was already becoming something of a legend among drummers.

'I'm sure Kenny would love to do it – just give him the drum book.'

'Sorry – there's not a drum book. It got lost while Sam Woodyard was with the band and he knew it all by heart – so it wasn't replaced.'

Kenny went on that afternoon with Duke's band without a drum book and played beautifully. 'How did he do?' I asked Duke afterwards.

'Great – he could play for me anytime he wanted.'

I found much later that he had made it clear in a subtle way to his band that Kenny would be welcomed in the permanent drum chair. This was the nearest that Duke ever came to stealing someone else's sideman – he was much too much of a gentleman to act otherwise. Anyway Kenny – if he ever knew about it – was loyal to us and the incident passed, but understandably our drummer never forgot the unique experience of playing with perhaps the greatest of the Ellington bands.

Another Ellington admirer was Gerald Lascelles, a cousin of the queen, who gave us a memorable night with the maestro. The Lascelles lived in an enormous mansion known as Fort Belvedere, near Virginia Water in Surrey. The place had a special place in history in that its previous occupant had been the Duke of Windsor (the abdicated King Edward VIII), who had resided there with Mrs Wallis Simpson before moving out of Britain. We were invited there for supper with Duke Ellington as guest of honour. We drove up the extremely lengthy driveway, expecting to see dozens of cars, but there were none. A servant opened the door and ushered us into the drawing-room, where we were greeted by Gerald and his wife Angela – and Duke. It was then that we realised that we were the only guests apart from Ellington himself and two other friends of our host's. The Lascelles obviously wanted the famous musician to themselves for an evening but felt in need of just one couple to keep the conversation going – us. The dinner went smoothly enough, and afterwards we were led into a room containing a grand piano. Duke sat down and strummed *Solitude* gently to the obvious pleasure of the Lascelles. Gerald, however, was quite knowledgeable about the Ellington repertoire and started requesting obscure items. Duke did well in response until it came to *Morning Glory*, a Rex Stewart feature from the forties. Duke managed the first sixteen bars without any trouble. Now I found an opportunity to get some information about the number direct from the source. 'It always struck me that the tune *Robbin's Nest* was inspired by – or perhaps plagiarised from – *Morning Glory'*, I said to Ellington.

'Yes', replied Duke, 'we were not at all pleased when we heard that tune.' He used the royal 'we', no doubt, to convey that it was beneath the dignity of someone of his stature to litigate against every cheapskate who stole an Ellingtonian musical idea – and there were legions of them.

He went on playing *Morning Glory* as far as the bridge – the middle eight as it is known in Britain – and came to a grinding halt. He had forgotten his own composition – understandable when one thinks of the thousands he wrote in his lifetime. It was my chance to show off. I strode up to the top end of the keyboard and confidently played the missing melody. Ellington quickly recalled the forgotten passage and augmented the notes I was supplying with strong Ellingtonian chords, nodding and smiling in recognition of my help, perhaps a little flattered that such an obscure piece of his work was known so far from its birthplace.

Not long after that Duke came to hear my band in our own club in Oxford Street, London. It was late in our last set when he arrived, but he sat there facing us in the front row, listening carefully. Towards the end of our sets we often played *Mood Indigo*, and I decided we would present our version for its composer's examination. Dick Hawdon played a beautiful trumpet solo, and in fact all the soloists managed to produce their best form – the great man's presence was inspiring rather than unnerving. Duke seemed to have that effect on people.

We finished the night with our traditional closer *Take the 'A' Train*. Ellington got up and we shook hands. Then he took me by surprise. 'Send me that chart of *Mood Indigo* – I'd like to use it.'

I assured him that I would, but I felt he was trying to flatter me. I never sent the arrangement – after all, what on earth would he want with my version when his own was the classic rendition? Later he repeated the request, but it wasn't till years after his death that it slowly dawned on me that Duke liked to ring the changes on his most obvious requests to avoid boring over-repetition, and he wanted my chart as part of this policy. It was three decades later when working with the Ellington band under the direction of Duke's son Mercer that

I finally realised this. The orchestra regularly opened their show with an arrangement of *'A' Train* in three-quarter time.

It was with Clark Terry, perhaps Ellington's principal soloist at that time, that Cleo and I struck up a very special friendship that lasted over the years. Not long after our New Jersey week in the States, Clark left Duke to join the trumpet section of the NBC *Tonight* show band, based in New York and led at the time by Skitch Henderson. He then freelanced in New York, and when I happened to be there I would sometimes go on his gigs with him.

When I did I crossed into another world, a world of which as a non-American I was not totally aware, although I occasionally glimpsed a little of it in magazines such as *Ebony*. Black society in the States, whether in the Deep South or the supposedly emancipated North, was segregated. The band I played in with Clark was black; the gig on one typical occasion was a black 'society' dance which included a fashion show featuring black models. I seemed to be the only evidence that human beings with pale skins existed – that is, until I climbed onto the bandstand, joined the saxophone section, and found myself seated next to the great Zoot Sims in the first tenor chair.

The band launched lustily into *Rockin' in Rhythm*, the first of several Ellington pieces that night, and I found myself loving every minute of it. Racial bigotry runs in both directions, however, and I couldn't help keeping a lookout for some belligerent glare from a member of the all-black throng who might have felt that my job should have been given to a black player. I saw no such looks. In those days at least, any white willing to be part of black society was usually accepted without question. I later noticed several white spouses of both sexes in the crowd. Crossing the colour line in the other direction was another matter.

New York later became a much more cosmopolitan city, but in those days it was not easy for a New Yorker to forget his colour, unless he was white. During the time I was recording *The Zodiac Variations* in New York I stayed at Clark's house in Bayside, Long Island. Sometimes as a break from writing I would go into Manhattan with my host for his nightly gig on the *Tonight* show. We would sometimes go by train and return by cab. One night, after several fruitless attempts to get a ride, Clark said, 'You hail the cab, and I'll stand round the corner.'

'Whatever you say – but why?' I asked.

'Cab drivers don't like driving to Harlem at night.'

'But we're not going to Harlem.'

'Cab drivers assume that everyone black goes to Harlem!' my friend retorted, as he dodged into a doorway at the first sight of an oncoming cab. I hailed it, it stopped, Clark emerged from the shadows – and we got home that night. What Clark did when he was alone I don't honestly know, but he generally accepted the handicaps of his skin colour with dignity and a sense of humour. And no racial indignities could take away his musical gifts, which surely make him one of the world's all-time great trumpet stylists.

Clark is the acknowledged inspiration of many fine exponents of his instrument the world over, from the legendary Miles Davis to Britain's Guy Barker, and particularly in his later years carried his influence into the world of jazz education with great success. Age brought Clark quite a bit of ill health but did nothing whatever to affect his music. In 1996 he came to London at my invitation to perform in the 'Jazz Encounters' series at the Wigmore Hall. He was flying in from Switzerland to Heathrow, and I drove out to the airport to greet him. I waited at the customs exit, but there was no sign of Clark. I began to think I had somehow missed him. Then I noticed a porter pushing a wheelchair away from the door, and something made me chase it to see who was being pushed.

It was Clark. A hat pulled over his eyes made him difficult to recognise, and all in all he presented a picture of frailty, indicating that his battles with eye trouble, diabetes, and some serious back problems had taken their toll. My only thought was to get him home as soon as possible – he was staying with us at our Wavendon home – and give him the opportunity to rest. We duly arrived, and Cleo and the two of us installed ourselves in front of the fire in our drawing-room. It was time for a moment's relaxation.

Not for Clark. He remained in the armchair, but reached to one side for his instruments. 'John, get your horns out – it's practice time.' Within a couple of minutes we were working on the pieces for the concerts (we were playing Wavendon and Nottingham as well as the Wigmore Hall), a process which went on for a couple of hours. His legendary musical agility was as effervescent as ever, and at the end of the session I felt a good deal more exhausted than he seemed to be.

But back to 1958. Our short season in New Jersey with the Ellington band drew to a close, and we returned to Europe for the less glamorous but necessary purpose of earning our keep in Britain. The experience had made me realise that we were a world-class band. Yet our recordings were as yet hardly representative of our class, and I resolved that over the next phase of its existence I would do my utmost as a composer to put that right.

11

And the band played on

The big band lasted on a full-time basis for about a decade, from 1953 to 1964, and in its various forms played in the region of a couple of thousand dates – dances, concerts, recordings and radio and TV airings.

It started as a conventional eight brass, five saxes and rhythm affair. Then in the late fifties the sax section was disbanded in favour of a 'band within a band' concept, with a five-piece small-band line up (three saxes, trumpet and trombone) surrounded by the conventional brass and rhythm configuration. In the early sixties I returned to more usual tactics with a sax, brass, rhythm pattern, but this time with somewhat smaller sections – three trumpets, two trombones plus tuba, and four saxophones, completed by my usual rhythm trio. A later band utilised a rather more complex mixture of saxes and brass, but this was to last for only a short while and for one major recording.

The bands abounded with memorable characters, and a whole book could easily be devoted to a listing and description of them all, so I can only select a handful. Good lead trumpet players are few and far between, and I was fortunate that my original choice in 1953 was one of the best. Derrick Abbott, a likeable Lancastrian, had had vast experience with other bands, and his air of authority commanded the brass section. We became good friends, more often than not driving to gigs together. Derrick eventually left and the lead trumpet chair was successively occupied by a number of players. Ron Simmonds was, like Abbott, vastly experienced when he came to me, and added a stamp to the brass sound which was hard to follow. He later went to Germany and played important roles in more than one of that country's large jazz-orientated orchestras during their heyday.

Both Abbott and Simmonds were by nature lead trumpet players. Two others who filled that post in bands of mine, however, possessed the rare dual ability of lead trumpet and jazz soloist. One of them, Leon Calvert, an associate of mine since Club Eleven days, could supply a well-crafted improvised solo and moments later switch to the rigours of leading a brass section – a talented and versatile man indeed. The other was Dick Hawdon, one of three brass players in my bands over the years whose careers started, like mine, in traditional jazz circles. Dick, a Yorkshireman, had more than a touch of his idol, the great American Clifford Brown, in his jazz playing, but he displayed a range more akin to that of a young Dizzy Gillespie than to Brown. This qualified him for the lead trumpet chair, and after a spell in the 'band within a band' format he graduated to that position with considerable success, featuring in both capacities on many recordings of that period.

Of the trombonists, two were from traditional roots. Keith Christie was a most gifted exponent of his instrument who first came to prominence with his clarinettist brother Ian in the Christie Brothers' Stompers. But his academic musical training enabled him to cross the demarcation line into more contemporary circles, and he was featured prominently both in the band and with his own splinter group, the Keith Christie Quartet, of which I was a part. This group also accompanied Cleo on one of her first solo albums, *Cleo Sings British*.

Trombonist Ed Harvey, also an early 'cross over', joined the big band direct from the Seven. A pensive soloist rather than a dynamic one in the Keith Christie mould, Ed contributed a number of his individual arrangements to the band's repertoire over the years, as well as his wry sense of humour – much as he had done in the Seven.

Our original lead trombonist was Maurice Pratt, a Tynesider with a wonderful command of his instrument. He was a great asset to the band, yet we parted company over a small disagreement, the nature of which I have forgotten. I think I was the one at fault, but it seemed to turn out as a bonus for Maurice, who went on to be one of London's most sought-after freelancers during an especially lucrative period for such specialists. Of the other trombonists, Ian MacDougall, one of three Canadians in my band at one time, eventually returned to his native land to be a prominent part of the brass world there. Tony Russell, who wrote a number of scores for the band as well as being manager, sadly died of Hodgkin's disease in 1970. Bass trombonist Garry Brown eventually became the band's manager after spending many years in the trombone section. Indeed in later years Brown profited from the experience gained and became a prominent booking agent. He followed my example by marrying a fine singer – Lorna Dallas. Bill Geldard was another of my trombonists who married within the profession, so to speak; he met and wed trumpeter Gracie Cole while she was playing at the same ballroom as us with Ivy Benson's band on the Isle of Man.

Of the sax players, Rex Morris and Alex Leslie, our original tenor sax soloist and baritone specialist respectively, come to mind. And then there was Danny Moss, a good-looking and fine-sounding tenor man who was the idol of the girl fans of the band, a position of which he took full advantage until his marriage to singer Jeannie Lamb. Danny had a distinctly romantic quality to his saxophone style, in complete contrast to the terse, monosyllabic tenor phrases which were a feature of the styles of Canadian Art Ellefson, his longtime colleague in our sax section.

George Tyndale was a fine tenor sax player whom I persuaded to take up the baritone after Alex Leslie's departure. His sculptured West Indian features dominated his amply built frame, and his good-natured grin made him a social favourite in the band. Vic Ash was another star, a clarinet specialist who had won polls on that instrument and who later migrated to the BBC Big Band.

Peter King joined our saxophone section in the early sixties and stayed for some time. It was difficult to find enough to keep this brilliant player busy in a working band like ours, but Peter stuck it out and contributed some great jazz to our music-making before going on to become an internationally known alto sax soloist.

My friend Bill Le Sage occupied the original piano chair, doubling on his newly acquired vibraphone as well as acting as band manager. When Bill left he was replaced by young Derek Smith, who later emigrated to the United States and became well known on the New York scene. Other pianists included Dudley Moore, who stayed about nine months, until his review *Beyond the Fringe* took off, and Dudley with it, to London's West End and then on to Broadway. He was succeeded by Alan Branscombe, a gifted musician who also played excellent vibes and fine alto sax. Alan, after nursing several musicians who were drug addicts through difficult periods, finally became a victim of hard drugs himself, and his musical performances became a shadow of their former selves. He died needlessly in the mid-eighties, and a great talent was lost.

Perhaps the longest-serving occupant of the piano chair was Dave Lee, my accompanist in South Africa. Dave joined with drummer Kenny Clare to replace Derek Smith and Allan Ganley, the original drummer with the big band. Allan, a friend since my 1949 visits to Paris, was at that time interested in small-band jazz, and lost no time in making his mark in that field. He was also beginning his lifelong interest in arranging and composing music. Later he was to develop this and become a most accomplished writer.

Dave proved himself a great asset to my big band, not only because of his strident piano style. His absurd sense of humour cheered us all during times of stress, and he turned out to be a good band manager when he eventually assumed this task. It was soon obvious that Kenny Clare was an important addition to our ranks. Critics had on occasions implied that my scores were too polite and lacking guts, and the arrival of our new drummer gave me an incentive to rethink my methods and add a dimension which somehow revitalised the band's sound. Kenny was a born big-band drummer. He earned the admiration of the great Kenny Clarke, who chose Clare as his co-drummer in the successful multinational Clarke–Boland big band, which became such an important part of the European jazz scene in the sixties.

All of these players and numerous others contributed in some way to the recording career of the Dankworth big bands. We made literally hundreds of visits to studios to record our music. In addition to the inevitable single titles we of course made albums. As I mentioned, the birth of my first big band coincided, within a few years, with the advent of the LP. Four of these, each one a concept album, I regard as especially good examples of the work of my big bands.

* * *

The first was *What the Dickens*, a concept album which set out to portray in music scenes and characters from the works of Charles Dickens. I am not a particularly well-read person, but my love of Dickens's work made him an obvious choice. I wanted to make this album a milestone in the band's history, and to draw attention to it decided to use a number of guest soloists. These included Peter King, Bobbie Wellins, Dick Morrissey, Tubby Hayes, Tony Coe, Ronnie Scott and Ronnie Ross in the saxes alone, all of them at the peak of their productive form at the time, so that putting several of them together on one track, *Dotheboys Hall*, was especially satisfying. My own duet with Hayes, *Dodson and Fogg*, performed without a rhythm section, also worked well, while Ronnie Ross made a brilliant portrayal of Sam Weller in *Weller Never Did*. Add the trumpet talents of Jimmy Deuchar, Dickie Hawdon and Kenny Wheeler, and the sum total was an album well received by public and critics alike. It has weathered comparatively well over the years and remains an interesting glimpse into the standards attained by the British jazz world in the early sixties. *What the Dickens* received an Ivor Novello Award, a rare honour for a jazz recording.

The second of a sort of trilogy of concept albums was *The Zodiac Variations*. Flushed by the success of the Dickens LP, I was anxious to go one step further in my desire to use guests on the album. I had gained a great deal of experience on the Dickens session in overcoming one big obstacle to the use of guests – their availability. I surmounted this problem by recording the performances of different artistes at different times and editing the results together. This practice later became widespread, and indeed an integral part of recording techniques, with the development of multi-track tape. But its use in conjunction with the simple splicing of recording tape (joining individual pieces of individually recorded tape together to give the effect of a single performance) had been confined to 'patching'. This meant that a written piece could be performed a number of times, then the best played parts of each performance could be cobbled together afterwards – a technique still widely used in classical circles.

I had used the facility in *Dickens* to string together performances by players who couldn't be there in the morning with others who couldn't be at the same place in the afternoon. But then it struck me – it doesn't have to be in the same place. Why not record one performance in London and the other in New York? I saw this as an opportunity to have some American guests play with my band without having to come to England, and put the proposition to Leslie Gould, head of Philips recording in London at the time. It was given the green light and a budget, and my fantasy started to be a reality.

*   *   *

However, I had started with an idea for the concept of the album. It was to consist of twelve tracks, each representing a sign of the zodiac, and feature as soloists only players born under that sign. This worked reasonably well with the writing for my own band, but considerably complicated the booking process for the seven-piece American unit I had decided on. My friend Clark Terry, who had agreed to book the band for me, was confused when we talked on the phone. 'John, I can't get Bill Holman for the date on tenor, but Jerome Richardson's available. He's a fine tenor player and he's excellent on flute as well.'

'Clark, I know he's great, but we can't use him.'

'Why's that?'

'He's not a Gemini!'

Clark bore the cross of having to deal with an eccentric Englishman quite nobly, and eventually came up with Lucky Thompson, a happy choice. He also recruited an old buddy and fellow Sagittarian, valve trombonist Bob Brookmeyer, two Scorpios in the form of Zoot Sims on tenor and altoist Phil Woods, while Leo was represented by bass player Chuck Israels. Capricorn drummer Osie Johnson completed the septet that assembled at a studio in New York in October 1964, and within minutes we were busy converting the notes on paper into sounds on tape. The players were at first mystified by the fact that some of the pieces stopped in mid-phase – sometimes even in mid-bar – but were quick to comprehend when I explained myself.

Later that month, back in London, the tapes from New York were put on the machines in the Philips studio in Stanhope Place, the tempos and sounds were carefully matched, and *The Zodiac Variations* were completed. A few careful operations on both sets of tapes with razor blade and joining tape, and the finished article was produced. And though I was the perpetrator of it all and planned every single edit, I now find it difficult to detect them myself – so good were they and so perfect were the matches of speed and ambience which the combined forces of musicians and studio technicians achieved. Critics were at the time suspicious of the complexities involved in the planning and making of *Zodiac* and the 'unnatural' nature of the system of editing and joining two separate sets of performances, and tended to dismiss the musical results. I think with the benefit of passing years, listening to the evidence again, that they may have been wrong, certainly in tending to overlook the many wonderful solo statements by the soloists, both British and American. I hope they might give it another hearing sometime in the future.

* * *

There was a long gap before my third exploration into the world of concept suites. The decision came with the idea of assembling a brand new band for a season at Ronnie Scott's. I sought inspiration in the world of pictorial art and called my series of pieces *The Million Dollar Collection*, a title long since made less meaningful by inflation in the art market. The pieces, each inspired by a specific painting, were unrelated either in thematic material or in style. Some were readily accessible, others more difficult on first hearing. Most of them presented technical challenges to the players, most of whom I had never worked with. Some I had not even heard. I was apprehensive when the time came for the first rehearsal, and I shared my anxiety with the sea of unfamiliar faces that confronted me. 'This is not easy music to play', I began. 'Don't get discouraged if it sounds a mess for a while.' I'm afraid I must have sounded like a schoolmaster lecturing a new intake of green-looking students.

We started and made our way through the first piece. It sounded more or less exactly as I had heard it in my mind while writing it, and the only person experiencing any real difficulty playing it was me. I realised at that moment that I was looking at a new generation of young players who, integrated with some very experienced older ones, represented new standards of ability in performance.

There were few problems with this new suite of mine that this band did not quickly overcome. Players such as Kenny Wheeler, Derek Watkins and Henry Lowther had no real problems with the trumpet parts, trombonists Mike Gibbs and Chris Pyne and reedmen Tony Coe and Tony Roberts dealt easily with their requirements, and percussionist Tristan Fry was as adept as pianist Laurie Holloway at coping with unfamiliar music quickly and brilliantly. Laurie, a lifelong friend, played with my sextet at a London club, The Cool Elephant, around this time. There he met Marian Montgomery, whose unique and prodigious artistry was being heard for the first time in London. Within weeks they were married, thus beginning a formidable and enduring musical alliance which immediately became an important asset to the British musical scene.

The album did not sell in great quantities, but it seemed to reach places that mattered all over the world. Many years later the Smithsonian Institution Jazz Orchestra, based in Washington, DC, included parts of it in their concerts. It remains for me a piece of which I am still quite proud.

*   *   *

Another extended work which came much later, for yet another Ronnie Scott's engagement with yet another big band, was received well in critical circles. Its style was considerably influenced by that of a fine writer, Mike Gibb, who had contributed some very interesting and original scores to our library. It was called *Lifeline*, and the album of that name featured some further newcomers to our fold – Stan Sulzmann and pianist John Taylor. In the trombone section next to Mike Gibb was Ken Gibson, an ex-composition student of mine at the Royal Academy of Music, where I had been invited to return to teach jazz both to aspiring sax players and would-be composers; Ken was a talented composer and arranger who subsequently assisted me with some film scores and contributed some fine pieces for the big band, particularly *Schmaltz Waltz* and *Fighting the Flab*.

These four albums cover most of the history of my big bands in the early and middle years. One other very important LP, issued under my name, I consider very much the property of the man who wrote and arranged all the music and was the featured soloist – Kenny Wheeler. The album was called *Windmill Tilter*, and my band of the time did the recording sessions, with a few additions. On the morning of the first day our bassist Kenny Napper rang me. 'John, I've cut my playing finger on a bread knife. It's not serious, but I won't be able to play. I've booked one of my students to do it instead.'

I commiserated with Kenny, but I cursed the luck which committed us to an untried bassist on such an important day. The student duly arrived at the studio. It was Dave Holland. It was probably his first important recording date, and he celebrated it by playing beautifully. Maybe he was inspired, not only by Kenny, but by guitarist John McLaughlin, Tony Coe, Mike Gibbs and the many other fine players on the album, which has become a collector's item.

But the recordings that meant most to the record companies were the hits, and they make another story.

Perspective III

The years of the sixties and their immediate predecessors were part of a period of strengthening and widening the jazz panorama. New shoots of innovation which had earlier begun budding now had the room and the life force to burst into flower and bear fruit.

The introduction of Cuban and Latin-American percussive influences, begun in the late forties (and in which Dizzy Gillespie played a leading part), was one example; the Brazilian bossa nova music was another, making a gentler impact, coupled with new approaches to harmony. It was possibly a case of Brazilian musicians and composers being influenced by American popular music and evolving their own style round these basics, and this in turn being heard by visiting jazz musicians and passed back into the language of the music with instant success. Who can be really sure in the complex alchemy of music?

A third major influence was to affect the course of jazz and give it new life in this period – soul music. This form of jazz, which had clear connections with American gospel music and its performance in churches, was to leave its mark on bands and arrangers throughout the period. Jazz musicians from pianists Horace Silver and Bobby Timmons to saxist Julian 'Cannonball' Adderley were examples of those who helped introduce the new material into the main fabric of jazz.

The long playing record was now the dominant source of jazz for its adherents. Not only did it give the artist longer performance spells; it also made possible a forty-minute sampler of perhaps nine or ten contrasting items from the repertoire of that artist. Where older jazzmen became famous for a single three-minute performance of one single tune – Louis Armstrong's West End Blues, *for example, or the Benny Goodman Sextet's* Air Mail Special – *the new way to emerge was via a whole set of performances all present on one LP.*

The Miles Davis Quintet was one of the earlier beneficiaries of this system. The quintet had so much to offer: Miles himself, whose playing from this period was to be an overwhelming influence on trumpet players all over the world; John Coltrane, who was to take over the mantle of the world's most emulated tenor saxist, first worn by Coleman Hawkins and then by Lester Young; Cannonball Adderley, since the demise of Charlie Parker in 1955 the spiritual leader of alto saxophonists; and Bill Evans, whose playing to this day has inspired countless fine jazz pianists. All of these players needed space to display their talents; replace this with the few short solo bursts they would have been allotted in the old recording system, and they might never have been truly appreciated. The LP changed all that, and made all four of them major names in jazz.

Other great practitioners of the music to emerge during these productive times were Sonny Rollins, an extraordinary tenor sax exponent, who made many highly original contributions to the role of his instrument; Charles Mingus, a bass player and composer whose work was of constant interest; and, augmenting the influential work of Bill Evans, two pianists, both non-American – the Canadian Oscar Peterson and the British émigré George Shearing. Peterson equated in some respects with the great Benny Goodman, in that both evolved a personal style by amalgamating the styles of previous exponents expertly into their own personal statement, assisted by prodigious technical facility. Shearing combined fantastic musicianship and breathtaking invention with an ability to make his music accessible to non-specialist ears. A new generation of players was exploring new improving tactics in jazz, where extemporising was up to now based largely on the harmonic content of the theme. These newcomers looked to the modal system, something that was prominent in early and medieval European music – and indeed was still a part of much ethnic music-making – but had been hitherto unexplored in any detail in jazz. Pianist Chick Corea, another Miles Davis ex-player, was prominent in this field and helped to open up yet another option for the jazz improviser.

Meanwhile the big bands, no longer subsidised by mass public popularity in the Glenn Miller sense of the word, were fighting a reasonably successful rearguard action. The Count Basie Orchestra went from strength to strength, and had become the yardstick of big-band perfection by the outset of the sixties. Ellington was still productive, and, although illness and later the death of his close ally Billy Strayhorn gave rise to fears that the Ellington well of invention might then run dry, Duke came up with a period of intense activity, most notably the sacred concerts, which were performed widely in Europe. The period even gave birth to at least one significant new band, that of Maynard Ferguson, a one-time member of the Stan Kenton trumpet section, in whose ranks many young jazzmen and arrangers won their spurs.

On the vocal front, Ella Fitzgerald and Sarah Vaughan were still active, the former enjoying a new lease of life as a result of the efforts of her manager Norman Granz.

In Britain great work was being done by West Indian alto saxist Joe Harriott, a pioneer of the fusion of jazz with Indian music; a prime force in saxophones was tenor man Tubby Hayes, who started his career as a fifteen-year-old jazz prodigy with tremendous talent on sax, flute and vibes. Both these players were to meet their deaths before the full value of their talents could be realised. Not so pianist Stan Tracey, however, whose highly individual style of playing and effective arranging were to endure and grow for decades to come. The same could be said for Cleo Laine, whose style at that time was maturing fast towards world class in the field of jazz singing. Norma Winstone was soon to be travelling the same road.

Jazz was holding its own. But the advent of rock-and-roll, typified by the enormous success of the Beatles in the early sixties, cast a shadow on the future well-being of jazz. Could it survive, or would it be submerged under the avalanche of the new wave in popular music?

We have since of course found that survive it could – and did. But the new developments were to leave their mark on jazz, just as had always been the case in the past.

12

That's entertainment

Jazz musicians tend to regard recording exclusively as an act of self-expression, unlike the record companies, who see it as just one stage in the production of a saleable product. In my recording heyday the companies with whom I and my band were involved looked very closely at the sales figures and, although jazz was not usually expected to vie with popular music from the sales point of view, the jazzman who sold records in large quantities was, so to speak, a piper in a much stronger position to call the tune. Indeed, the concept recordings just described would probably never have happened had it not been for my hit records. There were just two of them, but both made a big enough impact, firstly to make me and my band a household name in Britain, and secondly to convince several record companies that any subsequent recording I made could emulate those. Any band or performer of any sort who has proven already that they can produce music that sells in large quantities will have their own way in choosing their recording repertoire for a long time.

George Martin, our first recording manager, was always on the lookout for a way to broaden the audience for our music, although to his credit he never rejected anything that we wanted to record, however esoteric or inaccessible he personally considered it to be.

The 1950s were the years of live big-band broadcasts, and top bands such as ours had prime-time spots in thirteen-week long series. Since the shows lasted about an hour and a half, I was always looking for regular features to 'milestone' the show – a special feature for a guest artist, a composition by a foreign jazz composer and so on. These helped enliven the programmes and ring the changes; for there was always a danger that, because of our dedication to quality and our rejection of the worst stupidities of Tin Pan Alley, we might in fact become too solemn. And this would be unacceptable, since one thing many jazz musicians are known to possess is a sense of humour.

So I hit on the idea of taking a theme and playing it in the styles of various bands. As a result, every week *Three Blind Mice* was performed as if by a different band or artist – Benny Goodman, Gerry Mulligan, Stan Kenton and so on. We even went as far as Glenn Miller. George heard us one evening and phoned me the next day. 'Sounds like a good idea for a record, Johnny.' He was the only person in my social or professional life who called me Johnny, although that was how I was known to the general public; it didn't bother me then any more than it does now when older fans use the name. 'The problem is to make all those blind mice into a three-and-a-half-minute single.'

'I'll try to think of something', I said, far from convinced that I would. That night I lay in bed running one idea after another through my racing brain. Then it came – the story of three blind mice who lived in a recording studio: one called Benny Goodmouse (burst of Benny Goodman's music), one who used to live in a mill, so they called him 'Miller' (burst of romantic Glenn Miller sounds) . . . and so on. George looked after the technical side of piecing it all together and guiding it skilfully into the right section of the record market.

It was a major hit, and although it remained in the Top Twenty for around three months it became our most requested item on one-night stands for years afterwards. It significantly added to my band's reputation, opening up the whole of Britain to our music – and it did no harm at all to George Martin's image. He was fast gaining a reputation in his parent company Parlophone (a division of EMI) of being their most important man, a position which his later work with the Beatles consolidated to make him perhaps the world's most famous record producer.

Flushed by the success of *Experiments with Mice*, we issued further singles which we all considered candidates for equal success, but as is so often the case the Midas touch proved elusive. 1959 and 1960 went by and produced nothing in the way of hit material. Although the records continued to sell well, the sweet smell of extraordinary success was hard to forget.

However, the sales of *Mice* were enjoyed by a publisher to whom I had assigned the rights, and with whom I obviously had to share the spoils of victory. I began to feel that it was time to have my own music-publishing organisation for any future hits. I came to an agreement with David Dearlove, then a music manager for an important independent TV company, and we formed a company, opened an office in Denmark Street in London's West End and proceeded to compile a repertoire, keeping a special lookout for young composers.

One day David drew my attention to a collection of demos (demonstration discs and tapes from aspiring composers of new material, with which publishers and artists have been regularly deluged ever since the advent of recording) which he had received that morning. A young composer had spotted our company name plate while wandering past our new home in Denmark Street, then the undisputed home of London's Tin Pan Alley. 'Some tracks are better than others, naturally', said David, 'and you don't have to listen to them all. But there's one I'd like you to hear, and maybe record.'

I listened to the scratchy sounds of a piano plonking out a tune. I can't say I was really impressed by what I heard, but I saw David's eyes light up, and I knew he had a much better commercial instinct than I. If David thought it had potential then I must at least give it a try. The tune was called *African Waltz*, and it had, as its title might imply, a percussive element which married it rather unusually to a rhythmic beat more common to waltz time. It was, I suppose, a jazz waltz with a difference, and jazz waltzes were rare in those days. David Lindup was the other David who now came into the picture, and together we worked out an arrangement which preserved the basic character of the composition yet gave it an added air of individuality.

We recorded it the following week, and it was duly, and slightly reluctantly, issued by the record company in the popular release category, rather than the specialist jazz one. Whether that last factor had an influence on what happened subsequently I shall perhaps never know. The disc jockeys pounced on the record and within a week it had nudged its way into the Top Twenty – and in a couple more to the Top Ten. There it remained for much longer than *Experiments with Mice*, and with much greater worldwide acclaim. Over the next six months or so, dozens of cover records (versions of the same arrangement by other bands all over the world) were issued, the most important being the one by Cannonball Adderley in the States. Adderley's version, unlike any of the others, was made with my blessing. This in a way turned out to be a tactical mistake, although I doubt if a refusal on my part would have stopped it. The Cannonball record turned out to be a minor hit for the American saxophone star, while our own recording, issued rather belatedly in the US, was much less successful. However, if anyone was to pip us to the post I was glad that it was Adderley, whom I had admired as a jazz soloist for years.

Six months or thereabouts in the charts with *African Waltz* gave me another lease of life with the big band. (Its composer, by the way, was Galt MacDermott, who later became an internationally known figure with his score of the musical *Hair* and the song *Aquarius*.) With the good fortune to have two hit records in the space of three years or so, at a time when the big-band sound was receding rather than advancing, my band was able to survive while others folded. However, like other leaders of big bands before me – notably the great Duke Ellington – I was able to subsidise my own band from another source of revenue which was at that time growing rapidly – my income as a composer, which was now becoming considerable as a result of my introduction into the world of film music.

* * *

It started in a small way. The phone rang: 'My name is Karel Reisz.' The cultured ultra-English tones gave not the faintest hint of a childhood spent in his native Czechoslovakia. 'I've made a documentary about a South London youth club, and I'd like you to do the music.' The thought of music for films had only occasionally entered my mind, and then not with any great enthusiasm. I felt that music used as a background to filmed sequences was a humiliation for music of

JD with Dizzy Gillespie... and with Duke Ellington

With Anthony Field and Leonard Bernstein . . .   with James Galway . . .

David Lindup,
my compositional collaborator

and with Cleo Laine and Frank Sinatra

With Ray Charles . . . and with Clark Terry and Bob Brookmeyer

With Julian Lloyd Webber

Below: Our current rhythm section (*from left to right*): John Horler (piano), Malcolm Creese (bass), Allan Ganley (drums)

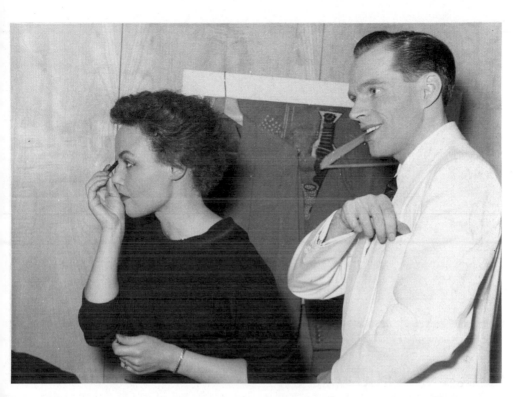

Early days with Cleo

Our young family - Alec and Jacqui

With Cleo and the children at home in Wavendon . . . and with Cleo outside Buckingham Palace

Envoi

any quality, and any composer agreeing to submit to such an indignity should be regarded with suspicion. However, Reisz was a persuasive person, and a dialogue over lunch in Soho won me over. He took me to a nearby cutting room in Wardour Street and showed me some scenes.

The effect was magical. Despite the clatter of the noisy Moviola playback machine and the tiny image it gave of the film, I heard music in my head – music different from any I had hitherto composed. The images had inspired me, and I raced home and feverishly scribbled down on paper the themes I had heard in that cutting room. The score was duly completed and recorded on a shoe-string budget at the National Film Theatre on the south bank of the Thames. I remember Karel himself carrying in the microphones to save a pound or two, and the film *We are the Lambeth Boys* went on to win an important prize at the Cannes Film Festival.

My film career had started at almost the same time as that of Karel Reisz, who went on to make many distinguished films, with *The French Lieutenant's Woman* perhaps the best known. The music for *Lambeth Boys* had worked well and we both knew it, with the result that I was booked to do Reisz's first feature film, a movie version of Alan Sillitoe's novel *Saturday Night and Sunday Morning*. Albert Finney was cast in the lead role for the first film performance of his career.

At almost precisely the same time I was discovered by another director, this time one who had already gained a reputation. Joseph Losey had already achieved some success in Hollywood when the McCarthy black list threatened to end his career. He came to Europe and thereafter made films in France and Italy as well as in Britain. He was nearing completion of a Stanley Baker epic called *The Criminal* (known in the States as *The Concrete Jungle*, but not to be confused with a 1982 film of the same name), and I accepted his invitation to supply a score.

Losey and Reisz were as different as two directors could possibly be. Their only common quality was their commitment to high standards. Losey's policy, in every facet of the film's making, was to delegate to the best qualified person available – scriptwriter, cameraman, designer, lighting director and indeed composer – and to leave them alone as much as possible. Reisz by contrast gave the impression that he would have dearly loved to have been able to write the score himself, and once a musical sequence was decided upon he proceeded to go through every second's worth with a stop watch and a fine toothcomb.

His discussions on the feel of the music for a scene would go something like: 'John, this scene starts with David standing and dreaming, not listening to what's being said. As his mind goes back – rather Debussy-ish perhaps . . . then flashback to the hospital, perhaps a touch baroque . . . then a Wagnerian flourish as the matron enters . . . then finally a Bach-like interrupted cadence, left in mid-air as the scene finishes.' As such a scene would probably last about forty seconds, this sort of thing always seemed like over-direction to me. Perhaps I should have ignored it, but I didn't and tried hard to please Karel, satisfy myself and serve the film well all at the same time. It could be the reason that, though I badly wanted to do an outstanding job for Karel – he had become a good friend – I never achieved it after *Lambeth Boys*, in spite of one further score for him – the film *Morgan*, starring Vanessa Redgrave (her first leading role) and David Warner.

Joe Losey left the whole issue of musical content completely to me. Apart from a cursory hearing of the theme or themes I proposed to use, his only concern was to involve me in the making of the picture, and the thinking behind it, as much as possible before I started work on my contribution. Thus I was whisked to studios in various parts of London as well as on location, whether it happened to be in the English metropolis or Amsterdam or Sicily.

Over the years I did four scores for Losey. The first, *The Criminal*, contained some quality music, but I was learning my craft and there were weaknesses as well as clichés. The other three were all to my mind good and effective scores for the job they were required to do. They were *The Servant*, featuring James Fox, *Modesty Blaise*, in which Monica Vitti and Terence Stamp starred, and *Accident*, which included roles for Stanley Baker and Vivienne Merchant. Coincidentally, Dirk Bogarde starred in all three of these movies. Of the three I think the score for *The Servant* was the most effective, and it is probably the best musical score of mine for any movie, to date at least. But the relatively high success rate of the Losey scores was to my mind due to the fact that Joe, while giving me every encouragement and opportunity to imbibe his own ideas, left me alone to make up my own mind about the way to handle the situation best.

In fact I believe it was the success of the score of *The Servant*, as well of course as the critical and box-office success of the picture, which led to a number of enquiries from other directors. The first came from John Schlesinger, who had just completed *Darling*, a film featuring Julie Christie in her first starring role. Schlesinger was a keen music lover and was anxious that the score had a different feel from fashionable movie scores which merely reflected current tastes in popular music.

I don't think I delivered what Schlesinger wanted, and in fact *Darling* was the only movie I scored for him. I wrote what I considered a good tune for the theme, to which writer Gene Lees supplied a good lyric (not incidentally used in the film) and which Sarah Vaughan subsequently recorded. However, I felt that a star of the film should record the song commercially. It was originally a man's lyric and the obvious choice was Dirk Bogarde. Dirk seemed to be in virtually every film I made during that period, and I had got to know him during a long period on location in Sicily for *Modesty Blaise*. I felt I could persuade him to record the number.

'But I can't sing', he protested. I managed to convince him that multi-track recording had made it easy to take the song line by line and extract a good performance from almost anyone. Moreover, he would not have the embarrassment of working in front of an orchestra. They would record the accompaniment and be sent home long before he arrived. 'It'll be a great thing for the film, and a new facet of your career', I assured him.

The recording date was set, and in spite of several attempts by Dirk to reverse his decision I eventually managed to get him to the recording studio. After a long and somewhat arduous session I was satisfied that we had a reasonable performance of my song. My opinion, however, was not shared by the press. Worse still, they lambasted Dirk personally for having the effrontery to believe he could sing, not me for having talked him into it against his better judgement. 'COME OFF IT, DIRK – WHO ARE YOU TRYING TO FOOL?' was typical of the headlines issuing from the lower-brow tabloids of the time. The Bogarde single was surely one of the big flops of the year.

I was so embarrassed I felt obliged, cowardly though it no doubt was, to avoid Dirk for a time. When I eventually saw him and was forced to mumble an apology he smiled good naturedly and passed it off as a joke. I had always liked Dirk, but appreciated him even more after the way he handled that episode so magnanimously.

Invitations to score other movies followed in rapid succession, some of the films good, some excruciatingly bad. One of the problems confronting a film composer is divining which films to take on and which to turn down. True, the movie is usually well under way by the time the invitation arrives, but judging quality from a very rough assembly of the footage shot thus far is not easy. A script is even less of a guide; so much can be added or taken away during shooting. Thus I make no excuses for picking a few duds as well as some classics among the many I have scored, in almost every class of film apart from musicals – horror movies, fantasies, jungle thrillers, serial murder mysteries, slapstick comedies, high drama – even cartoons.

When *The Servant* was nearing completion I arrived at Shepperton Studios one morning to see Joe Losey, Spike Priggen the producer, Richard Macdonald the designer and a few others on their way to a viewing theatre. They looked and sounded concerned, especially Priggen, as they had found something that would probably have to be reshot, and add accordingly to an already overstretched budget. We sat down on the plush theatre seats, the room darkened and the scene in question was shown. When the lights went up again the worried looks were still there. I confessed to them that I had seen nothing amiss. 'Roll it once more, please, Gary', said Joe. 'Look to the bottom right of the screen, John.'

I glued my eyes to that point. The scene was one of James Fox making a call on a public pay phone. There were the usual phone numbers and various graffiti on the wall, accompanied by the odd bit of visual art work. And then I saw it, meticulously and graphically drawn in white chalk – the unmistakable outline of an erect penis.

Such things were most definitely taboo in those days, and I walked away from the theatre with Richard Macdonald while the others got into a huddle to reschedule the shot. 'I bet they'd like to get hold of whoever it was who added that drawing. Do they have any idea?'

Macdonald sniggered in a way that had become characteristic of him. 'As a matter of fact it was me', he replied.

One day I had a message from my agent that a Hollywood producer named Henry Hathaway was trying to get hold of me. His name rang a bell immediately. His many credits included the block-busting epic *How the West Was Won*. He was also supposed to be just about the richest man in Hollywood. I duly went to Pinewood to see his movie called *The Last Safari* featuring Stewart Grainger. To say it was not the greatest example of the film-maker's craft would have to be the understatement of the century, but Hathaway's enthusiasm for my work and his insistence that the job was tailor-made for me eventually flattered me into taking the job. As I started to get to grips with the work it became apparent that he trusted me completely. He had no wish to hear anything of the score before it was actually recorded.

I decided to make the important opening sequence a quasi-ethnic piece, borrowing the sounds of *kwela*, an urban African style. This meant combing London for players, particularly percussionists, who could contribute the right authentic sounds. Such people were eventually unearthed and the day of the first recording session arrived. As the musicians streamed into the sound stage at the old Denham Studios I felt a sense of foreboding – was it all going to work? And then I noticed something unusual. Producers are normally to be found sipping coffee in the control booth while the recording engineers prepare the studio and adjust the microphones. But there was Henry, sitting a few yards away from the conductor's rostrum in the studio itself. He was seated, cigar in mouth, clad in an expensive-looking gabardine raincoat which he kept on throughout the day as he waited for the sounds to emerge from the assembled orchestra. A male assistant, almost identically garbed, sat next to him.

I started the orchestra, and out came the first bars. I was aghast. Ethnic music is always difficult to re-create, but this sounded to me quite abysmal. I had altogether failed to capture on paper the sounds I had heard in my head. I made adjustments and tried again, but several such attempts did little to help. After about an hour I felt quite despondent. The only thing to do was to give the band a break and hear the results so far. So I dismissed them and made my way to the control room, carefully selecting a route that avoided having to meet my producer. I was so conscious of having let the man down, after all his faith in me, that my cowardice got the better of my more admirable qualities.

But my avoidance tactics were unsuccessful. Hathaway strode purposefully across the floor, and it became clear that he intended to intercept me. I prepared myself for a burst of film producer's rage, the like of which I had so often seen acted out in Hollywood movies – maybe even one of his. I stopped in front of him sheepishly and awaited the eruption. 'John, that was marvellous, *really* marvellous', came the outburst. 'It's just exactly what I'd imagined – only much better!' I could hardly believe it – the man had a broad grin on his face as he slapped me on the back with a vigour that nearly winded me.

After that the sessions went like wildfire. He adored everything I had written, and by the time the third day of recording approached it became apparent that in spite of our slow start we would probably finish on schedule. I quickly sensed an air of complacency in the orchestra – things were going so very well. 'Now, guys, don't let's get sloppy – keep the concentration level up now we're in sight of the finishing line. Let's keep it moving.' I was quite pleased with this timely, well-crafted exhortation, which immediately brought a tight discipline back to the musicians, and looked across the studio for an endorsing smile from Henry.

I saw instead the first look of displeasure I had ever seen on the Hathaway visage. I was transfixed and puzzled, but the stalemate was broken, as Mr Hathaway's assistant approached my rostrum. 'John', he drawled in sotto voce tones. 'Henry wants you to know that he's not a pusher. If you'd like some more time on this score, he'd be very happy for you to take some extra sessions next week.'

I quickly realised my mistake. I had worked too often for budget-conscious British producers, straining to save every possible penny. But here was one of the old-school Hollywood legends, to whom over-spending a budget signalled a dedication to quality whatever the cost. Besides, he was enjoying himself. With great presence of mind I slowed things down dramatically and booked the musicians, there and then, for a further day's work the following week. They were naturally delighted, if a little puzzled that their very efficiency had initially caused displeasure. But the main objective was to keep Henry

Hathaway happy, and that is exactly what it did. We completed the two unfinished music cues on the subsequent session and re-recorded a few others for no reason at all. Honour was served, and we finally parted company with an extremely satisfied client.

13

There'll be some changes made

The band occupied a lot of my waking hours, but then there were also solo engagements and dozens of writing commissions throughout the fifties and most of the sixties, for films, TV themes, documentaries and commercials, as well as for plays and indeed the musical theatre. On top of all this I was often asked to present radio programmes, and on many occasions to write articles for newspapers and magazines. More than once I was even employed as a TV interviewer, and one of my most flattering assignments was to be the presenter for a Duke Ellington appearance at the Royal Albert Hall during one of his many visits to London. On this occasion his band was augmented by nothing less than the entire London Symphony Orchestra, and the show was covered by BBC TV.

TV work included the music for the original series of *The Avengers*. I would have continued my contributions were it not for a rather questionable ultimatum which was introduced into my contract regarding the publication rights of the music, to which I refused to be a party. I was also asked around this time to supply a theme for a pilot BBC science feature, a six-programme series which, as *Tomorrow's World*, turned out to have a life of over a quarter of a century. My music lasted for the first ten years or so, before it was replaced by something rather more metallic.

Commercials are by nature rather less memorable works in the long term (or, at least, usually deserve to be), but on looking through some of the dustier shelves of my music library in Wavendon some familiar names peer at me in their faded ink – Pepsi-Cola, Wilkinson's Sword, Camay soap, Robertson's marmalade. And indeed there was one memorable one – a choral score in quasi-plainsong. The lyrics, in Latin, have sadly been lost in the dust, but I seem to remember that the last line went something like '*gaudeamus in Ovaltine!*'. If I remember correctly, such a highbrow concept was targeted less at TV-addicted Latin scholars than the judges at the Cannes Film Festival, but it is too long ago to recall whether it had any success in either field of endeavour.

Those years were fertile ones for me in the world of musicals and plays containing music. I shared my work with such lyricists as Shakespeare, Congreve, T. S. Eliot – and Benny Green, with whom I have collaborated on at least two musicals and two ballets. The performers included Dame Sybil Thorndike, Nicol Williamson, Anna Quayle, John Neville, Helen Mirren, Michael Crawford, Annette Crosbie, Clive Revill, Alec McGowan and Robin Bailey, while my employers varied from the National Theatre and the City of London Festival to the Royal Shakespeare Company and the BBC.

Then there were my well-publicised flirtations during that period with symphony orchestras – or perhaps I should say the symphony orchestras' flirtation with me, since it was they who made the first overture (if that is an appropriate word). In 1958 I was offered a commission by the London Philharmonic Society to write a piece for my own band and the London Philharmonic Orchestra. Lacking experience at that stage in orchestrating for a symphony in full cry, I suggested a collaboration with a 'straight' composer. I felt that, between the two of us, we would surely be able to get the best out of the forces at our disposal. 'Any suggestions?' was the response as I enlarged on my proposal.

My mind flew back to a meeting the week before in connection with a Hoffnung concert in which I was taking part. It was usual to have a 'think-tank' to ascertain what was already in preparation and what remained to be dreamed up. Such meetings would normally involve perhaps composer Malcolm Arnold, conductor Norman del Mar and a couple of others as well as, of course, Gerard himself. On this occasion there was also Mátyás Seiber, the London-resident Hungarian composer, who was involved with one of the new pieces. I had exchanged a few words with him and we seemed to get along well.

'What about Seiber?' I ventured with a knowledgeable air – and Seiber it was decided to be. Thus our work together began, and although I would not claim that it was an easy partnership we somehow managed to cobble together between us a piece that was quite effective in its own way. Things went smoothly at the first run-through until one particular passage raised a problem. When jazz music is put onto paper it is common practice to write eighth-notes (or quavers) in normal style, and to leave the 'jazzing' element to the player. Symphony musicians, on the other hand, would always play the passage literally just as it was written. Whenever this discrepancy occurred we would hear a protesting high-pitched shout coming from the middle of the hall, where Seiber had positioned himself to get the full effect: 'No! No! Eet ees not jazz, eet ees "ta-ta-ta-ta"!'

Despite years in England, Mátyás had not lost his squeezed mid-European vowel sounds. He would then quakily sing the phrase, and our musicians would comply, though not without a well-concealed giggle or two. For years afterwards, when the question came up as to the interpretation of similar passages in more usual circumstances, any member of my band would be quite likely to ask of his section-leader, 'Ees jazz, or ees ta-ta, Derrick?'

'Oh, definitely ta-ta, Stan', would come the totally poker-faced but infinitely helpful reply.

About that time we were asked to perform Stravinsky's *Ebony Concerto*, which was originally written for the Woody Herman Orchestra (in fact we also recorded the piece for a small classical label, with clarinettist Gervase de Peyer as soloist). Our conductor for a Royal Festival Hall concert containing this work was William Steinberg, who in those days was being shared between the Pittsburgh Symphony and Israel Philharmonic orchestras. There is a passage somewhere in the middle section of the piece where a trumpet and baritone sax play together – yet not quite together (this is the only way I can explain it without getting technical). It can so easily be played incorrectly, and George Tyndale, our huge-framed, happy-dispositioned baritone player, an excellent musician with a great jazz talent and a mammoth sound – got it wrong.

Dr Steinberg was undoubtedly a fine conductor, and had guided the fortunes of none but the world's finest orchestras; consequently he was not accustomed to hearing wrong notes. Moreover, in addition to his qualities as a music director he would no doubt have enjoyed a brilliant career in Hollywood movies as a character actor should he have so desired – that is, if he were to specialise in one particular role, that of a classical conductor. His natural movements and body language were straight out of a thirties black-and-white saga about, say, a boogie-woogie pianist who wants to play Carnegie Hall, or something of that sort – one expected S. Z. Sakall or Eric Blore or Barry Fitzgerald to appear at any moment. Moreover, nothing would inspire Dr Steinberg more to give his best acting performance than a succession of wrong notes, and that is exactly what he was getting from George. I had a grandstand view: I was in the front row of the sax section, a good vantage point to watch the maestro's face changing gradually in colour and the little vein on his left temple beginning to pulsate. 'Vunce more, zat passage', growled the doctor, and we repeated it as directed. George, now flustered, with beads of heavy sweat forming on his brow, got it wrong again. And yet again.

Our maestro was now at the point of no return. I watched as his breathing got shallower and faster, as his eyes ascended towards the source of divine assistance, and as the knuckles protruding from the fists clenched at his side got ever whiter. An eruption was inevitable, and we all waited for it. Steinberg lowered his raised shoulders, straightened his tie and slowly turned to face us. But he had pulled himself together – this was no time for a Steinberg to lose his self-control. He now had the look of a saint about him, and his mouth was forced into a sickly exaggerated smile. He strolled slowly over to George with a calculated nonchalance, and lowered his smile on to the now alarmed musician. 'Vot ees your name, Meester Baritone?'

'Tyndale, sir – George Tyndale.'

'George, I have a vay to get zis music right. For quarter-notes I put my thumb down, and for half-notes I put it up – OK?'

George nodded assent, and on the next attempt the improvement was noticeable. The saxophonist's eyes were glued to the conductor's left hand, which rotated up and down, thumb rampant or drooping, according to the pattern of the music. And so on the concert that night, in front of several thousand people (a few of whom would have been perplexed, but most of whom would never have noticed), Dr William Steinberg – with the help of George Tyndale – added a dimension to the orchestral conductor's technical weaponry, conducting the ensemble with his right hand and employing the 'thumbs up-thumbs down' technique with his left. I just wish someone had been there with a camera.

At the time of the start of the big band in 1953 I had been a 26-year-old bachelor living at home with my parents. By 1966 I was happily married to a very successful professional artiste, and together we were jointly in possession of a beautiful Georgian country house – Nether Hall in the Buckinghamshire village of Aspley Guise – and two fine children, our son Alec, born in 1960 and destined to become an excellent musician in his own right, and daughter Jacqueline, born in 1963, a future singer and actress of great ability. Stuart, Cleo's son from her first marriage, joined us in the late fifties at Nether Hall to become an integral part of our household. His talents lay in a different direction, leading him to a successful career in graphic art.

Cleo's life in the world of music had started with my band, but by the time we were married in 1958 she had already begun a separate phase of it with a hit record which led to solo cabaret work, as well as to all sorts of other interesting engagements, including visits to the Edinburgh Festival in the roles of both singer and actress. This separation of our careers at this stage was no accident; we felt that because we had worked together for so long our joint presence had begun to be taken for granted – as if one of us was a sort of free gift bestowed on anyone who booked the other, so to speak. We therefore resolved to keep apart professionally for a while until our independence as artistes was fully established in the minds of the public.

Nevertheless we enjoyed immensely those occasions when we did share a stage, and by the late sixties had decided we had made our point about being separate entities. Consequently, when the opportunity came to do so, we began appearing as a team. Such a scheme had its advantages; an extra instrument added colour and variety to the vocal accompaniment, and my skills as an arranger could be more effectively used when I was on the spot to govern their usage, as, for example, at London's Camden Festival featuring a mixed programme of material ranging from Shakespeare to twentieth-century song, conceived by festival director Jack Henderson as a modern version of a lieder recital. Its warm reception by the critics led to a number of similar such engagements up and down the country. Our joint appearances were obviously popular with promoters, since they now had two names to promote instead of one. Moreover, in this 'chamber-music' formula our logistical requirements were simple for a local management to provide – just basic lighting, a simple sound system and a piano.

We played several smaller auditoriums around Britain, some of them in private homes or on private estates; and this put into our minds the idea of doing something similar ourselves one day – with one difference. We decided that if we put such a plan into operation we would also incorporate an educational programme, to enable us to pass on to future generations the benefit of our own experiences in music.

Our dream of a music centre of our own began to come true in 1968, when, after having realised that our lovely Nether Hall would not be suitable for public performances, we started casting our gaze about the neighbourhood for something that would work as a home for both us and our ideals. We needed a place with easy access, which somewhere in its grounds had a building that could conceivably be converted into a performance centre. We also wanted plenty of open space, not too near any neighbours, so that my sister Avril might establish a children's music camp.

We found it at the Old Rectory in Wavendon, a small village just two or three miles from Aspley Guise and Nether Hall. The house itself was hardly as attractive as our abode of the last nine years – its Victorian neo-Gothic was no real match for clean-cut Georgian lines – but we made our decision to go ahead on the strength of a stable-block which seemed as if it might fit the bill for our auditorium. And although the original purchase of the house and garden might have left us short of space for the music camp idea, the presence of twelve acres of fields adjacent to us (which we later acquired) seemed reassuring. So we bought the Old Rectory, and, after waiting just about a year for some alterations and improvements to be finished, finally installed ourselves in May 1969.

It seemed a good idea to get our own house in order – literally – before doing anything about our project. After all, the stable-block was in terrible condition and the idea of using it, as we intended, for music seemed remote; people whom we showed round the dilapidated edifice, telling them of our plans, tended to say, 'Ah, yes', and nervously change the subject – they obviously thought we were stark, staring mad. It was surely a moment to take a deep breath before proceeding, and I said as much to my spouse.

But Cleo would have none of it. 'If we don't take the plunge now we'll never get it started', she warned, and she was probably right. So what could I do but go along with this impulsive decision? We called up our friends and asked for their help to prepare The Stables for a party in October, when we could explain our idea to people who could possibly help us; within days the place was a hive of feverish activity, with painters, carpenters, plumbers, decorators and cleaners – all unpaid – buzzing in all directions at one and the same time.

The party finally took place in mid-October 1969. It started in motion a ball that would roll on, at ever-increasing speed, for the ensuing thirty years until The Stables' next phase of expansion and its true coming of age. Someday I hope to write a book devoted entirely to our Wavendon brainchild; just now it will have to suffice to say that, since its inception, we have seen thousands of music students and literally hundreds of thousands of music-lovers pass through our gates, to be taught or entertained – or both – by the countless musicians who have provided their services over the years.

Perhaps our greatest pleasure from Wavendon has always been our part in the success of our educational activities. Many of today's professionals attended our courses in their student days, and we are always naturally proud when one of our alumni goes on to a successful career in music. But I always warn incoming students that music courses are places for musicians – teachers and learners alike – to exchange ideas and thoughts. A musician is just as likely to hear something which will change his whole outlook on music in the coffee queue during break time from a fellow student as he is from an instructor. And that applies to the teachers too: music courses are learning experiences for everyone, not just the student body.

Our music courses outgrew the Wavendon building very early in their existence, and so memories of the first courses, with students staying with villagers and practising wherever they could, in the car park, in the loo, or wherever they were able to find a vacant space in our home, are confined to the first couple of years. Most of the courses grew to numbers which required more space than we were able to provide, and thus we migrated to nearby educational centres. Yet nothing will replace the fond memories of the very shortcomings of those first efforts of ours in music education.

Our concert programme was also intended to be an education of sorts – to the public. Our programmes were models of musical integration; every ticket buyer could be sure that, whatever style of music the concert showcased, it could be guaranteed to be the best of its kind. To list all of the fine artists who have performed with us would be impossible here, and to pluck a few of the more famous out of the pack would tend to suggest that their contribution was greater than that of the others.

One of our very first concerts will always remain in my memory more than any other. Cleo and I had invited three good friends, John Williams the guitarist, John Ogdon the pianist and Richard Rodney Bennett the composer, to join us as artistic directors; as well as their expertise in helping with matters of policy, all three generously offered their services on occasions for concerts.

A concert recital by John Ogdon was arranged for early 1970. By this time we had barely sorted out our infrastructure, and our sole assistance came from Milton Keynes Development Corporation, who supplied the services of Lavinia Dyer. Lavinia became our administrator, artistic co-ordinator, publicist and general manager rolled into one, and also ran our box office single-handed for over a year until we were able to accumulate some funds to employ others to help her.

The concert was not surprisingly sold out weeks in advance. The excitement mounted, and the day arrived. The winter sun was peeping bravely through as I extricated my Rolls Royce Silver Shadow from its shelter and drove to London at about midday. I arrived outside the door of John and Brenda's very grand home in Chester Terrace,

Regents Park, and as I got out a couple of snowflakes fluttered meekly down in front of me. The Ogdons and I were in the car and on our way back to Wavendon not more than ten minutes later, but now the snow was swirling merrily towards the windscreen as we sped along. By the time we turned into the driveway at Wavendon less than an hour had passed, but there was no doubt about it – we were witnessing a snowstorm.

The snow itself eventually eased off, and the concert seemed possible. However, Lavinia soon came running, or rather wading, over to the house from The Stables with the news that the storm had knocked out both the electricity supply and the phone lines. Worse still, it now began to freeze, with the result that many of our ticket holders would be unable to get their cars out of their own garage driveways. Concert time approached, and to our surprise a few vehicles managed to struggle to The Stables, discharging a few brave mortals, blankets tucked over their arms, who had decided that a John Ogdon recital was worth the risk of possible frostbite and/or a night in the car. But what of our artist – was it fair to ask him to perform in an unheated, unlit and probably half-empty auditorium?

John was a gentle and softly spoken man, but he answered the question with an uncharacteristic firmness which left us in no doubt as to what to do. The show was to go on. 'If people have made the effort to get here, the least I can do is make the effort to perform', was his view. And perform he did. In a Stables a little more than half-full – the rest of the audience had been unable to reach us – a dedicated band of blanket-shrouded concertgoers, who were just able to see the great man in the flickering candleglow which served as our only saviour from total darkness, listened enraptured. And how he performed! With an old woollen cardigan augmenting his concert tails, his chilled fingers caressing the cold ivory of the keys as only a virtuoso would know how, John produced one of the most moving performances we listeners could hope to experience in a lifetime. And The Stables, in the midst of one of its initial challenges, echoed to truly great music on that very memorable night.

A frequent visitor to our little auditorium was the great comedienne Joyce Grenfell. However, perhaps her most memorable visit was not to perform, but solely to make an appearance during a fund-raising fête in the Old Rectory garden. She arrived when the event was in full swing and joined Cleo, who was disposing of some of her discarded wardrobe in what was called Cleo's Clobber Shop. Joyce immediately disapproved of the low mark-downs Cleo had carefully pinned to the garments, and put new and higher prices on everything. 'Marking-up' merchandise that is not selling well is an ancient ploy used by Middle-Eastern traders, I believe. The ruse seemingly worked like a dream, as business immediately appeared to improve – perhaps it gave the stuff greater appeal to our more up-market patrons.

Joyce Grenfell made no secret of the fact that she loved performing at The Stables, and came on several occasions, usually staying overnight at the rectory when she did so. From the moment she stepped onto our tiny thrust stage, with perhaps a fifth of the audience directly in front and the remainder stretched out on both sides – a real challenge to any performer – Joyce took total command. She was one of the very few artists I have seen who could switch suddenly from the frivolous to the extremely serious, and even the touchingly poignant, with total success.

Joyce could and often did strain The Stables' roof with the laughter from her adoring audience, without ever reverting to 'blue' material. Yet contrary to some people's belief she was no prude. At a tribute to her life in entertainment, after her untimely death, her lifelong friend actress Daphne Oxenford shared Joyce's favourite joke with the audience. The story opens as a scruffy man elbows his way into a crowded railway carriage, coughing, sniffling and spluttering loudly and objectionably as he lowers himself into a seat. He then pulls out a grubby handkerchief and, with a noisy and unhygienic fanfare, blows his nose literally all over the compartment. Putting down his *Times* newspaper, a conservatively clad middle-aged gentleman peers over his horn-rimmed glasses at the offender and says: 'And now, sir, perhaps you might be good enough to oblige us with a fart?'

A great supporter of our cause has been Princess Margaret, who befriended us when we were appearing at the 1964 Bath Festival. Ever since attending our very first gathering to launch our efforts in 1969 she made a point of assisting in our various fund-raising activities. Her many visits to our home over the years, and ours to hers for that matter, have given us the chance to discover a very musical person, equipped with both a good ear and an excellent musical memory, and not only able to sing perfectly in tune but capable of leading a group of enthusiastic but untrained spontaneous singers with authority and gusto. The queen's sister quickly proved herself to be a genuine music lover in the least snobbish sense of the word, with preferences in every sphere of music. Which made it especially appropriate that she should espouse our cause, since our avowed philosophy – the driving force of Wavendon since the beginning – amounts precisely to hers: that all music of whatever style can eventually be placed into one of only two categories – good or bad.

Perspective IV

The future of jazz in the early seventies was far from clear. The trouble could be traced down to the fact that the word jazz meant (and indeed to this day still means) very different things to many self-professed jazz lovers. This of course had always been to some extent the case, understandable in view of the considerable number of new departures – and indeed new arrivals – on the jazz scene. But at this point in its history jazz was witnessing the upsurge of the avant garde.

It is difficult to pinpoint the precise beginning of the movement. It was obviously subject to some influences from the world of Western European classical music, where attempts to incorporate improvisation had long been made. Moreover, the atonal, unpredictable and indeed almost 'random' effect that young modern 'legitimate' composers were at that time achieving from music constructed on the tone-row system (closely associated with the work of Schoenberg) or by other similar methods was remarkably akin to the free-form improvisation being investigated by jazz musicians. The avant garde appeared to be a natural and logical development of the music, and few jazz musicians, composers or critics with a concern for the future of the music failed to take it seriously.

Free-form improvisation clearly demanded to be taken seriously. At its best it had much to offer – the immediacy of improvisations unfettered by the requirements of form and of underlying harmonic content, the freedom to change mood and perspective at will, plus the excitement of collective extemporisation. All of this was so much a part of early New Orleans jazz, yet rarely heard in the music after the advent of swing in the thirties.

At its highest level, free-form jazz could and sometimes did achieve all these things; a good free-form collective improvisation can be thrilling for performers and audience alike. In general terms, however, it has been performances by two or at the most three players which have seemed its most successful application; the more performers involved, the smaller the chances of a satisfactory outcome. One drawback of avant-garde free-form jazz improvisation is that it has been known to attract performers of dubious ability. Such players are easy to identify and weed out in more traditional music circles, but the avant garde can sometimes afford an effective hiding place for their lack of talent. As with other forms of contemporary art, the ancient story of the emperor's clothes (where his courtiers, because of a clever con by a dishonest tailor, found themselves praising clothing that in fact didn't exist) has its present-day parallels, and only some future generation will finally pronounce judgment on the merits of it all – valid art, or simply a confidence trick?

Free-form jazz posed a question then which I believe has since been answered. Its place in jazz appeared to be a large one, but the ensuing years have shown it to be a smaller niche than at first appeared likely. However, its advent, and its effect on the general pattern of jazz, made the answer to one question that the arrival of bebop had begun to pose absolutely definite: jazz was no longer a dance music.

Right up to the fifties the progress of jazz was inseparable from the world of dancing. No club which featured the music was ever without a dance floor. All the London clubs which featured the early British groups playing this style boasted at least a corner where dancers could practise their form of self-expression. More often, indeed, it was not a corner, but a considerable expanse of space right in front of the performers. The cavorting was energetic, exuberant and sometimes extravagant; but whether one took it seriously or not, there was not the slightest doubt that it was directly inspired by the music.

The seventies saw a new stage in the world of jazz – the sharp diminution of its role as a dance music, together with its rise as an independent form of musical expression, or, if you prefer, art music. Clubs featuring jazz found themselves in a quandary from which some have never quite suc-

ceeded in emerging – unable to decide whether they were to continue to be places of enjoyment, where patrons could dance, eat, drink and even talk at will. Should the new rule be that the music is all-important and should take precedence over all else during its progress? It is a question that has not so far been satisfactorily resolved – except by the advent of a phenomenon which did not exist until the thirties, but was now destined to become an important factor in the history of the music, the jazz concert.

Since the first major jazz event in a major concert hall in 1938, when Benny Goodman led a plethora of jazz greats into Carnegie Hall, jazz had slowly crept into the world's symphony halls. Nevertheless, the over-whelming majority of jazz performances were in clubs and other places where the music could be considered incidental to the general proceedings – a logical sequence of events ever since the early days of jazz in the bordel-los of New Orleans.

But in the years after World War II a new dimension was created in the jazz world, largely by the impresario Norman Granz, whose Jazz at the Philharmonic concerts at symphony halls in the United States were a runaway success. Indeed the formula was repeated in many other countries with similar results. Even though the Jazz at the Philharmonic concerts were formalised and controlled jam sessions with the emphasis very largely on the star names on the bill, it was to be only a matter of time before bands of all kinds, large and small, were appearing in the same concert halls and adding another dimension to the kind of audiences that jazz was now proving it could attract. My own experiences in Britain, with concerts in the Conway Hall in London and Birmingham Town Hall in the fifties with the Club Eleven band, formed part of this pattern; and later my big band found itself playing in a ballroom in Glasgow on the same night as a JATP concert featuring Dizzy Gillespie, by then a firm friend. I was unaware of his visit to Scotland until I noticed him playing in my trumpet section towards the end of the evening after the end of his own gig.

During the fifties and sixties, then, more and more jazz was appearing in concert form in suitable venues, and this led to yet another platform for jazz which was to blossom in the sixties and seventies – the jazz festival. Even though jazz festivals had begun to blossom in the fifties, the full bloom of the phenomenon was heralded by the spread of such events all over the earth's surface. Even when jazz was not in command of its own festival, its presence within the structure of general music festivals was coming to be an accepted feature of such activities. In fact my 1972 visits to the Perth and Adelaide festivals in Australia were to be the first of many such over-seas appearances for me throughout the world. These events also on occa-sion afforded opportunities for jazz musicians to combine forces with performers from other fields, a chance not overlooked by many jazz com-posers, such as Dave Brubeck, Gerry Mulligan, Mike Gibbs, Michael Garrick, Claude Bolling and many others. I myself added a number of pieces to this 'third-stream' repertoire, with an opera-ballet for the Bath Festival in 1964 and Escapade *for the Durham Festival in 1968, a piece which over the ensuing years has been performed by Kenny Wheeler, Tony Coe, Peter King and Guy Barker.*

This blurring of boundaries between jazz and other music forms was occurring in other areas of music. In the classical world any divergence from a strictly 'legitimate' path was then considered career suicide, yet the late sixties and seventies witnessed an increasing tendency for classical per-formers to experiment with other musical forms. Early in the field was the legendary violinist Yehudi Menuhin, for whom I wrote an early 'cross-over' piece for the Bath Festival in 1963. Guitarist John Williams was another early experimenter with the cross-over, together with flute virtuosi James Galway and Jean-Pierre Rampal. Then there were those who had already proved themselves in the world of jazz, such as pianist and conductor André Previn, trumpeter Wynton Marsalis, pianist Fred Hersch and clarinettist Eddie Daniels – following much later in the footsteps of the great Benny Goodman, perhaps the first great jazz-to-classical bridge builder.

And so it could be said that jazz had in one short period come of age and gained respectability. Yet it could be argued that at this point in time the music, presented with so many avenues of possible exploration and develop-ment, began to lose its momentum. In spite of the fact that much was still happening, with countless talented new musicians arriving on the scene almost every day, and thousands of new record albums heralding new per-mutations of ideas and trains of thought, something was missing. And the period to come would be the time of a search for a new direction for jazz. Time alone would tell, and my own experiences of jazz all over the world in the seventh and eighth decade of the twentieth century was to bear this out.

14

World on a string

The sun was being pretty merciless to the tarmac on the day we touched down at Perth airport in Western Australia early in February 1972, our first visit to the Antipodes. In fact neither the temperature, the light nor any of the other elements of the climate bore the slightest resemblance to those in the gloomy, misty Britain that we had left not so long before.

A brief glance by immigration at our sturdy hard-covered British passports, and we were through – in those days the gold-embossed coat of arms on its dark blue background was sufficient to get any Briton into the ex-dominion, without any need for visas and work permits. Very soon we were being met by our promoter's representative, David Vigo, and were installed in a pleasant but modest motel on the outskirts of the city, where we spent the rest of the day marvelling at the weather before travel fatigue and jet lag took over.

The next morning a visit to Winthrop Hall on the campus of the University of Western Australia (where that night's concert was to be held) proved something of a disappointment. The place was handsome enough, and obviously intended primarily for ceremonial occasions involving the academics; in fact it may well have been suitable for a number of functions, but percussive music was certainly not one of them – it had an echo which could compete with that of the Grand Canyon. But we installed ourselves and resolved to do our best.

We retired to the dressing-room, where I removed my instruments from their cases and checked them for travel damage, while Cleo extricated her stage dresses and began ironing, a therapeutic occupation which she invariably executes unaided by others, even today.

Our fellow traveller to Australia was our pianist John Taylor, whose gifts as an inventive jazz improviser were matched by his skills as a sensitive accompanist. However, John was suffering. He had received the necessary vaccinations for the trip in London before leaving, but had forgotten to bring the documentary proof of these to Heathrow with him. The result was that the injections had to be repeated at the airport before he was allowed to travel. The double dosage had caused his arm to swell alarmingly, and he was in considerable pain for some weeks afterwards – not the best state for someone who uses his arms extensively for his work. Nevertheless he applied himself uncomplainingly to the job in hand.

John strolled onto the stage to examine and test the piano, and soon we were applying ourselves to rehearsals with (and getting to know) our two Australian musicians, bass player Derek Capewell and drummer Graham Morgan.

Concert time: I felt nervous as I walked onto the stage and began playing our opening instrumental number. But I soon convinced myself that there was no real reason why I should be – the place, after all, was not high up in the league of world concert halls, either in size or in importance, and I was already a seasoned professional. Moreover, the audience was both attentive and welcoming, so I soon felt more at ease. The music started, the musicians were settling in nicely, and it was altogether a good prelude to Cleo's arrival on stage.

Enter Cleo, to warm applause.

Then, over the next ninety or so minutes, Shakespeare, Weill, Gershwin, Ellington, even Dankworth. Then Bessie Smith, Noël Coward, Cole Porter and more Gershwin.

Exit Cleo, to thunderous applause.

Re-enter Cleo to even more thunderous applause, and some shouting.

Exit and re-enter Cleo, and they're all up on their feet and roaring for more.

It was hard to take it in. We had played an almost identical programme to those which we'd performed for years in Great Britain, yet it had caused this extraordinary reaction. 'I didn't know that a standing ovation was customary in Australia', I muttered to someone backstage, as we walked off when the tumult had finally died down.

'It isn't. Yours is the first we've seen in this hall for years', came the reply.

It was then that it dawned on me perhaps for the first time that we were something special. I had of course always had my convictions about Cleo's extraordinary and unique talent, but they were tempered by a suspicion that I might have somehow misassessed them because of my proximity to the subject. Even the pronouncements of several eminent British critics, such as Derek Jewell, Benny Green, Peter Clayton, Max Jones, Michael Billington and several others, had not allayed my suspicions. Perhaps they were all, to a lesser extent, also involved with Cleo's artistry, personality and track record in a way that clouded their judgement. It took that smallish audience in Perth to convince me finally that Cleo's was a voice that should be heard all over the world. Our international career had begun.

After Perth it was back to the airport, and then on eastwards to Adelaide, then north to Brisbane. And finally the biggies, Melbourne and Sydney. In each of them our success story was repeated, with cheering and standing audiences and ecstatic press reviews on the following day. Our arrival in the east of Australia meant that at last we met Clifford Hocking, the Melbourne-based impresario who had been the instigator of this, our first Australian tour. Cliff, a sensitive, intelligent and knowledgeable man with a great love for the performing arts (none of which qualities are by any means automatically present in the make-up of a concert impresario), was naturally delighted that his hunch had paid off and that we were an immediate success with Australian audiences. And we started a long and lasting friendship with a man who was to play a large part in our careers in the ensuing years.

We said good-bye to Australia and prepared to fly home to England with a short stop-over in New York.

* * *

The unexpected success of our Australian tour made me determined not to lose the chance of being in Manhattan exploring the possibilities of an American debut for Cleo. What was needed was an agent or promoter, and I did the best I could to scour the scene to see what was available.

Our Australian visit had been negotiated and arranged by Basil Horsfield, a London-based agent who was then looking after this aspect of our career. Horsfield's specialist musical field was the classical and operatic world, so it seemed natural for me first of all to approach classical agencies. These all had major access to music festivals, and it seemed to me that Cleo's lieder style of recital would be appealing to them. I prepared myself to do rounds of meetings with representatives from the various agencies. I felt fairly confident, since Cleo had not long before made an appearance on the Tony Awards TV show which was widely shown in America, and for which she had gained some approbation in theatrical circles. Moreover, I had books full of her reviews from both England and Australia, and so felt I had a fighting chance of gaining agents' attention. At least they would certainly have heard of her, I reasoned.

I was wrong. I had to start from scratch and got practically nowhere. They all came to the conclusion from my descriptions and my evidence that Cleo was a cabaret singer, and that cabaret was not part of their stock-in-trade. They all felt unable to help; some of them at least were later to rue their decision not to take us on.

Our friendship with Duke Ellington and devotion to his music led us to meet other friends and devotees of the great man, among them Anita Porter. Anita's southern drawl sounded especially warm in New York, where people can be tough and abrupt. I told her of our plight of being unable to find a Cleo Laine ally in the whole of the Big Apple. 'Perhaps Ron Delsener might be interested', murmured Anita.

'Ron Delsener? I don't think I'm familiar with his work', I replied. I had somehow picked up this very American way of politely saying 'never heard of him'.

'He's a rock promoter who's just done something at Madison Square Gardens.'

'Well, that doesn't sound exactly as if it's what we're looking for. But I'll go and see him all the same if I can find him.'

I sought out Ron Delsener the next day and found myself facing him over a large desk in an office in midtown Manhattan. I gave him my spiel and waited for the reaction. 'I think I get the picture. What you've got is a *class* act, John', said Ron with a twinkle. The word 'class' contained a number of diphthongs absent in the English pronunciation, and lasted about twice as long. It sounded more like 'claa ... aay ... ahh ... ss'.

'That's exactly what it is', I replied instantly. A positive response like his was worth hanging on to.

'Then you need a *classy* place to do it in. What about Alice Tully Hall at the Lincoln Center?'

The Alice Tully Hall it was – on Friday 22 September 1972. The arrangement with Ron Delsener was that we should share equally both the expenses and the profits, should there be any. For Ron it was to be an interesting exercise. For us it was to be a crucial debut in the spiritual capital of the largest English-speaking nation in the world.

Leaflets were printed, press kits were prepared, and every possible interview opportunity was arranged. Nevertheless, soon after the first ads appeared and the box office opened it became apparent that we were not going to fill the thousand-seater (or even half fill it) by ticket sales alone. Delsener 'papered' the event heavily with complimentary tickets, and made sure that all the most influential New York critics were invited. Musically the concert was to be almost identical to the Australian ones: our loyal pianist, John Taylor, was still with us, and we recruited bassist George Duvivier and his fellow American drummer friend Bobby Rosengarden to complete our accompanying quartet.

The concert went smoothly, and as it drew to a close we were prepared for a similarly enthusiastic reception to those we'd had in Australia. But of course we had underestimated the Big Apple's capacity for ovations. The demonstration of approval that followed

Cleo's closing number was perhaps the most generous, the most adoring and certainly the most noisy that we had ever received in our careers. To say that the audience went wild would be a totally inadequate way to describe the scene, since the cliché has become an ordinary one, and this was certainly an extraordinary ovation. Our audience was now totally committed to us, and encore followed encore with even more thunderous applause.

A post-concert champagne party was the scene of much excited talk among our supporters. The concert had gone extremely well, and the general verdict was that the press would be good. Ron Delsener wended his way through the throng to me. He seemed happy.

'How did we do?' I asked.

'The show was great', answered Ron, 'the crowd loved it.'

'And – how did we do, businesswise?' I tried to choose words that sounded like the Americanese that Ron seemed to use.

'I'll send you the details later. But the bottom line is – you owe me $150.'

It seemed cheap at the price. I knew lots of artists who would have gladly paid ten or even a hundred times that price for a New York debut. I wrote Delsener a cheque there and then. 'Where do we go from here, Ron?' I asked.

'You should be doing Carnegie. But don't look at me – I've had a bad time with my promotions lately. All I can handle at the moment is what I consider to be sure-fire money makers, and nobody can make money at Carnegie Hall – the overheads are far too high.'

I said I understood, and thanked Ron Delsener for his help so far. We shook hands and promised to keep in touch. I sauntered across the room among a sea of faces. Most of them were unfamiliar to me, but virtually all greeted me with smiles and congratulatory nods. Then I saw a face that made sense yet took me completely by surprise. It was Cliff Hocking, our Australian promoter. He had flown in specially for the occasion.

'Terrific show, John.' Typically, he mentioned a few sections of the evening which had particularly pleased him. He was something of an expert on our repertoire, having seen so many of our Australian concerts. 'You know, this success should be followed up. I hope Ron Delsener is going to do that. If he isn't, just say the word.'

'I think the word's already been said', I replied. 'Ron turned the idea down. But be practical, Clifford. If it's Carnegie you're thinking about' – and here he nodded vigorously – 'we drew only a few hundred paying customers tonight. How do you expect to turn that into thousands for a place as big as Carnegie?'

'John, you two obviously know how to put a concert together and satisfy an audience. Why not concentrate on getting that part together for Carnegie, and leave the worry of selling out the hall to me?' It seemed a fair proposition: Cliff Hocking Pty Ltd had certainly done a fine job of filling concert halls in Australia. So it was decided to go for a Carnegie debut the following April, in the spring of 1973.

Over the next few days the press reports made it clear that we had made a great start to our American campaign. The *New York Times* was the first: 'The British, who have been dropping one rock group after another on us for years, have been hoarding what must be one of their national treasures', wrote John S. Wilson. Later on that week *Variety* proclaimed, 'Years from now there's going to be a small group of theatre and music buffs who'll be able to quiet any discussion by commenting, "But I was at the American debut of Cleo Laine, back in 1972".'

We basked in the glory briefly before returning to London. It had been a memorable few days.

*   *   *

The atmosphere was entirely in contrast to our Alice Tully Hall experience. Carnegie Hall has an air about it which goes along with its image as the world's most famous concert venue; it sends an immediate message that it is not to be taken lightly.

I imbibed some of the atmosphere as I walked towards the stage for rehearsal on the afternoon of 26 April 1973. On a wall I noticed a picture frame containing an object rather than an image; it turned out to be the baton used by Tchaikovsky when he conducted there at the turn of the century. I gulped.

The evening came, and with it concert time. Our preparation for the event was good and rehearsals had gone well. All we had to do was keep our nerve, a challenge which would not, I felt, pose much of a problem to Cleo, never one to be unduly troubled by apprehensions of any sort. The performance was under way. I had changed the programme significantly from the Alice Tully Hall night, as I guessed that many of the same critics would be at this concert. But all the ingredients of the debut were there – the a cappella start, together with its lack of key preparation, which mystified as well as entranced the audience, followed by a mixture of poetry settings (John Donne, T. S. Eliot, W. H. Auden, Spike Milligan), standard material (Richard Rogers, Cole Porter, Noël Coward, Johnny Mercer), jazz archive items (Bessie Smith, Duke Ellington), music from contemporary sources (Carole King, James Taylor) and of course the inevitable Shakespeare, which had become a speciality ever since the album *Shakespeare and All That Jazz*, for which Cleo had a five-star rating in the US jazz magazne *Downbeat*.

From the very outset it was clear that the audience was on our side. The word had got around since Alice Tully, and our friends had brought their friends, and they their friends too. At the end of it all we experienced easily the greatest ovation in our lives. The crowd not only stood; they cheered, they clapped, they waved, they jumped, they threw flowers onto the stage, in fact they indulged in every extreme that I imagined previously to be confined to Hollywood movies. Encore followed encore, and when in the end it subsided our exhilaration was complete.

The next day it became apparent that the press shared the fans' fervour. Cleo Laine had not only become the darling of concertgoers, she had become a news item: *Newsweek* magazine gave substantial space to the concert, while *Time* magazine almost went further, and reliable sources told us that Cleo's face would soon be the subject of a much coveted cover portrait on that famous publication. But bigger news intervened: the Watergate affair broke. Richard Kleindienst, the US attorney-general, resigned on 17 April, and shortly after in a televised address to the nation President Nixon accepted responsibility for the incident. It was big stuff – a scandal of proportions seldom reached in US politics – and Cleo missed the front page.

For the rest of 1973 we travelled the United States, spreading out first across the eastern seaboard – Boston, Philadelphia, Washington, DC – and then into the Midwest – Detroit, Cleveland, Chicago.

Virtually everywhere the press was the same; nobody could understand why Cleo had not been heard before in North America. '. . . one
of the true stellar entertainers in the world', trumpeted the *Chicago
Tribune*. The *Boston Globe* wrote, 'she not only has marvellous wit . . .
but also a deeply affecting poignancy that had her audience's eyes
brimming with tears . . . to hear Cleo Laine for the first time is one of
the rare experiences.' The *Detroit Free Press* drew attention to an
'extraordinary voice, swooping from resonant lows all the way to an
incredibly strong and clear F above high C, a lofty region where few
singers can survive.'

In October 1973 we were booked for a three-week season at the
Rainbow Grill, a cabaret-cum-jazz room on the sixty-fourth floor of
the Rockefeller Center in New York; it was deemed a good tactical
move to increase our profile in the metropolis before our second
Carnegie Hall concert that year, which was to be within a week of our
Rainbow residency.

Business at our first season was extremely brisk, but our three
weeks included the Jewish holiday Yom Kippur, a notoriously bad
time for show business in view of the large (and usually supportive)
Jewish population in New York. Knowing of this possible low point,
Hamilton Whyte, then in charge of British Information Services in
New York, organised a party to boost our morale on a night when
attendance was expected to be bad. He phoned to make the booking –
and was told the place was sold out. He transferred his attentions to
another night, and thus started a friendship of many years' duration.
Later he was knighted and became the high commissioner at
Singapore, which later gave us a good excuse to go to that far-flung
corner of the ex-empire.

Another would-be party was turned away from the Rainbow Grill.
The maître d' came up to me one night and explained that Elton
John had intended to bring a group of friends until he was told that
the place had a sacrosanct dress code (tie and jacket), which most of
his friends could not honour. The attitude of the grill was one of
intransigence, and so one night we joined Elton at his own party
instead on another floor of the Rockefeller Center after our own gig
had ended.

But many New Yorkers did get in to see us: Lena Horne and Tony

Bennett turned up on the same night, while on other occasions I saw saxophonist Paul Desmond (composer of *Take Five*) and Irving Caesar (lyricist of *Tea for Two*), among many other celebrity visitors.

And again the press was so good it was hard to believe. The *New Yorker's* listing of events of note declared that the 'lack of exposure in this country remains a major puzzlement in the realm of jazz and popular music . . . she and her husband John Dankworth, a prolific and respected composer, have had a [long] musical relationship, and it shows; he sets Shakespeare to music, and she turns Kern into poetry.' And Richard Dyer wrote later in the *New York Times*, 'Earlier on the first night I saw Cleo Laine I'd done time at the City Opera . . . then [she] came out at the Rainbow Grill and sang, flicking her voice easily through the fascinating traceries of Dankworth's arrangement; in those three minutes I found more vocal, more musical pleasure than in three whole hours at the opera.'

It all amounted to a suitable build-up to our Carnegie concert, which was to be recorded to produce the first of three albums we made there between 1973 and 1983. It was destined to sell magnificently, in quantities previously unknown to us for an album, and help immensely with the trail-blazing nationwide appearances which ensued. But there was still much work to be done; America is a vast nation, and a New York success by no means guarantees an audience in even the other major centres. As we walked away from the stage area at Carnegie that October night, with stage hands, recording engineers, agency people and friends smiling and applauding after what was becoming a typical New York reception for us, I nudged Cleo and whispered in her ear: 'Don't let this go to our heads. We've still got plenty of half-empty halls to face in our career.'

I was right, and during the following weeks we had, together with many moments of exhilaration, just enough disappointments to keep our feet firmly on the ground – such as at Grand Rapids, Michigan.

The local promoter, obviously impressed by our New York debut and the resultant press material, had expected a turnout of 'pop' dimensions, and had accordingly booked a 4000-seater aircraft hangar-styled place in which to pack them all in. This proved unnecessary. Whether it was the fault of the advertising, or the uncompromising hate the citizens of Grand Rapids harboured for the ageing, uncomfortable venue, or just lack of interest, we will never know, but I walked out that night to an audience of just short of four hundred spattered about over the several thousands of seats before us. I invited them all to the front and we gave them the concert of their lives. Nevertheless, it demonstrated that, though we had made phenomenal progress, there was still a long way to go.

So on we went to the West Coast: San Francisco and finally Los Angeles.

Our compatriot Leonard Feather had established himself as perhaps the world's most respected jazz critic as a result of his writings for the *Los Angeles Times*, as well as his classic reference work *The Encyclopaedia of Jazz*. Leonard and his wife Jane welcomed us to the LA jazz circle and took us on the round of clubs as well as throwing a party for us. Our concert at the Santa Monica Auditorium, a vast building much more pleasant than but comparable in size to our Grand Rapids venue, was respectably full on the night. On the afternoon arrival at the place, however, I was in for a few surprises.

We drove to the security gate and the guard directed us to the rear of the theatre, which looked uncompromisingly shut. The driver nevertheless drove determinedly, at a rather alarming speed in the circumstances, towards a closed door. At the very last second, however, it rolled upwards to admit us, and moments later we came to a screeching halt literally on the stage. I got out and surveyed the scene. The technical director introduced himself: 'What d'you think?' he asked. I didn't like to tell him I was disappointed; the stage was literally on the same level as the audience seating, and the floor of the building was totally flat; how anyone sitting further back than row five could see anything at all was a mystery – a periscope would be the only answer. I couldn't avoid mentioning it in the end, and it brought a frown to his hitherto beaming face.

'Well, I'll have to see what I can do to fix that. Hold on a minute.' He disappeared to the side of the stage, and did something at a switchboard. A low murmuring rumble permeated the building, and the seats facing me a few feet away began to disappear downwards. Within half a minute I was looking at a completely raked ground floor equipped with a gentle slope which gave every seat a satisfactory view. It seemed typical of the sort of technology I had subconsciously expected in movieland, and the transformation was one of the parlour tricks sprung on unsuspecting first-time users.

That year, 1973, saw the deaths of Betty Grable, Pablo Casals, Lyndon B. Johnson, Noël Coward and W. H. Auden. It saw the birth of our career in the United States, and was one of the most memorable years of my life.

All in all it was quite a year. We hardly noticed the rise of Harold Wilson to become prime minister, although we were certainly aware of the fall of Richard Nixon, since our presence in the States around that time made it impossible to avoid. Other happenings coincided with this special year – Solzhenitsyn was turned out of the Soviet Union; Patti Hearst turned out to be a bank robber. Juan Peron, president of Argentina died, but then so did the archduke of jazz, the wonderful Duke Ellington. Cleo and I, saddened at the loss of such a great champion of jazz, joined countless other musicians and fans in a memorial service at St Martin-in-the-Fields church in London, on 12 June 1974.

The following year might well have been the most active. My diary of 1974 shows us to have been in New York in January (24th–27th) for a Benny Goodman TV Special. Then Holland in February (23rd Amsterdam; 24th Rotterdam; plus five other venues), back in England to Chichester in early March (9th, 10th), then to Los Angeles for a *Tonight* TV Show (18th) and on to Vancouver for another TV with Oscar Peterson (20th). Then three San Francisco Bay area dates (21st–23rd), Hollywood Bowl (27th), Washington, DC (29th) and Chicago (30th). April saw us in Philadelphia (2nd) and Detroit (5th, 6th) and back in London for the Royal Festival Hall (15th). June brought our first trip to Iceland (13th), and July saw us back in the States for Cleveland, Minneapolis, Chicago, Los Angeles (Hollywood Bowl and more TV) and Philadelphia. In August we paid our first visit to Israel, which still had the previous year's six-day war on its minds; we visited Tel Aviv, Caesarea and Jerusalem. Our return to Britain took us again to London's Festival Hall (24th) and a late-night series at the Edinburgh Festival (29th, 30th, 31st). October came around to herald yet another Carnegie Hall concert (2nd), then Vancouver (4th) and Seattle (6th), followed by the San Francisco area (10th, 11th, 12th), the Los Angeles area (13th, 15th, 16th), Oklahoma

(18th), Chicago (21st), Minneapolis (26th), Philadelphia (28th) and Washington, DC (30th). November looks a little more logical geographically, with most dates on or near the Eastern seaboard – Burlington, Vermont (2nd), Raleigh, North Carolina (3rd), Detroit (5th–7th), New Jersey (8th, 9th) and a season at New York's St Regis Hotel (11th–30th) before returning to Britain. Two concerts there, both near home, preceded our annual Christmas concerts in The Stables theatre at our home in Wavendon.

A very happy occasion which took place that year was being chosen, with Sarah Vaughan and Dizzy Gillespie, as guests for a jazz TV series with the great Canadian pianist Oscar Peterson. The series was recorded in Vancouver, and was a joy musically. I had an inward smile when I presented my arrangements for the great pianist's attention. Oscar was seldom required to sight-read, and it was no surprise to hear him struggling a little with the charts. It was somehow reassuring to realise that not even Oscar Peterson was perfect. My chief recollection of Peterson's trio, however, is – the grunting. Oscar grunts when he is improvising, much like classical pianist Glenn Gould and fellow jazzmen Lionel Hampton. But the trouble is that so does Louie Bellson, the trio's drummer on that occasion. The Danish bass player Niels-Henning Ørsted Pedersen does not, thank goodness, otherwise the constant drone which accompanied their efforts would have been even louder. I found it off-putting at first, but soon got used to it and enjoyed blowing with these greats immensely.

On the evening before the show we went out to eat with Bellson and Pedersen. I caught sight of a belt the drummer was wearing, a gorgeous affair in bright red leather with a splendid multicoloured buckle. 'I like your belt, Louie', I said. He responded immediately by ripping the admired article from the loopholes of his pants and presenting it to me. I have still got it. I knew it would be pointless to protest, because the same thing had happened with Clark Terry some years before, when I admired a cap the trumpeter was wearing. It seems to be an American jazz musician's way of being friendly, although I, a reserved Englishman, tended to be embarrassed by it. Moral: if you indeed find it embarrassing, then don't admire other people's clothes. And if you're short of clothes, try admiring other people's!

Admiration is something I possess in abundance when it comes to the work of Benny Goodman. I, of course, had worked with Goodman before, but in 1974 it was Cleo's first time, and she felt honoured; the man was a perfectionist and had the reputation of associating with only the best in musical circles.

Part of the videotaping was to be done at Carnegie Hall, where a big band containing many of Goodman's original players had been assembled. I wandered onto the stage there, clutching my alto sax (a standard clause in the contract prohibited me from playing clarinet, presumably to preserve Benny's exclusivity on that instrument, but it was hardly a necessary precaution in my case since I would never have dared put the instrument to my mouth in the presence of my all-time idol). One of the handful of arrangements for Cleo that I had supplied ideally required the use of a bass guitar, an instrument I felt I was unlikely to find in a band like Goodman's. Still, as some string bass players play guitar as a double, I felt it worth enquiring of the bassist, whom I did not recognise. I asked him the all-important question, and he replied – very apologetically – in the negative. I assured him it was not important and there the matter ended. I enquired about his identity, and went cold when I was told that it was Slam Stewart, who was regarded by a certain generation of jazz enthusiasts as perhaps the best-known jazz bassist in the world. To have asked such a renowned specialist if he played the bass guitar seemed to me about as tactful as asking Art Tatum if he also played the accordion, or a grand prix motor-racing champion if he did anything on a motor-bike. I don't know if the redness of my face showed, but I hoped it would die down by the time we taped.

Later we recorded some more material at Benny's beautiful colonial home near Stamford, Connecticut. Most of the music was taped in a studio separated from the house, and we trudged through a light coating of January snow to get to it. The musicians present in addition to Benny, Cleo and myself were Richard Davis (bass), Bucky Pizzarelli (guitar), Grady Tate (drums) and the redoubtable Hank Jones (piano). The room was distinctly chilly during one of these sessions, but, since Benny could be resentful of anything which interfered with the progress of the rehearsals, no one dared mention their discomfort. Eventually Hank, with fingers on the point of freezing up, had to break silence. 'Don't you think it's getting a wee bit cold in here, Benny?' he ventured.

'Why, yes, Hank, it sure is getting chilly. Just run the arrangement once more without me, guys – and I'll be right back', said Benny. He disappeared as the music began and, a few minutes later, as the final bars were reached, re-entered the studio – resplendent in a thick green sweater.

Another overseas trip that year got us acquainted with the ultra-strict security arrangements practised by El Al, the airline taking us on our first-ever visit to Israel. Cleo found herself sitting next to a tough-looking gent clutching a holdall which, he later confided to her, contained a sub-machine gun. He was a guard in civilian clothing, a feature of all Israeli civilian airliners in those days; these were times when hijacking was always considered a risk, and we were frankly relieved to arrive.

Our first concert was in the Mann Auditorium in Tel Aviv. As it drew to a close I wondered whether we would get our now customary American-style standing ovation. The last notes died, and I was pleased to see many people standing. But on looking again – no, they were beginning to move along towards the aisles as they clapped. They were presumably standing to leave. But then – another surprise. They reached the aisles, but instead of turning towards the doors they came towards the platform. And there they stood applauding us, a mass of humanity around the stage, which reminded me of our early days with the big band in the British ballrooms, when the fans would gather in their hundreds around the bandstand. It was all very exciting.

Our next concerts were in the beautiful amphitheatre at Caesarea, one of the most memorable and idyllic settings for music I have ever experienced, though the start was not propitious. As we approached the stage I noticed in the middle a peculiarly shaped canvas bundle which turned out to be a small, wizened baby grand piano. Tony Hymas, our pianist for the tour, tried a few notes and quickly found it to be in tragic condition and quite unacceptable for our purposes. I quickly found the man in charge. 'When is the piano for tonight's concert arriving?' I asked.

'It's already on the stage', came the reply.

'I beg to differ. That piano is virtually unplayable for any purpose, let alone for the accompaniment of an international singing star.'

'But, Mr Dankworth, we are a small country and in the middle of a music festival. There are no other pianos available. Please be reasonable. Daniel Barenboim played that piano last week and made no complaints.'

This I knew was a lie, which angered me. But I retained all the cool I had learned from experience is needed to deal with such situations. I adopted my most reasonable tone of voice. 'Well, of course, I understand if there is no other piano to be had in the whole of Israel. It is, as you say, a small country. We must just sit down together, get out our diaries and reschedule the concerts for dates when an acceptable piano is available.'

The man paled. 'B-but we can't do that – both concerts are sold out.' He was clearly highly alarmed by the thought. 'All those disappointed people.' He searched my eyes for a sign of relenting and found nothing but a stony stare. 'Well, I'll get on to the office and ask if they can find a piano.'

'A first-class Steinway', I corrected.

'A first-class Steinway', he repeated.

Less than an hour later a first-class Steinway was delivered to the stage and tuned. Tony Hymas was happy, I was happy, Cleo was happy, and she sang particularly well that night in the perfect acoustics, to the delight of the capacity audiences. Sometimes being intransigent is the only way.

The periods in Britain contained, in addition to the performance dates, a number of recording sessions, the most important for Cleo being of *Pierrot Lunaire*, the Schoenberg work which she had been requested to study and perform. This remains to my knowledge the only existing version of this work in the English language, a phenomenon which remains inexplicable in view of the fact that Schoenberg himself declared that ideally the piece should be performed in the language of the listeners, and indeed made some alterations to the original score in order to accommodate a translated version.

1974 seemed a specially active and eventful year, but it is not untypical of the level of activity Cleo and I have sustained over virtually all of the following period, with annual multiple visits to North America interspersed with trips to Australia, New Zealand, Japan, Europe and the many other parts of the world which show enough interest in our work to warrant a visit. We count ourselves fortunate to have the opportunity to go regularly to the United States and Canada. It provides a wonderful feeling of energy, an air of bustle and industry which is inspiring. Even though it is no longer the only source of the best exponents of jazz, it is certainly still the ambition of every jazz performer to make his or her mark there, and I feel proud to have done so.

15

Trains and boats and planes

While we went to North America as a duo, we were anxious to continue to prove that we each still had separate careers. Although I was frequently, but not inevitably, involved in Cleo's recording career, I played no part whatsoever in her classic recording of *Porgy and Bess* with the great Ray Charles. This was the brainchild of Norman Granz, the jazz-loving impresario who had done so much to raise the profiles of a number of top jazz artistes – Ella Fitzgerald, Oscar Peterson and Count Basie among them.

The recordings were made in Los Angeles, and an orchestra star studded with famous jazz names – Joe Pass, Lee Ritenour, Buddy Childers, Harry Edison, Jimmy Cleveland, J. J. Johnson, Benny Powell, Britt Woodman, Bill Perkins, Jerome Richardson, Bud Shank, Ernie Watts and Vic Feldman – was present. It was a thrilling time for Cleo, and the event did a great deal to increase awareness of her abilities among parts of the American public who were not familiar with her work.

Yet another extended break from our double act came when she was invited to join the team for a workshop production of a new musical by Rupert Holmes called *The Mystery of Edwin Drood*. The workshop attracted backers, and the production first went on in 1985 in the Delacorte open-air theatre in Central Park, New York, a dramatic arena usually reserved for the works of William Shakespeare. It was so successful that it went to Broadway the following autumn. The Broadway production was a big hit and eventually won the Tony Award for the best musical of the year. Cleo was also nominated for a Tony in the best supporting actress category, and, although she failed to convert this into an actual trophy, she was more successful with another type of award at almost precisely the same time. We were both delighted to hear that she had won outright a Grammy Award for our joint Carnegie Hall tenth anniversary album. This followed three previous nominations for Grammies in various categories, and Cleo was delighted to have made it. In fact it was the first occasion on which a British singer had received a jazz Grammy, a feat which at the time of writing has not, to my knowledge, been repeated.

Meanwhile I was busy with other projects. This often entailed arranging for and conducting symphony orchestras, something which I have found myself doing with increasing frequency, since our American success has inevitably led us to engagements known as symphony-pops concerts. These events, common in America, but for many years rare outside, are looked on by symphony orchestra managements as rich sources of revenue for their annual 'serious' programmes, and are the regular stock-in-trade of all but the most highbrow American orchestras. Here my academic training stood me in good stead; true, I had had no academic training in either conducting or orchestrating, but my Royal Academy background had given me a good understanding of orchestral musicians, and these concerts provided excellent opportunities for me to hone my skills as an orchestrator. The pattern of such concerts was that I usually did the first half instrumentally, while Cleo joined the orchestra for the post-intermission section.

Soon I started presenting instrumental pops concerts in my own right and acquired a contract with a classical company to record symphony pops both under my own name and in conjunction with guest artistes such as trumpeters Al Hirt and Dizzie Gillespie.

As time went on I became convinced that symphony pops could be a success in Britain, and approached the London Symphony Orchestra to suggest a summer pops season. In the summer of 1985 the first London symphony pops series got under way at the Barbican Centre. My strategy from the start was to see that the orchestra itself became the star of the show, even though there might well be one or more guest artistes involved.

The series met with considerable success, and a more ambitious second season was planned. But there were snags. My recipes for success had been based largely on the phenomenal achievements of the famous Boston Pops Orchestra, whose events regularly sold out months in advance. Circumstances in London, however, were considerably different. For instance, the Boston venue was furnished with tables at which the sponsors and their guests sat drinking, whereas that was impossible at the Barbican. In Boston the orchestra was virtually the sole star; minor guest soloists were brought in to play repertoire concertos, and major guests were employed only on quite separate television series that the orchestra taped annually. Moreover, Boston is a city with far fewer competitive events than London, which is, after all, one of the great music centres of the world.

In London there were no pre-event 'sellouts', and, instead of a number of small and willing sponsors in the form of corporations who bought small blocks of tickets, we had one overriding sponsor, the *Daily Mail*. To retain the interest and indeed the sponsorship of this newspaper we were compelled to listen to their suggestions regarding guest artistes, and this continually forced me to compromise the policy which I felt to be the right one. I later regretted this, since the paper eventually withdrew their sponsorship in any case. Nevertheless, over the ensuing five years the series contained some memorable and significant concerts, including appearances by dozens of internationally famous guest artistes, including George Shearing, Marian McPartland, Clark Terry, Paul Tortelier, Barry Tuckwell and many others.

From the outset I wanted to prove that good music of any sort could co-exist in one programme, and the initial concerts seemed to bear this out. Consequently I found myself conducting Dvořák as well as Lennon and McCartney, Walton as well as Ellington. This proved to be my eventual undoing; I had no experience as a conductor, and since the programmes came hot on the heels of each other I really had no study time on scores which I knew very inadequately. Consequently,

I know now that I made a very poor job of conducting some of the works that deserved much better.

But by this time the hopes that I had entertained at the beginning of the venture were turning to disillusionment. The dates and duration of the series changed alarmingly every year according to the availability of the Barbican Centre; successive sponsors and eventually the orchestra management increasingly wished to influence the content of the programmes, and the London Symphony Orchestra, with its established pecking order of principals, proved something of a problem when it came to tackling the stylistic requirements of popular and jazz-orientated music. This was in sharp contrast to organisations such as the Boston Pops, whose principals in each section are carefully chosen for their special pop background and skills. Theirs was a quality that the London Symphony Orchestra, enthusiastic though it was, could not match.

I became acutely aware of the problem during an evening dedicated to the music of Duke Ellington, to which I contributed a number of symphony scores. The orchestra sounded distinctly below its best in pursuit of such classics as *Satin Doll* and *Take the 'A' Train*. Indeed the naked truth was brought home to me some time after, when I transcribed an arrangement of *Caravan* (which I had previously done for the LSO) for use by my own big band. (Paradoxically, the LSO's symphony recording of this arrangement later won a Grammy nomination for me in the orchestration category.)

I had similar 'pops conductor' directorships with both the Rochester Philharmonic and San Francisco Symphony orchestras around this time. One of my greatest thrills with the latter orchestra was conducting for Ella Fitzgerald in 1991. She was already ailing from a number of problems springing from her diabetes, and I had to lead her onto the stage – her eyesight had never been very trustworthy. Even though her voice was long past its best, Ella still had the ability to mesmerise an audience, and it was a sheer joy not only to conduct the orchestra in conjunction with her own Los Angeles-based trio, but at the same time to weave in some saxophone obligatos behind her. It was a wonderful night for me, spoilt only by the fact that I was told by the orchestral manager on no account to go overtime. As I led her off to the deafening applause of the enormous crowd, Ella asked if she could do one more tune. I told her that I had been given strict instructions that the concert was not to overrun, and she accepted this without a further murmur; it is a decision which I had to make, and for which I have never been able to forgive myself. I really should have let her go on. It turned out to be one of her very last major public appearances, and certainly her last symphony pops date. A few thousand dollars in orchestra overtime would have made it the bargain of a lifetime.

The conclusion I drew from this whole period of my life, flirting with the notion of being a pops conductor, was that it was a corner of the music profession which requires not only a set of skills which I did not at that time possess, but, more important, a temperament to go with it. Conducting a symphony orchestra is a tremendous responsibility, one of which I am quite capable provided I know the music thoroughly. But orchestral conductors in general, and particularly symphony pops conductors, have to be good sight-readers, quick at assimilating new material, and able to cope with the enormous work-load which all that entails. I felt, after a number of years of attempting to juggle with all these requirements, and to fulfil them, that I was not quite cut out for the job. This has not precluded my conducting and creating symphony pops concerts. But it has taught me to stick to my own style, and never to undertake to conduct music which I feel that a modestly talented classical conductor could do far better than I. Thus when I fashion a programme completely of my own creation, I really enjoy myself with a good symphony orchestra.

Perhaps the most enjoyable times I have ever experienced in the symphony pop mode have been with the excellent New Zealand Symphony Orchestra, with whom I have toured on a number of occasions. When assimilation of an idiom is at stake, the more repetitions one can do of a concert, the better the players can absorb the language; and each time I have toured New Zealand we have done the same concert in up to twelve different venues. Consequently, after a usually more than adequate rehearsal period, the excellent NZSO has shed all stylistic inhibitions by about the fourth or fifth concert, and the remaining appearances have become plain sailing, with the atmosphere resembling that of a long-established specialist jazz orchestra.

Cleo and I continued with our visits to America, and our appearance at the Newport Jazz Festival at Avery Fisher Hall in New York in July 1975 was specially exciting. The artist preceding us on the bill was no less than the legendary pianist Thelonious Monk, whom I was sadly unable to hear – it was to be perhaps his last major public appearance. For this occasion I had gathered together a big band to do the opening half of a concert in which Cleo would provide the second section. The band included trumpet players Red Rodney and Jimmy Nottingham, together with reedmen Frank West, Cecil Payne and the legendary Eddie 'Lockjaw' Davis, once of the great Count Basie Band. Our own rhythm trio completed the line-up. They included drummer Kenny Clare, bassist Brian Torfe, then at the beginning of a notable career, and Paul Hart, who faithfully performed duties on both piano and violin for many years during our American touring days. Paul, then a youngster of about twenty-three, remains perhaps the nearest thing to my conception of a genius among all the musicians with whom I have worked.

I suppose for that concert I tried the impossible – to form a big band, rehearse it and get it to realise my expectations in the space of two days. As a result I'm not sure that it sounded very good. However, it was a wonderful experience playing with all those musicians. The band was assembled and led by my old friend, trumpet virtuoso Clark Terry.

Another highlight was our appearance at the 1980 Kansas City Women's Jazz Festival. Cleo had been invited for obvious reasons, and we men were invited to accompany her in spite of our sex. We shared the bill with Marian McPartland, JoAnne Brackeen and Carla Bley, and there was also a reunion appearance of an extraordinary all-women's band known as the International Sweethearts of Rhythm. This group toured the States extensively in the forties, making a number of recordings and creating something of a name for themselves. They had been recobbled together for this occasion and were introduced by Leonard Feather. They sounded fine.

Though the festival was a noteworthy event, it is sad that an all-women's festival need even be considered in the world of jazz, usually so far ahead of world thinking. The absence of large numbers of women in jazz remains inexplicable to me, particularly as by the end of the twentieth century we have come to see women comprising a large minority in symphony orchestras and even sometimes forming the majority of the total strength. Jazz is beginning to show signs of catching up, but it still has a long way to go.

However, festivals such as these always provide an excellent opportunity for meeting other jazz musicians, and although Cleo and I both knew numerous American jazzmen from their visits to Britain, the American jazz festival circuit widened our circle of musician friends immensely.

Gerry Mulligan was one. He had been engaged by the Rochester Philharmonic Orchestra to do a concert which I was to conduct. To discuss the arrangements, we agreed I should go to his home in Darien, Connecticut, just a short train journey from Manhattan. Intending to buy flowers for Gerry's wife, Franca, on the way, I arrived at Penn Station in Manhattan in good time. To my horror all the florists were shut; it was Saturday morning. In fact the only shop I could find open sold knives, cutlery and kitchenware. I went in and wandered hopelessly around looking for a suitable present. A carving set seemed a bad bet, since I had a suspicion that the Mulligans were vegetarians. My eyes finally alighted on a wall barometer, which I eventually bought as a rather strange substitute for a bouquet.

As I descended from the train at Darien station, I glimpsed a waving, bearded Gerry standing by his car in the parking lot. A short drive and we were chez Mulligan, where Franca gracefully accepted my strange present. Soon we were in Gerry's gigantic studio music room, in which a Synklavier, then the doyen of music synthesisers, took up a large proportion of the floor space. There we two ageing musicians plonked ourselves into comfortable seats and talked.

We talked of the past, the present and the future. We talked trivialities and profundities. We talked of music, both basic and complex. We talked of methods of synthesising music, ways of playing music, systems of writing music. We talked of our own strengths and weaknesses in music, our regrets and our dreams about music, and anything else that came to our minds. It seemed no time before we were summoned for an evening meal, and an early night left us fresh next morning to continue our soul-search and our preparations for the forthcoming symphony evening.

For me it was a memorable weekend, one of those rare occasions when I felt I really got to know someone whom I had long admired mostly from afar. Gerry was a volatile man who did not suffer fools gladly, and he had a reputation among other musicians for occasional bouts of testiness whenever his pursuit of perfection was challenged. Underneath all this, however, was a very warm heart indeed, coupled with such a good sense of humour that on the rare occasions when he lost touch with that admirable quality one could readily forgive him. The fact that he obviously liked my work and said so was something that made me feel very proud indeed, since I considered him then, as I do now, one of the great jazzmen of all time.

We did little work on actual musical detail during that weekend, but made a point of planning the sequence of events on the forthcoming programme most meticulously. When we had completed these preparations to our satisfaction I bade my farewell to the Mulligans and returned to New York, where I immediately began the orchestrations which I had promised.

Gerry Mulligan's complex personality on some occasions exuded total authority and on others a complete lack of confidence in himself. Once he was guest artiste on a recording Cleo was making of his composition *Walking Shoes*, for which I was the arranger. Gerry eyed the baritone sax part I gave him with a worried look which quickly turned to one approaching suspicion. I had allocated him a 32-bar improvised solo on his composition, preceded by a two-bar break. 'What's that?' said Gerry, pointing to the break indication on the page.

'It's a two-bar solo break, Gerry – you know, like the Original Dixieland Jazz Band used to do', I quipped. I was anxious to keep that sense of humour of his going. Gerry was worried and obviously didn't hear it.

'But the previous section is in a different key', he returned.

'Yes, you modulate during the two bars', I explained. I was tempted to add 'like the Original Dixieland Jazz Band', but felt it wasn't the right moment to continue that analogy.

'Well', said a frowning Gerry, 'I'll try it on the next run-through, but promise me you won't record it', he pleaded.

I agreed. However, unknown to me the recording engineer did in fact press the appropriate button. The whole performance was recorded with Gerry playing a two-bar modulatory break into his solo which has become one of the gems of my record collection, a masterly stroke of genius which couldn't have been bettered had he subsequently tried a hundred times.

My friendship with Gerry Mulligan, as is so often the case, resulted from meeting for professional reasons. However, a chance encounter that might easily never have happened was the beginning of Cleo's and my friendship with the great pianist Chick Corea and his wife Gayle Moran. Gayle was spotted walking away from one or our outdoor Hollywood appearances and persuaded to retrace her footsteps and come backstage to meet the singer she had admired enough to wish to hear in the flesh.

We were invited back to their lovely quasi-'olde worlde' home in an affluent area of the city not far from Hollywood Bowl, which I found in a strange way reminiscent of our beloved Old Rectory in England. One of our subsequent visits there was at a lavish St Valentine's Day party, the brainchild of Gayle, who was an avid collector of heart artefacts. Every guest was requested to wear something with a heart motif, and I chose a pair of socks, which seemed appropriate. Chick had assembled a Mozart-sized orchestra so that he could offer a Mozart concerto with himself as soloist for dinner music. It was a joyful reading of the work, with the soloist's eyes sparkling with glee as he added some rather impudent jazz-influenced improvisatory turns in the written cadenza. It was altogether a wonderful evening.

Later Gayle, Chick, Cleo and I performed together at Detroit's Meadow Brook performance arena, an experiment which we all enjoyed immensely; and later still we were invited to Chick and Gayle's wedding ceremony. I accompanied Cleo on the piano for my own setting of Shakespeare's *Shall I Compare Thee to a Summer's Day*, and then Herbie Hancock joined us to provide piano playing of a different class in a version of Gayle's favourite song, *My One and Only Love* – a romantic occasion.

*   *   *

One day we got a surprise phone call from the actor Sam Wanamaker, with whom we had collaborated many years previously to assist with his life's ambition, the establishment of a Shakespeare Globe Centre on the south bank of the Thames in London. He had remembered our willingness to help raise funds and was seeking our help again. He had arranged a series of visits throughout the United States targeted at the wealthiest sections of that opulent nation. Several of the concerts were to be at ambassadorial homes and residences of the rich, while others took place in country clubs and superior hotels. The idea was to provide a smattering of Shakespeare in music and drama, followed by an appeal by Sam in search of funds. We played in the homes of the Gettys in San Francisco, the Wyatts in Houston, the Wrights' ambassadorial residence in LA, as well as in less domestic but similarly opulent surroundings in Chicago, Denver, Pittsburgh, Boston, New York and Houston.

I remember the last-mentioned occasion particularly well. We had all given of our best in the fifty-minute lightweight pot-pourri of Shakespeare-related material, and the audience had lapped it up. Sam sprang onto the platform in his normal jaunty way. He made his impassioned speech as usual, somehow subtly underlining on this occasion that he was looking for big money. The rumour had got around that anything less than half a million dollars was unacceptable.

When it was over, I climbed down from the stage and happened to be passing Sam as three little elderly, bejewelled and blue-rinsed ladies approached him diffidently. I heard one of them say: 'Mr Wanamaker, we understand that you're only interested in really big donations, but if we three girls got together and rustled up a half a million dollars, would you make an exception and take our individual cheques totalling that amount?'

I watched Sam's face carefully. It didn't slip one millimetre. I couldn't eavesdrop any further, but as I walked away I heard Sam reluctantly agreeing to bend the rules (just this once) entirely to give these three supporters the pleasure of a small donation. Sam Wanamaker always thought big.

Cleo and I later performed in a marquee on the Globe site, just after the foundations had been laid and basic construction had commenced. It was the first performance anybody did on that site as far as I know. After our show Sam came up to Cleo and me and said: 'Cleo and John, I think we three are going to see this thing to its finality – and all the work we've put in over the years will have paid off.' Our efforts were trivial compared to his, but we felt somehow part of it all. We didn't know when he said this that Sam had only a few more months to live. He obviously did, but was hoping to be able to hang on for the crucial day. We were deeply grieved when we heard the news that he hadn't made it.

In my early days as a schoolboy admirer of Benny Goodman I only dreamt of one day playing at Carnegie Hall, the scene of that historic 1938 Goodman concert. I scarcely imagined that one day I would be unable to count accurately the number of times that I had played in that hallowed venue. Yet, as I write, this is the case. One such appearance, however, will stay in my memory a long while. On 6 September 1989 the whole place had been taken over by Nissan Motors, who were in the process of launching their new luxury car, the Infiniti. Since they were convinced their new product represented perfection, the concert they staged was called 'The Seal of Excellence', or something of that nature. The bill included the Katherine Dunham Dancers, violinist Itzhak Perlman, the jazz trumpeter Wynton Marsalis, a Japanese violin prodigy whose name escapes me, plus Cleo and myself. It was our first meeting with Marsalis, who declared himself an admirer. In fact he later reinforced this in a roundabout way by choosing the name E. Dankworth as a pseudonym on a recording session in which he was contractually not allowed to participate.

It was our first meeting with Perlman, who announced his intention of playing a piece by Kreisler, which to my astonishment brought a roar of laughter from the audience. For a split second we all wondered what on earth caused the merriment, then realised that everyone present was connected in some way with the automobile industry, and the only way to spell and interpret the word which Perlman had just uttered was – Chrysler. Giving unpaid publicity to a rival motor manufacturer was not Nissan's intention that night, but I think their directors saw the funny side.

*   *   *

Our first Australian visit, which led then to America, resulted in performances across the world – Iceland, Israel, Bermuda, Singapore, New Zealand – in places we had never been before and in new musical circles. Cleo duetted with Ray Charles, Dinah Shore, Mel Tormé, Joe Williams, Michael Feinstein, Sarah Vaughan; I jammed with Chick Corea, Ray Brown, Tom Scott, Oscar Peterson, Zoot Sims, Gerry Mulligan, Mark Whitfield, and my fellow British expatriates Marian McPartland and George Shearing. At a conservative estimate we must have travelled half a million air-miles since that first trip to perform together in the States. It could be closer to a million.

So it is with a regular routine of travel and music that I have interspersed the writing of these chapters. I suppose I am well past the age of conventional retirement, but I nevertheless keep on applying myself to the only activity in my life to which I can lay claims to special skills.

I suppose I will continue to do so for the forseeable future.

Perspective V

As the world turns the corner into the new millennium, jazz nears the end of its first century of existence.

Living, as we do, in the midst of an avalanche of music-making of widely varying types (some would begrudge the use of the word 'music' in the description of a great proportion of it), it is extremely hard to see what the future holds for jazz. In one sense the continued use of the word in most of the world's languages is a comfort (it has been employed to name everything from perfumes to basketball teams over the years), but frequently this has little to do with the qualities of the music, only the public perception of those qualities. Yet somehow jazz music continues, at the time of writing at least, to be used in situations when 'high fashion' music is not appropriate, yet 'lasting appeal' music is. The air of respectability that jazz has acquired more recently has luckily not made it so respectable that it has come to represent establishment, pomposity or stagnation, all of which might be connected by some listeners to classical music.

The position of jazz seems to be an ideal one on the face of it. It is not governed by the senseless world of current style which pervades and pollutes popular music, or by the motives of power and greed which make such music highly suspect in terms of integrity and frequently devoid of any real worth. Nor is it part of an established hierarchy so that it is cloistered and protected, partly as a museum-piece and partly as a status symbol, in the way that its classical counterparts, especially in opera, are pampered and mollycoddled. Jazz has reached the stage when its presence is realised in such quarters to be inevitable and perhaps faintly desirable, even though it may be held at arm's length by some of their number.

In spite of its virtual disappearance from media reportage, jazz has continued to spread itself across the earth's surface, with world-class practitioners coming from every corner of the globe. True, the home of jazz is still considered to be the United States, and as far as one can predict this situation could prevail for another decade or so; but radical and seemingly unbelievable changes can and often do occur in a short space of time – we see such things in almost every field of human endeavour, be it sport, art, fashion or food; it could well include jazz. The fact that there are legions of non-American jazz musicians who are little known outside their home countries is a pity; making a reputation of some sort in America is still a necessity, or at the very least an enormous fillip to a jazzman's career, even in his homeland. Yet those Europeans and others who feel hard done by should remember that the same problem applies to many Americans. If you happen to live and work in San Francisco, say – or Houston or Cleveland or Seattle – your only way to major success is to move to New York, still the jazz capital of Mother Earth. To stay in your hometown is to court anonymity, however good you are. But the day will surely come, particularly as a great new field of influence, the Pacific Rim, comes into its own, when European, Asian, African and Australian jazz musicians hitherto unknown will find themselves playing alongside their American counterparts on equal terms.

Musicians of my generation are often asked the age-old question – where is jazz going in future years? How will it change, and what new factors will influence it? It would take someone much braver than I to predict its future course. Perhaps 'foolhardy' might be a better word than 'braver', since those who made forecasts and pronouncements in the past have so often looked foolish in the fullness of time. However, certain things become apparent to a working musician such as myself which could possibly escape the attention of a non-player. Most of these revolve around technical factors – firstly, instruments. Electronics have of course become part of jazz, and players such as Chick Corea and Herbie Hancock have amply demonstrated their ability to use electronic keyboard sounds effectively. Likewise electronic 'wind' instruments such as the Lyricon and its Yamaha equivalent have sounded good in the hands of players such as Tom Scott. But the intro-duction of a new instrument to jazz demands unshared devotion and commitment as well as talent – as Lionel Hampton demonstrated with the vibraphone, Gerry Mulligan with the baritone sax and Toots Thielemans with the harmonica. Thus the impact made so far by these new instruments is minimal.

Strangely, something that had been with jazz for many years, albeit in less sophisticated form, has made a bigger contribution to its progress – amplification. For instance, improvements in amplification have helped the tremendous advance of the flute and the enormous step forward in the role of the double bass. Moreover, the violin and even the string quartet have become viable and valid forces in the jazz world, and the harmonica and the steel-pans can these days take as prominent a part in a jazz performance as a saxophone or trumpet. Perhaps the only area of jazz where amplification is of dubious assistance is in the realm of the big band. One has only to watch a young sound technician at a rehearsal equipping a big band with chandeliers of microphones to wish one could have taken him – just once – to a Count Basie concert of the fifties, when the only mike in sight would be centre-stage, well to the fore of the band. This would be used for instru-mental soloists (who left the band and stepped up to it), for singers and for announcements. The band balanced itself – as indeed do most big bands – and produced a marvellously controlled, wholesome acoustic sound.

It is far more difficult to predict changes and movements in the content of the music itself, either by composers or by the performers. Composers in jazz have in general showed signs of slowing down any trend towards atonalism, minimalism or any other influence leading away from access-ibility, and moving back to a new classicism with renewed respect for and reference to the earlier leaders of jazz thought – Duke Ellington, Fletcher Henderson, Ed Sauter, Gil Evans and so on. All in all, jazz composition has progressed intelligently and logically along paths which bode well for its future.

It is the jazz instrumental soloist who will, I believe, be the subject of the greatest role change. The music in its early days drew its practitioners from the ranks of musicians who were either self-taught or had an extremely rudimentary musical education. For a while this tended to add to the music a certain style which readily distinguished it from the poker-faced efforts of better-trained but less motivated musicians to capture its spontaneous feel.

But some of the more effective resources of more formal music – particularly the use of dynamics – have tended to be underused in jazz, especially since the advent of amplification. Despite the immaculate dynamics and the mesmerising effects created by the Basie band (and later by the Thad Jones–Mel Lewis ensemble) using close juxtaposition of very loud and extremely soft passages, small bands and individual soloists rarely seem to employ such tactics. Perhaps the increasing numbers of academically trained newcomers into the jazz world will reintroduce to the music a vanishing art among the younger generation of jazzmen – the knack of playing softly and still swinging.

Another aspect of jazz which could surely adopt new tactics (and here the composer could play a crucial role) is in the way jazz improvisation is disciplined. Fluency in improvisation has in the past two or three decades leapt ahead with seven-league boots. Chord progressions, modulations and extremes of tempo which would have been deemed unplayable by the players of a generation or so ago are being handled with ease by even the fledgling youngsters of today. The incredible increase of facility in this skill is probably due to its having been honed to an enormous degree by academic methods, coupled of course with the natural advance of technical standards. Surely, with such extraordinary dexterity at the fingertips of so many excellent musicians, it is time to guide improvisation away from being fluent but often meaningless doodling, which explores harmonic content but never thematic material, into a new phase when themes, motifs and key phrases become as much a part of improvisation as they have for centuries of written music, jazz included. The extemporiser would be given by the composer not only chord structures with which to work, but themes and other material to reiterate, reconstruct, dissect and transpose at will, as well as specific rhythmic instructions to complement similar patterns occurring elsewhere in the music.

Attempts by composers to bring this technique into jazz have been made in the past – I have on occasion experimented with it myself – but only a major work featuring extensive use of these techniques stands a chance of persuading jazz musicians to take this new requirement seriously. It is a development on which jazz exponents will have to focus their attentions soon if they wish to retain the music's dominance as the leading showcase for the improvising musician. It is a wonderful experience to be left breathless with admiration at the dexterity of a skilled improviser in full flight, *but machine gun-like delivery of an endless cascade of notes can pall with repetition; many young players are guilty of these offences. Only with more considered and better controlled musical content can improvisation continue to play a major part in the progress of jazz.*

In spite of the confusing and somewhat tawdry world of commercial music (and this description to my minds fits some areas of the so-called classical field), jazz continues to attract the lion's share of the world's most gifted young musicians. Of all those youngsters who are drawn to music as either a hobby or a profession, those who seek to perfect their instrumental skill further usually find their way to the music academies – and the world of classical music. Of every dozen or so of these youngsters perhaps one finds that simply playing other peoples' music gives insufficient satisfaction, and turns either to composing or to improvisation (which of course amounts to instant composition) – or both. He or she will then find, no matter which of these activities is selected as favourite, that there is vastly more opportunity to interact in jazz than in the classical world. No wonder that jazz attracts the cream of young musical ability – the challenges, the excitement of creation combined with improvisation far outweighs the offerings of a classical career. Small wonder that so little of real interest comes from the tired world of contemporary classical composition; the exceptional talent is in another sphere of music. Yet (and I suppose not surprisingly, given the prejudice existing in the world of formal music) the jazz fraternity is starved of financial help, not to mention media exposure, while their classical counterparts are, in relative terms at least, richly endowed.

After my half century as a professional music-maker (and a half century of being appalled by such injustices) the final irony of it all has just recently become clear to me. Those stout defenders of the status quo, the minders who jealously guard the territory of Western European music culture, are protecting the wrong music.

Jazz is the real classical music. As the Old World approached the final bend into the finishing straight of the nineteenth century it was already apparent that the age of the New World was on the threshold. America, once a disparate set of European colonies planted by British, French, Spanish, Dutch and Portuguese adventurers, had now become a series of nations, one of which was already waxing powerful and influential, a subcontinent in itself which would go on to supplant the old superpowers with its own brand of persuasive dominance.

The New World was taking over, and it was a natural and inevitable sequence of events that it would produce the significant music of the coming age. So, in the same way that Western European classical music had emerged as a musical style from the combined effects of French, Spanish, German, Italian and English music and musicians to form an identifiable and lasting entity, so the combined musical influences of the nations and races contributed to the American melting-pot. French military marches, English hymns, Irish dance tunes and African drum rhythms all made their mark, and out came a fresh, vital, compelling new musical language to match a new way of life.

Interestingly, as the new music matured, in its turn it paid homage to – and learned lessons from – some major figures in the European music world of the time. Thus Debussy, Ravel, Delius and Stravinsky all had their effect on jazz, which in turn made a significant mark on the music of at least three of them. But from then on jazz took over the world music initiative – the new guard replaced the old. Of course the change was resented by many, often for social and political reasons rather than musical ones. Jazz, even more than the USA itself, seemed to those in power to be a harbinger for social change of a less than desirable nature. Such a view was taken by the Nazis, who in the thirties effectively banned the music and even the word from Germans.

The bans have long disappeared. But a certain old guard resistance is still there in some high places, and the threat that jazz poses to them is still very real in their minds. It is of little use trying to explain to them that their fears are really groundless; jazz has since its beginnings been an instrument of goodwill and peaceful and gradual change rather than anything really revolutionary. An amalgam of origins, of styles, of methods, its attitude to race and ethnic background has always been all-embracing, and its view of society classless. Only its musical standards have remained from the outset unswervingly devoid of compromise – only the best will do.

I once said, early in my career – and I was widely quoted – that jazz was the journalism of music. What I meant was that, while a great symphony or concerto might be compared to a great novel as an important product of a particular year or decade, jazz was the musical commentator portraying the mood of a given day or even hour. (Perhaps the extensive quotation of that viewpoint was owing to its obvious appeal to the journalists who reported it – except perhaps those who had written novels.) But all these years later, after having spent a lot of my life working in and studying both worlds, I have changed my views, even reversed them.

I had it all wrong. The classical world, while continuing to preserve (and perhaps overexpose) the music of the past, has little or nothing of serious consequence to do with the present. Most new work that does emerge self-consciously from its loins is performed brilliantly by musicians who are frequently only too aware of its paucity of invention and overall lack of distinction. Classical music circles abound with hypocrisy; concert promoters pander to the wishes of the lowest common denominator. It all equates very closely with the attitudes of the worst sections of the national press. Hence I now realise I was wrong with my early allocation of the journalism metaphor to jazz.

Jazz on the other hand has acquired all the ingredients of genuine musical progress – considered prepared musical statement combined with opportunity for intelligent spontaneous virtuosity. It can be spiritual, cerebral, motivating or moving. It can evoke tension, relaxation, laughter, tears. Surely jazz is truly the music of the era, combining stature, dignity and emotion with the highest musical ideals. The musical world will one day realise this, and begin devoting to jazz the respect and attention it truly deserves.

Epilogue

What, then, do I feel I have gained from all those miles, all those airport lounges, all those hotel lobbies, all those concert halls with their widely varying audiences? What have I learned from sharing the limelight with so many world-famous musicians and illustrious orchestras at all those hallowed venues? Now that I have performed my compositions and orchestrations to so many millions of listeners in one medium or another, now that I have talked and compared notes with musicians of so many nationalities and ethnic backgrounds – well, in short, has it been worth while and, if I had my time over again, would I do things differently?

Perhaps I should deal with the last of these points first. I would be a pompous fool indeed if I claimed that nothing I did during all those years was to be regretted. I have made countless mistakes which caused me profound regret. Yet I also recognise how often I have been lucky. I think that the ability to recognise this is an important factor in one's mental well-being in a career such as music. Being in the right place at the right time is something over which we often have no control, yet it is sometimes a crucial factor.

The professional sportsman or athlete can often judge success by discernible achievement measured by a stop-watch, a tape-measure or a scorecard. No one can deny such evidence of a person's ability, however popular or otherwise that person might be to the public. There is by contrast no such way of calibrating musical talent; thus it is inevitable that while, by and large, musicians with talent succeed and those without it do not, some of lesser musical ability nevertheless make more progress than their more talented counterparts. Some members of our profession find it difficult to cope with this fact of life and emerge as unhappy and bitter people – and thus become their own worst enemies. When I see some hopelessly dim 'megastar' being lauded to the skies and enjoying celebrity status, I cope by reflecting that, though I often see inferior musicians in a better position than I, there is also the other side to the coin: I can think of many instances of musicians of greater ability than myself who have had none of the good fortune I have been lucky enough to have experienced coming my way.

And of course all of us living in countries where we can pursue our careers in relative peace have something to be thankful for; whenever I see the results of a massacre on television, or see someone hurrying along a street to avoid being hit by a sniper, I ask myself – is one of them a jazz fan, or maybe even a musician on his way to a gig? Every jazz lover who has been blessed not to be caught up in that sort of world must be truly grateful.

Living and working mainly in the Western world has enabled Cleo and me to bring up a family in spite of a heavy touring schedule. I suppose it was inevitable that any offspring of a union such as ours would have a strong involvement with music, but we resolved to do nothing that would influence their own judgement on a choice of career. Alec and his sister Jacqueline frequently spent their school holidays travelling on tour with us, often to exotic overseas locations. Thus they were initiated at an early age into the intricacies of life on the road, and spent many evenings at our performances in America, Canada and elsewhere listening to – and sometimes being critical of – the work of their parents.

Later Alec started playing himself – first the cello, then the clarinet and finally the bass, on which instrument he began his playing career at some of the very places where he had previously been a spectator. Since those early days he has truly made his mark as a fine musician, touring and sometimes recording with many well-known artists. His success in the British Jazz Awards as this country's premier bassist has enabled him to conquer fresh fields, and nowadays I am sometimes asked by younger jazz enthusiasts if my name is connected in any way with that of Alec Dankworth – which I guess is the inevitable fate of an ageing father of an increasingly well-known son.

Alec and I have made several recordings with our own fourteen-piece group known as the Generation Band, assembled from some of Britain's most talented jazzmen of three generations. The GenBand has also provided concert support for both Cleo and daughter Jacqui, whose career as an actress, which started in the mid-eighties, preceded her decision to make singing her main preoccupation. However, her spells with the Royal Shakespeare Company and the British National Theatre played, I believe, a large part in giving Jacqui a self-assurance and a charisma on stage which serves her well in her singing performances. In her appearances with Field of Blue, her own ensemble co-led by musician-composer Harvey Brough, these qualities readily came to light, coupled with a charmingly unique vocal delivery and a great sensitivity. Jacqui and I have performed together on two extended tours with the New Zealand Symphony Orchestra, and these experiences confirmed my own verdict that my daughter has star quality.

Alec and Jacqui have both long ceased to reside at their parental home in Wavendon, and of course their presence is missed; so it is fortunate for us that our annual Christmas concert season at Wavendon Stables quite often acts as an occasion for reuniting us. Whether they are there or not, we are delighted that both have their own musical worlds, and we are proud to enjoy our common love of music together with them whenever the opportunity arises.

But, of course, we oldies are often away working ourselves; our careers seem to get busier rather than otherwise as the years go on.

How have we weathered the storm, Cleo and I, and coped with the wear and tear? Several things have contributed to our travel longevity. Firstly, excellent tour management, initially by Elliot Ames, then later and for many years by Kurt Gebauer, who also became our very efficient business manager, and later still by Jim Zimmerman. For many years we have been protected like royalty – from queues, ticket counters, baggage claims and all the hassles of air travel. We are usually whisked from hotel to airport by limousine (our luggage having been taken there long before us) and spirited on arrival to an airline club, leaving us little to worry about. We almost invariably travel first-class or the nearest available equivalent, which we have found reduces travel fatigue enormously. It is our one luxury which we consider a necessity, and we are convinced that it has enabled us to enjoy much longer-than-average careers.

In Britain, where travel is by and large less of a trauma, with only rare visits to airports, our life is simplified by the services of Sheila Gray and Becky Stevenson, both of whom make the procedure of UK engagements as smooth as feasible. And the incomparable skills of our musicians – drummer Allan Ganley, pianist John Horler and bassist Malcolm Creese – all contribute to making our work a pleasure, with Malcolm giving us additional assistance in the touring management department.

One other thing, which is also always part of the answer to the question 'What is your recipe for a long-lasting marriage?' The answer – two bathrooms. We have several times turned down occupancy of a hotel's finest suite, complete on one occasion with grand piano, because it did not have two bathrooms. Nothing in my experience can remove the cause of marital friction more successfully than two bathrooms, and nothing can lead more quickly to disharmony and eventual conjugal disintegration than one.

I have as I write no thoughts about retiring. Cleo seems to be of the same mind – we would both prefer to keep going as long as we have the stamina. The question of retiring would be quite a different story if we had not spent our lives earning our living pursuing our hobby. But as things are, what on earth would we do if we stopped?

So, in short, we intend to go on as long as our energies and our bodies allow us. If, however, one day in the far and distant future, you see some little cottage, or bungalow, tucked away in a corner of Devon, or northern California, or Hawkes Bay, New Zealand, or any other of a dozen places we like, and by chance hear jazz music emanating from the open windows and see a couple of bikes outside with JD and CL on the saddlebags, it may well be us. If so, you can be sure that, however small our abode, it will be a longish, thinnish place so that we can each get to opposite ends and steer well clear of each other during our periods of verbal fisticuffs.

And of course it will have two bathrooms.

*   *   *

The globe keeps turning – and the musical world keeps revolving with it. I have been privileged to witness (and play a minor part in) one complete revolution of the wheel of jazz music, running as it did concurrently with my own lifespan. The succeeding turn of that wheel is just beginning; indeed I hope to contribute a bit to its next revolution before I finally withdraw (I hope gracefully) from the arena of jazz, that unique form of self-expression which has played such a huge part in my own passionate affair with the sounds of musical endeavour.

Discography

1948	*Ladybird/Mop Mop w/Victor Feldman Quartet*	Esquire

Johnny Dankworth Quartet

1949	*Lover Man/Bremavin*	Esquire
1949	*Body and Soul/Second Eleven w/Johnny Dankworth Quartet*	Esquire

Johnny Dankworth Seven (singles)

1950	*Lightly, Politely/Marmaduke*	Jazz Parade
	Strike Up The Band/Little Benny	Jazz Parade
	Sam's Song/Haunted Ballroom	Esquire
	Seven Not Out/Cherokee	Esquire
	Get Happy/Perhaps	Esquire
	Don't Blame Me/Lament & Wild Dance	Esquire
1951	*Stardust/Marching Through Georgia*	Esquire
	Blue Moon/So in Love	Esquire
	The Slider/I Hear Music	Esquire
	Leon Bismark/Webb City	Esquire
	Lush Life/Mr & Mississippi	Esquire
	Allen's Alley/Strictly Confidential	Esquire
	It's no Sin/Wedding of Painted Doll	Esquire
	Stomping at The Savoy/MYOB	Esquire
1952	*Very Thought Of You/Got You under my Skin*	Esquire
	Bopscotch/Our Delight	Esquire

1953	Two Ticks/Moonflowers	Parlophone
	Honeysuckle Rose/Swinging	Parlophone
	Easy Living/I Get a Kick out of You	Parlophone
1954	Runnin' Wild/Ooph-e-dooph	Parlophone

Johnny Dankworth and his Orchestra (singles)

1954	'S Wonderful/Younger Every Day	Parlophone
	The Slider/Talk Of The Town	Parlophone
	My Buddy/The Jerky Thing	Parlophone
	Ain't Misbehavin'/I Got it Bad	Parlophone
	I Got Rhythm/I Know You're Mine	Parlophone
1956	Experiments With Mice/Applecake	Parlophone
1958	England's Ambassador of Jazz (LP)	Roulette
1959	Bundle from Britain (LP)	Top Rank
1961	African Waltz/Moanin' (single)	Columbia
1964	From Seven on (LP)	EMI
1962	Big Band Sound of Johnny Dankworth (LP)	Roulette
1962	Dankworth & the London Philharmonic Orchestra (LP)	Society
1963	What the Dickens (LP)	Fontana
1964	Zodiac Variations (LP)	Fontana
1967	The Million Dollar Collection (LP)	Fontana
1967	John Dankworth and his Music (LP)	Fontana
1969	Windmill Tilter (LP)	Fontana
1972	Full Circle (LP)	Philips
1973	Lifeline (LP)	Philips
1974	Movies and Me (LP)	RCA
1979	Octavius (LP)	Sepia
1979	Kite Flight (LP)	Sepia
1979	Telford's Change/Serenade for Strings (single)	BBC Records
1980	Starburst (LP)	Grosvenor
1981	Prelude to a Kiss (LP)	Sepia
1982	Fair Oak Fusions (LP)	Sepia
1983	Metro (LP)	Sepia
1983	Gone Hitchin' (LP)	Sepia
1984	Johnny Dankworth 1953–58, featuring Cleo Laine (LP)	Retrospect
1986	Bop at Club II (LP)	Esquire
1986	Get Happy (LP reissue of 1950–1952)	Esquire
1986	Symphonic Fusions (CD)	Pickwick
	[Crossing over the Bridge (USA release)]	MCA Classic
1988	Innovations (CD)	Pickwick
	[Misty (USA release)]	MCA Classic
1988	Echoes of Harlem (CD)	Pro Jazz
1989	Jazzin' the Pops (CD)	Pro Jazz

1989	*The Vintage Years (CD)*	Sepia
1989	*Dizzy Gillespie – the Symphony Sessions (CD)*	Pro Jazz
1990	*Live at Ronnie's (CD)*	Sepia
1991	*The Johnny Dankworth Years (CD)*	Roulette

The Alec and John Dankworth Generation Big Band

| 1994 | *Nebuchadnezzar (CD)* | RSJH |
| 1995 | *Rhythm Changes (CD)* | RSJH |

List of Films

Feature films as composer/Music director:

1960   *Saturday Night and Sunday Morning* (d. Karel Reisz. Also composed song 'Let's Slip Away'; lyrics – David Dearlove)
The Criminal (d. Joseph Losey. Also composed song 'Thieving Boy'; lyrics – Alun Owen)

1963   *The Servant* (d. Joseph Losey. Also composed song 'All Gone'; lyrics – Harold Pinter)

1965   *Darling . . .* (d. John Schlesinger)
Return from the Ashes (d. J. Lee Thompson)
Sands of the Kalahari (d. Cy Endfield)

1966   *The Idol* (d. Daniel Petrie)
Modesty Blaise (d. Joseph Losey. Also composed title song; lyrics – Benny Green)
Morgan, a Suitable Case for Treatment (d. Karel Reisz)

1967   *Fathom* (d. Leslie Martinson)
Accident (d. Joseph Losey)
The Last Safari (d. Henry Hathaway)

1968   *Salt and Pepper* (d. Richard Donner)
The Magus (d. Guy Green)
I Love You, I Hate You (d. David Hart)

1969   *The Last Grenade* (d. Gordon Flemyng)

1970   *Perfect Friday* (d. Peter Hall)
The Engagement (d. Paul Joyce)
10 Rillington Place (d. Richard Fleischer)

Short films as composer:

1959   *We are the Lambeth Boys* (d. Karel Reisz)
1961   *Hamilton in the Music Festival* (d. John Halas)
1962   *Hamilton the Musical Elephant* (d. John Halas)
1964   *Top Flight* (d. Julian Spiro)
1965   *A Game Called Scruggs* (d. David Hart)
        The World at Three (d. Frederic Goode)

Feature film performances:

1958   *6–5 Special* (as himself. d. Alfred Shaughnessy)
1961   *All Night Long* (as himself. d. Michael Relph)
1963   *The Servant* (as himself. d. Joseph Losey)

Short film performances:

1955   *Parade of the Bands* (as himself. d. Michael Carreras)
1968   *Music* (as himself. d. Michael Tuchner)

Stage productions as music composer:

1964   *Twelfth Night* by William Shakespeare (City of London Festival)
1967   *A Soldier's Fortune* by Thomas Otway (Royal Court Theatre, London)
        A Midsummer Night's Dream by William Shakespeare (Edinburgh Festival, and later Saville Theatre, London)
        Sweeney Agonistes by T. S. Eliot (Globe Theatre, London)
        Boots with Strawberry Jam by Benny Green and John Dankworth (Playhouse Theatre, Nottingham)
1968   *Edward II* by Christopher Marlowe (Old Vic, London)
1971   *A Man of Mode* by George Ethereges (Aldwych Theatre, London)

Television:

1959   Composed theme for *The Voodoo Factor* (ATV serial)
1961   (onwards) Composed music (with David Lindup) for *Survival* (Anglia TV series – approximately 90 episodes)

1961   Composed original theme for *The Avengers* (ABC series). Appeared in
         One Man's Music (ATV series)
1962   Composed music for *The New Ark* (Anglia TV documentary)
1963   Appeared in *Experiment – Improvisations* (ATV series)
1964   Composed music for *Lyrics by Shakespeare* (Rediffusion)
         Composed theme (with Mike Vickers) for *Search For A Star*
         (Rediffusion series)
         Composed Associated-Rediffusion's London call-sign
         Composed theme for *Three after Six* (Rediffusion series)
1965   Composed theme for *That's for Me* (Rediffusion series)
1966   Composed theme for *Tomorrow's World* (BBC-1 series)
         Composed theme for *The Frost Report* (BBC-1 series)
1968   Composed music for *Pippa* (London Weekend documentary)
         Composed music for *The Helicopter* (BBC-2 documentary)
         Composed music for *Ooh La La* (BBC-2 series)
1969   Composed theme for *Bird's-Eye View* (BBC-2 series)
1970   Composed music for *The Enchanted House* (Granada series)
1971   Composed music for *The Canterbury Tales* (BBC-2 Series)
         Composed *Musica in Camera* for the Open University (BBC-2)

Commercials:

Since 1961 Dankworth has also composed the music for the following
British radio, television and cinema commercials: Apollo Super Soap, Bass
Export, BBC-2, Betty Crocker Cake Mixes, Big S, B.O.A.C., Bovril, British Rail,
Cleveland Discol, Cossack Vodka, Dip, Driway Raincoats, English Rose
Nylons, Esso, D. H. Evans, Escort Cigarettes, Fropax Quick Frozen Peas, Ilford
Films, Knights Castile, Lucky Strike Cigarettes, Mackintosh's Week-End,
Marlboro Cigarettes, McVitie and Price, Michelin X Tyres, Moussec, National
Dairy Council, Nescafé, Omo (an arrangement of the title song from *Modesty
Blaise*), Ovaltine, Philips Snow Queen Refrigerators, Players Admiral
Cigarettes, Prestige, Robertson's Golden Shred, Robertson's Gollicrush, Skol
International, Viota Mixes, Viscount Cigarettes and Wilkinson Sword. He
has also scored an Australian radio commercial for Super Sheep Thread
(1961)

Radio:

1961   *The Sunday Market* by Johnny Dankworth, Ned Sherrin and Caryl
         Brahms (BBC musical play)
1962   Composed theme for *The Dales* (BBC serial)

Musical Works:

1956   *Conducted Tour*
1964   *Zodiac Variations*
       Lysistrata (with Benny Green. For Bath Festival)
       What the Dickens
1967   *Tom Sawyer's Saturday* (for Farnham Festival)
       City Sequence (with Caryl Brahms. For the opening of the Queen
       Elizabeth Hall, London)
1968   *Sextet* (for Belfast Festival)
1969   *Folk Mass for Choir and Congregation*
1970   *Palabras* (for the Northern Symphonia Orchestra)
1971   *String Quartet* (for the Alberni String Quartet. First performed at
       Playhouse Theatre, Harlow)
       Life Line (for Aldeburgh Festival)
       Seasons (for the Royal Philharmonic Orchestra and Magna Carta.
       First performed at the Royal Albert Hall, London)
1972   Untitled piano concerto for small chamber orchestra (for
       Westminster Festival)
1992   *Worship Songs Ancient & Modern* ('Everlasting love', 'Light of the
       world', 'They killed him as a common thief')

Dankworth's many other compositions include *Itinerary of an Orchestra* (with David Lindup, 1956), *Improvisation for Jazz Band and Symphony Orchestra* (with Mátyás Seiber, 1959), a number of songs written with Steven Vinaver, Ned Sherrin and Caryl Brahms for the BBC television series *That Was The Week That Was* (1963 onwards), *The Million Dollar Collection* (1967), *Escapade* (1967), *Hideaway* (with Don Black, for the film BOOM!, 1968), *Grace Abounding* (1980), *The Diamond And The Goose* (1981), *Suite For Emma* (1985), (this four-movement suite was specially composed for Emma Johnson, who became the BBC 1984 Young Musician of the Year at the age of seventeen), *Reconciliation* (for Silver Jubilee of Coventry Cathedral, 1987), *Woolwich Concerto* (for Emma Johnson, 1995), *Live '95'* (commissioned by BBC Radio Live '95', 1995), *Bulletrain* (commissioned by BBC Live '95', 1995), *Dreams 42* (String Quartet for 1997 Kidderminster Festival), *Double Vision* (1997 World Premiere by BBC Big Band at BBC Proms)

Publication: *Sax from the Start, 1996*

Index